MANIPULATION OF
THE AMERICAN VOTER

Recent Titles in the
Praeger Series in Political Communication
Robert E. Denton, Jr., *General Editor*

MANIPULATION OF THE AMERICAN VOTER

Political Campaign Commercials

Karen S. Johnson-Cartee
and Gary A. Copeland

Praeger Series in Political Communication

Westport, Connecticut
London

Library of Congress Cataloging-in-Publication Data

Johnson-Cartee, Karen S.
    Manipulation of the American voter : political campaign
commercials / Karen S. Johnson-Cartee and Gary A. Copeland.
        p.   cm.—(Praeger series in political communication, ISSN
1062–5623)
    Includes bibliographical references and index.
    ISBN 0–275–95588–5 (alk. paper)
    1. Advertising, Political—United States.   2. Television in
politics—United States.   3. Presidents—United States—Election.
I. Copeland, Gary.   II. Title.   III. Series.
JK2281.J64   1997
324.7′3—dc20   96–20688

British Library Cataloguing in Publication Data is available.

Library of Congress Catalog Card Number: 96–20688
ISBN: 0–275–95588–5
ISSN: 1062–5623

First published in 1997

Praeger Publishers, 88 Post Road West, Westport, CT 06881
An imprint of Greenwood Publishing Group, Inc.

Printed in the United States of America

The paper used in this book complies with the
Permanent Paper Standard issued by the National
Information Standards Organization (Z39.48–1984).

10 9 8 7 6 5 4 3 2 1

Copyright Acknowledgments

The authors and publisher gratefully acknowledge permission to reprint the following advertisements.

"Kerry 'Shattered' Ad" and "Kerry 'No AK47 Needed' Ad" used with permission of Bob Kerry.

"Flippo 'Bio' Ad" used with permission of Ronnie Flippo.

"Bachus 'Hogwash II' Ad" used with permission of Karen Johnson-Cartee.

"Campbell 'American Dream' Ad" used with permission of Ben Nighthorse Campbell.

Every reasonable effort has been made to trace the owners of copyright materials in this book, but in some instances this has proven impossible. The authors and publisher will be glad to receive information leading to more complete acknowledgments in subsequent printings of the book and in the meantime extend their apologies for any omissions.

To Dr. Fred Eichelman and Dr. Dan Nimmo, two men who encouraged female students to excel in a time when it was neither fashionable nor rewarding to do so. And to my parents, Edsel and Betty Johnson, for what I am today, and what I will be tomorrow is the result of their years of love, patience, and support. And to my husband Michael who loves politics almost as much as I do.

Karen Johnson-Cartee, Ph.D.

To Uncle Leonard Knaffle and the memory of Aunt Juanita Knaffle who valued knowledge, scholarship, and education not only for their children and grandchildren but for all.

Gary A. Copeland, Ph.D.

Contents

Political Advertising Transcripts

NOTE: Titles may not be those given by the political consultants.

Series Foreword

Those of us from the discipline of communication studies have long believed that communication is prior to all other fields of inquiry. In several other forums I have argued that the essence of politics is "talk" or human interaction.[1] Such interaction may be formal or informal, verbal or nonverbal, public or private, but it is always persuasive, forcing us consciously or subconsciously to interpret, to evaluate, and to act. Communication is the vehicle for human action.

From this perspective, it is not surprising that Aristotle recognized the natural kinship of politics and communication in his writings *Politics* and *Rhetoric*. In the former, he established that humans are "political beings [who] alone of the animals [are] furnished with the faculty of language."[2] And in the latter, he begins his systematic analysis of discourse by proclaiming that "rhetorical study, in its strict sense, is concerned with the modes of persuasion."[3] Thus, it was recognized over 2,300 years ago that politics and communication go hand in hand because they are essential parts of human nature.

Back in 1981, Dan Nimmo and Keith Sanders proclaimed that political communication was an emerging field.[4] Although its origins, as noted, dates back centuries, a "self-consciously cross-disciplinary" focus began in the late 1950s. Thousands of books and articles later, colleges and universities offer a variety of graduate and undergraduate coursework in the area in such diverse departments as communication, mass communication, journalism, political science, and sociology.[5] In Nimmo and Sanders' early assessment, the "key areas of inquiry" included rhetorical analysis, propaganda analysis, attitude change studies, voting studies, government and the news media, functional and systems analyses, technological changes, media technologies, campaign techniques, and research techniques.[6] In a survey of the state of the field in 1983, the same authors and Lynda Kaid found additional, more specific areas of concerns such as the presidency, political polls, public opinion, debates, and advertising to name a few.[7] Since the first study, they also noted a shift away from the the rather strict behavioral approach.

A decade later, Dan Nimmo and David Swanson argued that "political communication has developed some identity as a more or less distinct domain of scholarly work."[8] The scope and concerns of the area have further expanded to include critical theories and cultural studies. While there is no precise definition, method, or disciplinary home of the area of inquiry, its primary domain is the role, processes, and effects of communication within the context of politics broadly defined.

In 1985, the editors of *Political Communication Yearbook: 1984* noted that "more things are happening in the study, teaching, and practice of political communication than can be captured within the space limitations of the relatively few publications available."[9] In addition, they argued that the backgrounds of "those involved in the field [are] so varied and pluralistic in outlook and approach. . . . It [is] a mistake to adhere slavishly to any set format in shaping the content."[10] And more recently, Nimmo and Swanson called for "ways of overcoming the unhappy consequences of fragmentation within a framework that respects, encourages, and benefits from diverse scholarly commitments, agendas, and approaches."[11]

In agreement with these assessments of the area and with gentle encouragement, Praeger established the Praeger Series in Political Communication. The series is open to all qualitative and quantitative methodologies as well as contemporary and historical studies. The key to characterizing the studies in the series is the focus on communication variables or activities within a political context or dimensions. As of this writing, nearly forty volumes have been published, and there are numerous impressive works forthcoming. Scholars from the disciplines of communication, history, journalism, political science, and sociology have participated in the series.

I am without shame or modesty, a fan of the series. The joy of serving as its editor is in participating in the dialogue of the field of political communication and in reading the contributors' works. I invite you to join me.

Robert E. Denton, Jr.

NOTES

1. See Robert E. Denton, Jr., *The Symbolic Dimensions of the American Presidency* (prospect Heights, Ill.: Waveland Press 1982); Robert E. Denton, Jr., and Gary Woodward, *Political Communication in America* (New York: Praeger, 1986); Robert E. Denton, Jr., and Dan Han, *Presidential Communication* (New York: Praeger, 1986); and Robert E. Denton, Jr., *The Primetime Presidency of Ronald Reagan* (New York: Praeger, 1988).

2. Aristotle, *The Politics of Aristotle*, trans. Earnest Barker (New York: Oxford University Press, 1970), p. 5.

3. Aristotle, *Rhetoric*, trans. Rhys Roberts (New York: The Modern Library, 1954), p. 22.

4. Dan Nimmo and Keith Sanders, "Introduction: The Emeregence of Political Communicvation as a Field," in *Handbook of Political Communication*, ed. Dan Nimmo and Keith Sanders (Beverly Hills, Calif.: Sage, 1981), p. 11-36.

5. Ibid., p. 15.

6. Ibid., pp. 17-27.

7. Keith Sanders, Lynda Kaid, and Dan Nimmo, eds., *Political Communication Yearbook: 1984* (Carbondale: Southern Illinois University, 1985), pp. 283-308.

8. Dan Nimmo and David Swanson, "The Field of Political Communication: Beyond the Voter Persuasion Paradigm," in *New Directions in Political Communication*, ed. David Swanson and Dan Nimmo (Beverly Hills, Calif.: Sage, 1990), p. 8.

9. Sanders, Kaid, and Nimmo, *Political Communication Yearbook: 1984*, p. xiv.

10. Ibid.

11. Nimmo and Swanson, "The Field of Political Communication," p. 11

Preface

In a speech delivered to the Civil Liberties Union in Honolulu, Hawaii on April 22, 1990, former Democratic presidential candidate Michael Dukakis explained his failed candidacy in this manner:

I said in my acceptance speech at Atlanta that the 1988 election was not about ideology but about competence. I was wrong. It was about phraseology. It was about 10-second sound bites. And made-for-TV backdrops. And going negative. I made a lot of mistakes in the '88 campaign, but none was as damaging as my failure to understand this phenomenon, and the need to respond immediately and effectively to distortions of one's record and one's positions. (Butterfield, 1990, part 1, p. 23)

Dukakis's words mirror the frustration of those who have been ill-prepared for the changes in modern American political campaigning. In order to successfully compete in modern campaigns, candidates and their advisers must be thoroughly grounded in the strategies and tactics associated with this new style of media campaign. This research text is designed to prepare readers—whether researchers, students, political leaders, journalists, consultants, or the interested political observer—with a thorough grounding in modern American political campaign knowledge. Political campaigning remains an art form, but this political artifact is ruled by a morass of competing, often conflicting research and theories that ultimately produce either a successful or unsuccessful campaign. This book takes the reader through this body of research, exploring the patterns and commonalities within the multidisciplinary field of political communication studies. But most importantly, this research text is designed to educate the consumer of political advertising, for as

Michael Dukakis has stated, the manipulation of the message is the key to victory in contemporary American politics. Understanding how and why political advertising works is the key to being an informed citizen.

As researchers and as practicing political consultants, the authors have drawn upon their divergent backgrounds in compiling the literature for this work. Karen Johnson-Cartee has graduate degrees in mass communication and political science, with an emphasis on political communication. Gary Copeland has graduate degrees in speech communication, with emphases on mass communication effects, broadcasting aesthetics, and social psychology. They have worked in numerous local, state, and federal election campaigns, and in 1992, they served as political media consultants to the Aruban Democratic National party on the island of Aruba. This book marries the research of scholars and academicians in mass communication, speech communication, psychology, sociology, political science, commercial advertising, and marketing with the work, research, and practical knowledge of countless political consultants.

To understand contemporary political campaigning, it is necessary to take an interdisciplinary approach. The professional field of political consulting has learned to draw on all of these research traditions in order to construct contemporary campaigns. Academicians and scholars would do well to follow their lead.

The rationale for this work is similar to that used in *Negative Political Advertising: Coming of Age* (1991a); many of the concepts first presented there will be further developed in this work. In this earlier work, the authors traced the evolution of negative political advertising during the age of television. In the present work, the authors focus on the political campaign commercials of the last four general election cycles, the 1988, 1990, 1992, and 1994 campaign seasons.

Acknowledgements

The authors would like to express their thanks to a number of friends and colleagues who have provided assistance and support throughout this project. We are indebted to Julian Kantor, the archivist at the University of Oklahoma Political Commercial Archives, who provided invaluable assistance to us in locating particular examples of campaign ads. A very special thanks to Rosie McMahill who worked as a graduate research assistant for this project. Her sleuthing skills in the library made this project far easier than it might have been without her. In addition, her editing skills made this a far more readable work than if it had been left to our own devices.

We would also like to thank our Aruban friends, Mirurgia "Uka" Marchena, Willem Vrolijk, and Mario Enrique Croes, who gave us fresh ideas about our own culture and opened a world of learning opportunities for us in theirs. Karl "Charlie" Nessmann and Walter Schludermann provided insight into European politics and support at the Universität Klagenfurt, Austria. This work reflects the long hours of brainstorming about U.S., Dutch, European, and Aruban politics that have helped cement our friendships, renewed our intellectual growth, and given us fresh insights into our own political culture, Southern and otherwise.

We would also like to thank the members of New South Coalition, especially Judge John England, State Representative Charles Steele, Willie James "Dino" Forte, and Maxie Thomas, for a thorough introduction to minority politics in a traditionally white state. And the catfish fries weren't bad either.

We would each like to thank those who were particularly helpful to us personally. Karen would like to recognize the Dean's

Office in the College of Communication at the University of Alabama, because for most of the summers, she was missing-in-action. Although there were weekly Associate Dean sightings, she recognizes that the following individuals had to work harder because she was not around as much: Mary Ann Shargo, Dinah Walton, Cecilia Hammond, Jim Oakley, Dolores Rhodes, Gail Leonard, Charlotte McNabb. Charlotte, Dolores, and Gail deserve special thanks because Karen could never have done her job without their support, help, and friend-ship. Their loyalty, hard work, and assistance are deeply appreciated. We would like to thank our significant others, Michael Cartee and Susan Copeland, who tolerated our many idiosyncrasies, long hours, and grumpy personalities during the summers of 1993, 1995 and 1996. Cully and Mary Clark, Dolf and Valtra Zillmann, Allison and Jim Taaffe, Jeremy Butler, Ken Goodwin, and Beth Bennett have provided support and encouragement when our morales were low and our hearts weak. We appreciate their friendship more than they can know. And we thank our parents, Edsel and Betty Johnson and Thurman and Wanda Copeland, who have given us the will and determination to work hard and to dream.

Introduction

Political campaigns are not in the same league with commercial advertising campaigns. Tony Schwartz told CBS News that "On Election Day, you have the equivalent of a one-day sale with each customer allowed in the store for one or two minutes and you have to sell a majority or plurality of the market or you're out of business" (Dalrymple, 1988, p. 5). Every word, every visual, every event must be carefully strategized and developed for maximum effect. As campaigns have become increasingly media affairs rather than party affairs, it is little wonder that so much attention has been focused on political advertising in the last thirty years.

In *Negative Political Advertising: Coming of Age* (1991a), we identified four strategies that political campaigns have traditionally used in the construction of political advertising: supportive (positive) ads; negative ads; reactive response ads; and proactive inoculation ads. Our use of the term *strategies* is deliberate. Political consultants and politicians make strategic choices as to the persuasive messages used in the construction of political advertising. We endorse Fisher's (1970) view that "A communicator perceives a rhetorical situation in terms of a motive, and that an organic relationship exists between his perception and his response to that circumstance; his perception determines the characteristics of his discourse and his presentation" (p. 132).

In this book, we provide a narrative analysis that examines the *motives* of intent behind the communicated messages in modern American television political campaign advertising. "Motives are names which essentialize the interrelations of communicator, communication, audience(s), time, and place" (Fisher, 1970, p. 132).

Minded behavior exists in all forms of human communication, and analysis of such behavior is central to undertanding the science and art of modern polispots; that is, broadcast political commercials.

Schutz (1962, 1967) distinguishes between "because of" motives and "in order to" motives. *Because of motives* are variables in life that "cause" or "lead" the individual to act in a certain way (that is, persona lity, race, religion, social class, and so forth). However, an awareness of these "causes" alone is not enough to understand people's behavior. A person is more than a set of characteristics; he or she is a minded animal. "People project their actions, plan, and anticipate meaning for those proposed actions" (Combs, 1973, p. 54). Thus, individuals have "in order to motives." *In order to motives* create goal-seeking and goal-achieving behaviors. Accordingly, this research takes the position that political advertising construction is minded behavior; therefore, it should be analyzed as such. Similarly, Fisher (1970) argued that reasoning or the study of reasoning in communication should not be limited to the analysis of argumentative prose.

In this work, we provide the reader with the means necessary to analyze political commercials. Indeed, we provide the motives behind the advertising strategies and tactics used in contemporary politics. Political advertising as a science and as an art is a manipulative business. We hope to provide the keys to unlock the mystery as to how and in what ways millions of voters are manipulated each campaign season. We do not hold an elitist view, for we believe that all voters should be given the opportunity to participate fully in our political system. By providing this advertising analysis, we hope to contribute to the education of the American voter.

POLITICAL ADVERTISING AS POLITICAL SHORT STORIES

In 1991 we maintained that political advertising should be viewed as modern-day political short stories. Through the ages, humans have used the short story form as a means to pass on cultural history, values, and norms. These cultural short stories were passed down for a reason: they socialized individuals in successive generations. We clearly recognized this view when we wrote that

All short stories have a beginning, a middle, and an end. They present, either explicitly or implicitly, age-old conflicts: person versus person, person versus self, person versus fate, and person versus nature. Through conflict resolution, the short story is said to ultimately reveal truth. Indeed, James Joyce called the short story an epiphany because of the revelations that emerged through its thematic conflict resolution. (Johnson-Cartee & Copeland, 1991a, p. 34)

Fisher's later work (1984) built on Alasdair MacIntyre's (1981) belief that "man is in his actions and practice, as well as in his fictions, essentially a story-telling animal" (p. 201). In 1984 Fisher proposed the narrative paradigm that presented a "theory of symbolic actions—words and/or deeds—that have sequence and meaning for those who live, create, or interpret them" (p. 2). Fisher writes:

The idea of human beings as storytellers indicates the generic form of all symbol composition; it holds that symbols are created and communicated ultimately as stories meant to give order to human experience and to induce others to dwell in them to establish ways of living in common, in communities in which there is sanction for the story that constitutes one's life. (p. 6)

Ultimately, the rhetorical composition, whether short story, news story, or political ad, "may be justly characterized as producing a real-fiction. . . . The fiction is not hypothetical; its author wants and intends that it be accepted as the true and right way of conceiving of a matter; and, if he is successful, his fiction becomes one of those by which men live" (Fisher, 1970, p. 132). "Fiction is a generic term that encompasses in whole or in part persona, fantasy theme and rhetorical vision, social reality, political myth, and ideology. This is to say that each of these concepts is a symbolic construction that exerts persuasive force in the making of persons, community, and the nation" (Fisher, 1980, p. 122).

Fisher (1984) also identified the presuppositions underlying the narrative paradigm:

(1) humans are essentially storytellers; (2) the paradigmative mode of human decision-making and communication is "good reasons" which vary in form among communication situations, genres, and media; (3) the production and practice of good reasons is ruled by matters of history, biography, culture, and character along with the kinds of forces identified in the Frentz and Farrell language action paradigm; (4) rationality is determined by the nature of persons as narrative beings—their inherent awareness of narrative probability, what constitutes a coherent story, and their constant habit of testing narrative fidelity, whether the stories they experience ring true with the stories they know to be true in their lives. (pp. 7-8)

Note that Fisher's analysis of the presuppositions underlying the narrative paradigm mentions the work of Frentz and Farrell (1976) who identified symbolic acts as "verbal and/or nonverbal utterances which express intentionality" (p. 340). They maintained that symbolic acts possess propositional, expressive, and consequential force (p. 340). *Propositional force* refers roughly to the semantic meaning of the act; *expressive force* refers to a manner of delivery that contains meaning within it; and *consequential force* is the "effect the act has on another actor" (p. 340). When symbolic acts are placed within the context of an episode that is a "rule-conforming sequence of symbolic acts generated by two or more actors who are collectively oriented toward emergent goals" (p. 336), then they may be said to have *episodic force*. Episodic force specifies "the communicative function of acts within the overall sequential structure of an episode" (p. 340). Meaning, then, rests not within the individual symbolic act but within the episode itself.

In 1985 Fisher explained that the "narrative paradigm goes beyond traditional social scientific theories . . . in that [it establishes] the concept of narrative rationality, which provides principles—probability and fidelity—and [gives] considerations for judging the merits of stories, whether one's own or another's" (p. 349). Fisher also refined his concepts of narrative probability and fidelity:

Narrative probability refers to formal features of a story conceived as a discrete sequence of thought and/or action in life or literature . . ., i.e., it concerns the question of whether or not a story coheres or "hangs together," whether or not the story is free of contradictions. Narrative fidelity concerns the "truth qualities" of the story, the degree to which it accords with the logic of good reasons: the soundness of its reasoning and the value of its values. To test soundness, one may, *when relevant*, employ standards from formal or informal logic. (Fisher, 1985, pp. 349-350)

For Fisher, "narrative rationality . . . is an attempt to recapture Aristotle's concept of *phronesis*, 'practical wisdom'" (1985, p. 350).

Fisher (1984) summarized his ontological approach: "The materials of the narrative paradigm are symbols, signs of consubstantiation, and good reasons, the communicative expressions of social reality" (p. 8). An analysis of political advertising must recognize that the ads contain reasoned, intended, persuasive acts presented in a narrative form that ultimately reveals a theme behind the composition of verbal and nonverbal symbolic acts contained within the ad. The *theme* is the underlying meaning behind the political symbols within the ad. Symbolic acts contained within a given political ad must be analyzed as part of the ad's totality. They should also be analyzed in light of the other political advertising and political communication messages disseminated by the political campaign.

Kirkwood (1983) highlighted a particular form of narration, the *parable*, or teaching story, which "is used primarily to teach, guide, or influence listeners" (p. 6). Indeed, political advertising may be viewed as parables. When one teaches, guides, or influences others, one may be said to be persuading them. Aristotle identified three means of *pisteis* (persuasion):

rational arguments [*logos*]
ethos: the presentation of the character of the speaker
pathos: the playing upon the feelings of the audience.
(Wisse, 1989, p. 5)

Root (1987) argued that Aristotle's means of persuasion may be used to understand strategies of modern-day advertising that Combs and Nimmo (1993, pp. 145-147) used to analyze commercial advertising. Root's strategies can be used on political advertising as well. In Chapter 5, we provide an analysis of the persuasive appeals used in political advertising.

SOCIOLOGY OF RHETORICAL CHOICE

Our approach is grounded in the sociology of rhetorical choice that Simons and Aghazarian proposed in 1986: "The goal of a sociology of rhetorical choice, as we conceive it, is to make sense of the actions of persuaders, as opposed to the reactions of their audiences" (p. 45). The sociology of rhetorical choice, they believe, has great utility:

Being better able to understand rhetorical choices should then place us in a better position to assess past performances and guide subsequent rhetorical efforts. We assume that amid the flux and uncertainty of rhetorical action, there exist levels of stability and predictability—made so by the very nature of rhetoric as a practical, pragmatic enterprise. (p. 45)

The sociology of rhetorical choice is "rules-oriented," for it attempts to make generalizations of the "'as a rule' variety that is intended to cover types of practices, namely, genres rather than specific acts" (Simons & Aghazarian, 1986, p. 46; see also Cushman, 1977; and Shimanoff, 1980). It is important to understand that rules "are expressions of human choice, and can thus be violated" (Simons & Aghazarian, 1986, p. 46).

In *Negative Political Advertising* (1991a), we presented both descriptive and prescriptive rules concerning negative political advertising. Descriptive rules are acquired by examining "evidence linking recurrent patterns of rhetoric to roles and situations, the researcher attempts to make explicit the generally tacit rules by which rhetors operate" (Simons & Aghazarian, 1986, p. 46). Prescriptive rules "are judgments by an observer of what actions are called for in a given situation—called for in the sense of being appropriate or efficacious, but not necessarily wise or just" (Simons &

Aghazarian, 1986, p. 46). Simons and Aghazarian point out that such rule analysis is very useful in the study of campaign politics, and it is in this situation that

Study of roles and recurrent rhetorical situations provides evidence not only of what rhetors are *likely* to say and do, but also of what they probably *ought* to say and do, in ways that are not suggested either by extending the logics of literary theory and criticism or by relying exclusively for rhetorical prescriptions on behavioral studies of message effects. (p. 48, emphasis in the original)

It is important to remember that political campaign prescriptions are "time-bound and culture-bound" and should always be reevaluated before being used as guidelines in the construction of political messages. In addition, researchers should not claim that because an approach has worked in the past for a particular situation, it should automatically be used. The sociologist of rhetorical choice would be aware of alternative ways of accomplishing goals and would know that political consultants may place their own "signatures" on a given ad strategy. In other words, political consultants must be constantly on the alert for transformations of the rules. On the other hand, it is safe to say that political consultants choose from a repertoire of relatively stable political advertising strategies and tactics implying

that the standard forms are learned, limited in number and scope, slowly changing and peculiarly adapted to their settings. . . . [The execution of the choices, i.e., the performances are not] necessarily frozen, regimented and stereotypical. . . . Nevertheless, a limited repertoire sets serious constraints on when, where and how effectively a group of actors can act. (Tilly, 1979, p. 26, as quoted in Simons & Aghazarian, 1986, p. 56).

In our analysis of the sociology of rhetorical choice associated with political advertising, the strategies used by political consultants are the supportive ad (positive), the negative ad, the reactive response ad, and the proactive inoculation ad. We recognize that other researchers have presented various other typologies (cf. Biocca, 1991; Burke, 1969; Devlin, 1986, 1987; Diamond & Bates, 1988; Gronbeck, 1985, 1992; Johnston, 1991; Kern, 1989; Payne & Baukus, 1988; Smith & Johnston, 1991; Tinkham & Lariscy, 1991, 1993).

FOUR STRATEGIES OF POLITICAL ADVERTISING

The four political advertising strategies and their substrategies operationalized in *Negative Political Advertising* (p. 211) are:

I.   *supportive [positive] ads* designed to position the candidate on the issues
     and increase the perceived ideal personal leadership qualities of the
     candidate,
     A. identification spots,
         1. name recognition spots,
         2. biographical spots,
         3. campaign films,
     B. mythical character spots,
         1. everyman spots,
         2. heroic spots,
     C. issue spots,
II. *negative ads* designed to question the opponent's suitability for office,
     A. direct attack spots,
     B. direct comparison spots,
     C. implied comparison spots,
III *reactive response ads* that serve as a reply to the opposition's negative ads,
     A. proactive inoculation spots
     B. Reactive spots
         1. silence,
         2. confession/redemption,
         3. sanctimonious admission
         4. denial/campaign attack,
         5. counterattack
         6. refutation
         7. obsfucation,
         8. counterimaging,
IV. *proactive inoculation ads* that are used to undermine, deflect, and reduce the
     power of anticipated negative attacks.

Positive and negative ads form the central thrust of campaign
strategy, for they provide the reasons why the voters should vote for
a particular candidate and against another. Reactive and inoculation
ads are used as necessary to combat candidate liabilities.

1

Positive Political Advertising

Political advertising, whether in the form of handbills, pamphlets, badges, buttons, bandannas, banners, posters, street signs, radio spots, newspaper ads, or television ads, is as old as the American republic (Hart, 1956; Jamieson, 1984, 1986; Rosenberg & Rosenberg, 1962; Washburn, 1963, 1972). The need to "spread the word" about candidates and parties was as keen in 1797 as it is 200 years later. Until recently, the majority of political advertising produced was positive. Positive ads are designed to position the candidate on the issues and to increase the perceived ideal personal leadership qualities of the candidate. It was not until the early 1980s, when national consultants began to experiment with negative political advertising, that we began to see a decline in the use of positive ads. Although negative political advertising is a significant part of our political campaign history, the campaign typified by a dominantly negative approach is a relatively recent phenomenon (see Johnson-Cartee & Copeland, 1991).

GOALS OF POSITIVE ADVERTISING

The current reliance on negative political advertising has not eliminated the use of or need for positive political advertising. Today, approximately 30 to 40 percent of most national campaigns can still be characterized as positive. In many local electoral races, the dominant strategy still remains positive political advertising (see Johnson-Cartee & Copeland, 1991a). Positive polispots continue to be used for six primary reasons:

1. To improve the candidate's name recognition.
2. To develop or improve the candidate's association with positive leadership characteristics.
3. To demonstrate similarity (homophily) with the voters.
4. To develop the heroic image of the candidate.
5. To develop or improve the candidate's association with issues positively evaluated by the voters.
6. To link the candidate with positive figures or groups.

Many political consultants, however, do not have a favorable view of positive polispots. While consultants recognize the effectiveness of positive polispots in reaching these six goals, they often remind candidates that positive spots are simply not persuasive. In a world where the majority of voters are independents, the central focus for most consultants and their clients must be on creating ads that can persuade. Yet, the concept of positive political ads has remained popular with the nation's voters. Voters often recall positive spots, because these spots make them feel good or give them a warm feeling (Katz, 1988).

POSITIVE ADVERTISING MODES

We have identified three varieties of positive polispots: identification, mythical character, and political issue spots as detailed in Figure 1.1. These forms of positive political advertising are not mutually exclusive. Rather, political consultants often choose to utilize one or more of these forms in crafting their messages.

Figure 1.1
Modes of Positive Political Advertising

| Identification Spots |
| Name recognition |
| Biographical |
| Campaign Film |
| Mythical Character Spots |
| Everyman |
| Heroic |
| Issue Spots |

Identification Spots

Early during a primary or caucus race, candidates work to define themselves in terms of who they are and what they believe. Such ads have traditionally been called identification (ID) spots (Diamond & Bates, 1988; Payne, Marlier, and Baukus, 1989). Because candidates often have regionalized or localized constituency bases, they may be relatively "unknowns" within the political arena they have entered. For this reason, often the campaign's first media goal is to develop name recognition for a candidate who needs to expand his or her constituency base. This has been done in a variety of ways. We have identified three variations of the ID spot: name recognition spots; biographical ads; and campaign films.

The most fundamental form of identification spots is the *name recognition spot*. The common denominator of all name recognition spots is that the sponsoring candidate's name is repeated over and over again. Repetition invites memory. Name recognition spots are used almost exclusively by challengers who usually have low name recognition or by incumbents in low-level, low-visibility races where the successful politician must remind voters of the candidate's name and incumbency status.

Name recognition spots may make a game of the candidate's name by repeating the candidate's name over and over, or they may misuse and abuse the candidate's name. When Ed Mezvinsky ran for Congress in Pennsylvania, his campaign ran an ad with voters trying to say his name. The spot ended with the statement: "People aren't sure how to say Ed Mezvinsky's name, but we are sure of what Ed Mezvinsky will stand for in Congress" (Rossen, 1984, p. 11). In the 1960 presidential campaign, John F. Kennedy used a jingle to highlight his name.

The 1960 Kennedy "Kennedy, Kennedy" Ad

Video	Audio
Close up of Kennedy. Leadership for the 60s poster. Black and white animated ad. Kennedy posters, Kennedy signs.	Singers (chorus) [VO]: "Kennedy, Kennedy, Kennedy, Kennedy, Kennedy, Kennedy, Kennedy, Ken-Ken Kennedy for me, Kennedy, Kennedy, Kennedy, Kennedy. Do you want a man for president who is seasoned
Vote Democratic sign. Vote for President Kennedy sign.	through and through. But not so doggone seasoned that he won't try something new.
Slide: A time for greatness. Slide: Vote Democratic. Poster: Kennedy for President. Poster: Leadership for 60s. Photograph of Eleanor Roosevelt and another of Kennedy. Photograph of Harry Truman. Kennedy for President poster.	A man who is old enough to know and young enough to do. Well, it's up to you, it's up to you, it's strictly up to you. Do you like a man who answers straight? A man who is always there. Well measure him against the others, and when you compare,

Elderly people, Black people,	you'll cast your vote for Kennedy,
Mixed White group	change that's overdue. So it's up
	to you, it's up to you, it's strictly
Campaign buttons appear with	up to you. Kennedy, Kennedy,
each Kennedy with a big one at	Kennedy, Kennedy, Kennedy,
the center of screen, the buttons	Kennedy, Kennedy for me.
make an X like the X made on	Kennedy, Kennedy, Kennedy,
a ballot. Portrait of Kennedy	Kennedy, Kennedy, Kennedy,
family.	Kennedy, Kennedy, Kennedy!"

Song spots were very popular during the 1956 and 1960 presidential campaigns. The most famous is the "We Like Ike" song written by Irving Berlin for Dwight Eisenhower's presidential campaign. Song spots were used into the 1970s. During the 1992 campaign, song spots were used extensively against incumbent congressmen who had been involved in the House Banking scandal.

Another form of identification spot is the biographical ad. *Biographical ads* (bio-ads) are short histories of a candidate's life. Sam Donaldson has called such ads *resume spots* (Kaplan, 1987). According to Gronbeck (1989), the majority of ads that appear during the caucus and primary periods are biographical ads. Gronbeck maintains that bio-ads often foreshadow the political strategies that will be used in the general election campaign. As he states, "we can learn much about the character traits and ideological positions candidates hope to project; bio-ads are the self-portraits that candidates hope will hang in the minds of the voters" (Gronbeck, 1989, p. 360). Bio-ads are particularly important for candidates with low name recognition and for those who need to reframe their public image. According to Gronbeck (1989):

The central engine for bio-ads, . . . is mythic portraiture that can heighten and empower these advertisements. More specifically, mythic structures can organize material drawn from a candidate's life in ways that create a larger-than-life portrait. That portrait associated desirable qualities and an ideological orientation with the candidate; those qualities include character traits and impressions of both viability and electability. (p. 351)

Gronbeck (1989) points out that the most successful bio-ads are those in which a homology exists "between candidates' portraits and voters' self-perceptions" (p. 362). In other words, the ads are much more likely to be successful when bio-ads highlight those components of American life, whether real or mythical, that voters have stored within their mental images of the world (see Brummett, 1988; Fisher, 1970; Schwartz, 1972, 1976).

In 1992 the Clinton presidential campaign aired several biographical ads. These ads related a tale of a fatherless, poor boy from Hope, Arkansas who, through "work, faith, and a good education," was standing at the door of the presidency, knocking to get into the Oval Office. A reading of Clinton's biography is akin to viewing an old 1940s propaganda film. The mythical components of his life appear almost larger than life; in effect, it is a life more appropriate to the movie screen than to a political candidate's simple biography. Interestingly enough, the ad even called the voter's attention to the mythical elements in Clinton's life and described his life story as being "as old as the American Dream." The ad concludes by revealing Clinton's mission or heroic quest.

The 1992 Clinton "Family" Ad

Video	Audio
Black and white footage of old photographs of Hope, Arkansas.	Announcer: "It's a story as old as the American Dream. And it begins in a small town called Hope.
Photographs of parents and grandparents.	His father died just before he was born. And his mother and her family struggled to give him better
Photo of Clinton as a child.	opportunities. To teach him that with hard work, faith,
Clinton meeting President Kennedy as a Boy's State Representative.	and a good education— anything was possible. Bill Clinton—he worked his way
Photo of young Clinton studying.	through Georgetown, a Rhodes Scholarship, Yale Law School.
Clinton being sworn in as governor of Arkansas.	Then went home to Arkansas not to chase dollars but to try
Clinton at table talking with voters.	to make a difference for others.
Clinton with children.	Education reform, job creation,
Clinton with workers.	changing people's lives for the better.
Clinton talking with a family.	That's the work of his life.
Clinton kissed by an elderly lady.	That's why he's running for president."

The ad is a classic American parable. The fatherless boy, the town called Hope, the struggling mother, the noble grandparents, the strong foundation in the American work ethic, the abiding religious faith, the dedication to education, his exalted achievements at the finest institutions, the almost religious rejection of material goods, his political successes are all stereotypical components of the American Dream. Furthermore, Clinton's stated mission is a reiteration of the Christian love ethic.

Another form of identification ads is the *campaign film*. In 1934 campaign films were first aired in California theaters during a gubernatorial election. This practice became widespread and climaxed with the 1948 presidential election (Jamieson, 1984). Although campaign films are still used today, they are usually presented at national political conventions where the party hopes the television networks will broadcast them to people's homes. Political campaign films resemble an "image mosaic," which Nichols (1981) defines as:

The whole is organized not as a narrative but poetically, as a mosaic. Only the parts have a diegetic unity. Between sequences editing seldom establishes chronological relationship; sequences follow each other consecutively but without a clearly marked temporal relationship. The whole thus tends toward poetry (metaphor, synchronicity, paradigmatic relations)—an all at once slice through an institutional matrix re-presented in time—rather than narrative. (Morreale, 1991b, p. 211)

According to Morreale (1991b), "the political campaign film is organized more by the oral logic of epideictic televisual communication than by the linear, formal logic of deliberation more characteristic of print media" (p. 193). The campaign film "implicitly argues that it represents social reality, and, in this way, it implies a course for future action. It does so by creating a favorable psychological image, by fostering an impression of attitude and not by persuading with logical arguments, information, or 'facts'" (p. 193) Morreale (1991a) identifies a number of prominent American mythologies that have played significant roles in the development of recent political campaign films: the Rebirth Ritual, the American Dream (materialism and moralism), the Western or Frontier myth, and the Myth of the Presidency (see Chapter 4 for an analysis of these and other American political mythologies).

Mythical Character Spots

Political consultants frequently make use of the cultural myths from American society. Voters may not be consciously aware of these myths, but they understand sufficiently to interpret them through stored political images that recognize the patterns and themes associated with significant political mythology.

While political consultants like to define or reframe their candidates in terms of heroic myths, consultants are well aware that there are basic contradictions within the political psychologies of the majority of Americans. A natural tension exists within American politics: Americans like for their candidates to be similar to themselves; yet, they also want their candidates to excel in some particular area of character that they themselves do not. This tension, which we call the Everyman/Heroic conflict, is one of the many paradoxes of political leadership in the United States. For this reason, American political advertising uses both everyman and heroic ads.

The term *everyman ad* is an allusion to the medieval play, *Everyman* which chronicled the pilgrimage of man toward death. In the play, Everyman was surrounded by friends very much like himself who exhibited the range of human frailties. Goodman (1961) maintained that the play's enduring popularity rests in its realistic representation of familiar life experiences and human behaviors. Because of this realistic portrayal, the viewer readily identifies not only with "everyman" but also with the host of friends and acquaintances in the play (e.g., 1992 Wilson "Square Dance" Ad). Goodman wrote:

By creating characters whose reasoning is psychologically sound and whose behavior is recognizably realistic, the author manages to engage the interest and sympathy of his audiences. Everyman, for instance, lonely and terrified in the face of death, is thoroughly understandable and moving; while the figures who surround him and display various human weaknesses, also evoke pathos and pity. Such characters are not arid personifications but possess genuine and fundamental attributes common to all of us. (1961, pp. 63-64)

During the 1988 presidential caucus and primary season, General Alexander Haig ran an Everyman spot that bordered on the bizarre. Haig had a real identity problem among even Republican voters. His aloofness and imperial manner made voters question the authenticity of the man portrayed in his many leadership appeals. Haig's unforgettable gaffe while he was secretary of state during the Reagan assassination attempt, where he declared to the nation that he "was in control," had left many voters a little fearful about the man behind the "uniform." Haig sought to repair his credibility factor with an Everyman spot.

The 1988 Haig "Alexander Haig Eats Pizza, Too" Ad

Video	Audio
Camera up on Haig shaking hands with clerk in pizza parlor.	(Music under Audio.)
Cut to Haig taking a slice of pizza and eating it. Pulls	Announcer [VO]: "Former Secretary of State

cheese with teeth. Clerk laughs. Haig passes pizza to aide.	Alexander M. Haig, the man with the best credentials of anyone to be president is also a lot more like you than you think.
Haig looks at camera and winks.	Vote for him."

(*Source*: Payne, Marlier, & Baukus, 1989, p. 377)

During the 1986 Senate Campaign in South Dakota, Incumbent Jim Abdnor made sure that his constituents realized that he took a South Dakota approach—a no-nonsense, common-sense approach—to real problems. In addition, he highlighted his unpolished, everyman image through light self-deprecatory humor. In the following ad, notice that Abdnor admits that he is not a flashy speaker and that he can't dance very well. Roering and Paul (1976) found that the ad sponsor's disclaimer of superiority on some attribute(s), significantly increased the believability of what the sponsor claimed as superior (see also Smith & Hunt, 1978).

The 1986 Jim Abdnor "Bio" Ad

Video	Audio
Jim Abdnor walking through a farm field.	Narrator [VO]: "Jim Abdnor, he's South Dakota, through and through. From humble beginnings, he worked his way up to become our U.S. senator.
Jim Abdnor sitting on front stoop of porch, wearing checked farm shirt.	Jim Abdnor [SOT]: "Once I realized that I didn't have the talent to make it as a major league baseball player, the only thing I ever dreamed about as a kid was to some day serve my state and my country. Now, I know that may sound corny, but it's true.
Abdnor addressing a rally. Talking with people in crowd.	Narrator [VO]: "Jim Abdnor today is known for his effectiveness, his honesty and for putting South Dakota first."

Abdnor back on porch.	Abdnor [SOT]: "God didn't make me a flashy speaker. That's for sure. But we got a lot of flashy speakers in Congress, and if speeches solved problems, we wouldn't have any problems."
Abdnor in working clothes talking with workers, with children, with children's baseball team. Abdnor walking down Capitol steps talking with people. Scene of congressional hearing.	Narrator [VO]: "A lifetime of service because South Dakota is like his family. In Washington, they like Jim Abdnor and they trust him."
Abdnor back on porch.	Abdnor [SOT]: "So, I'm not a great speaker. Heck, I'm not a great dancer either. But I'm a great fighter for South Dakota."
Abdnor at rally shaking hands.	Narrator [VO]: "Jim Abdnor, he's more than a senator. He's a South Dakota institution of integrity."
Abdnor back on porch.	Abdnor [SOT]: "Come to think of it, I'm not such a bad dancer."

The other type of mythical character spot is the heroic ad. According to Combs (1980), "every culture appears to have certain qualities in their leaders, and has an ideal conception of achievement in public roles." For example, the early Greeks "conceived a hero as a person who pursued honor through chosen actions. This was usually a superior individual who understood tasks and risks, standing up for principles or against forces that most people would not" (p. 92). In the United States, political heroes personify the word "ambition." To work hard, to succeed, is the evidence of heroic virtues—the evidence of American nobility.

Political leaders have ambitions, careers, and a conception of ideal role perfor-
mance; they take initiatives, seek dramatic encounters, try to accomplish things.
Their actions make a difference; they believe that they control events, and that
their power stems from the force of their personality rather than their official
position. (p. 93)

Warner (1976) emphasizes that the American heroic myths are closely linked with American materialism: "The myth of ultimate success and the creation of the symbolic role of the successful man who rises from lowly beginnings to greatness and final heights is a necessary part of the apparatus of our social and status system" (p. 207). Frequently, these heroic ads may also be biographical ads in that they show the evolution of the political leader's fortunes over the leader's life time.

In 1990 Ronnie Flippo, a Democratic congressman from Alabama's Fifth Congressional District, made an unsuccessful gubernatorial bid during the Democratic primary. After fourteen years in the House of Representatives, Flippo had accumulated a sizable campaign war chest, and his moderate views made him a popular contender for the traditionally Democratically held governorship. Even so, during the primary, he had to get by some equally well-financed Democrats such as the head of the state's powerful teacher's union, Dr. Paul Hubbert, and the state attorney general, Don Sigelman. Flippo hired Struble and Totten Communications, a well-known Washington, D.C.-based media consulting firm which produced a series of advertisements portraying Flippo's life and rise to promise as the embodiment of the American Dream. They gave particular attention to his hard work and ambitious character. These early bio-ads resulted in a 6 percent increase in statewide polls (Whillock, 1991).

The 1990 Flippo "Bio" Ad

Video	Audio
Flippo is standing before a rustic brick wall in a home, and he is holding a photo of his mother.	Flippo [SOT]: "The worst thing you could say to Momma was one of her kids was lazy."
Black and white photo of Flippo as a young boy.	Narrator [VO]: "An ironworker's son, Ronnie Flippo's father died when Ronnie was only seven."
Flippo, talking head.	Flippo [SOT]: "My mother had eight kids to take care of so we all had to pitch in."
Black and white footage of boys working to get the fires ready in old-fashioned pot-bellied stoves. Footage of boy sweeping church.	Flippo [VO]: "My brother Harold and I would get up and go build the fires at Wheaton's school. Then we'd go to Arnold's grocery to stock shelves. But sweeping out the church was the best job."
Black and white graduation	Narrator [SOT]: "After high

photograph.	school, Ronnie became an iron
Black and white marriage photo.	worker. He and Fae started a
Photo of iron construction.	family. Critically injured on the
Photograph of Florence State	job, Ronnie fights back. Studies
College diploma.	accounting and graduates, top in
	his class. A successful small
Photograph of Flippo working in	businessman; Ronnie first serves
a suit, at the Legislature.	in the State Legislature."
Footage of him working in	"And today is recognized as one of
Congress, talking with an elderly	America's most effective
woman, working with small	congressmen. Ronnie Flippo:
children.	Pride in the past. Vision for the
	future."
Ronnie Flippo talking.	Flippo [SOT]: "A new day is
	dawning in Alabama."
Alabama flag.	Flippo [VO]: "A day when
	Alabama"
Flippo talking at rally.	Flippo [SOT]: "Steps into the
	sunshine of the 21st century."
Super: "Flippo for Governor."	Narrator [SOT]: "Ronnie Flippo,
	Alabama's next great governor."

The success of the early Flippo bio-ads was not repeated by the remainder of the campaign's advertising. Whillock's (1991) book chapter "Death at the Hands of Consultants" (pp. 55-73) carefully documented the disintegration of the Flippo campaign . In a state marked by its acceptance of negative political advertising (Copeland & Johnson-Cartee, 1990; Johnson-Cartee & Copeland, 1989a, 1989b; Johnson-Cartee, Elebash, & Copeland, 1992; Johnson-Cartee, Copeland, & Elebash, 1992), Struble and Totten had designed a positive media campaign (Whillock, 1991). The Flippo campaign went down in obscurity.

Some heroic ads demonstrate that the political leader has uncommon personality traits, that is, he or she possesses a superlative amount of some desirable trait. Shyles (1988), in his study of candidate imagery (personality characteristics), used a Delphi panel to examine personal characteristics. He found that the personal characteristics most often used in the 1984 presidential primary campaign were altruism, competence, experience, honesty, leadership, personality and strength. Twenty-eight percent of all personality characteristic mentioned belonged to the experience category. The competence category received 24 percent and the honesty category 15 percent.

Patriotism and courage are two very popular emotional appeals used in heroic character ads. In the 1986 U.S. Senate race in Alabama, Jeremiah Denton, an incumbent Republican, made use of his nearly eight years of captivity in a Vietnamese prison during the Viet Nam War.

The 1986 Denton "Hero" Ad

Video	Audio
Black and white photo of Denton as a POW.	Narrator [VO]: "It seems so long ago and so far away, but Jeremiah Denton's tortuous experiences as a prisoner of war have proven to be an example of courage and leadership that none of us should soon forget. Even in captivity, Jeremiah Denton has shown himself to be an authentic American hero. Daring to communicate to the outside world by blinking his eyes in Morse code. Incredible as it may seem after being shot down and then spending seven and one-half years in a Vietnamese prison, Jeremiah Denton was still thinking of others first. Stating simply upon his return: 'We are honored to have had the opportunity to serve our country under difficult circumstances.' Patriotism, duty to be sure. And now as a U.S. senator from Alabama, he continues to demonstrate that he is a man of untiring energy and uncompromising dedication to traditional American values. Alabama's own Jeremiah Denton. More than just a senator."
Super: Jeremiah Denton Footage of POWs marching through Vietnamese streets with guns pointed at them. Close-up of rifle. Footage of Denton being interrogated by Vietnamese.	
Denton blinking his eyes in Morse Code. Plane flying low over jungle of Southeast Asia, smoke behind it, falling down. Denton walking down plane's steps, greeting military officers on the POW's return, saluting officers, smiling	
Denton salutes. Photo of Capitol.	
Photo of Denton. "More than just a Senator." White on blue.	

In a 1994 Pittsburgh, Pennsylvania mayoral race, Jack Wagner ran an heroic ad that highlighted his military record in Viet Nam. The ad is unusual in that it shows Wagner speaking at a Veteran's banquet where his emotions clearly show through.

The 1994 Wagner "Courage" Ad

Video	Audio
White print on black background, "April 29, 1993." Wagner talking at a banquet at a lectern. Super: "Pittsburgh Veteran of the Year."	Wagner [SOT]: "I'm accepting this award on behalf of marines from Hotel Company, 2nd Battalion, 9th Marines that died on May 19th, 1967. You see, I was in a squad in Viet Nam with 12 marines. And on that day seven died, three of us were wounded, and two were not wounded, but I'm sure carried with them mental scars for the rest of their lives.
"The courage to fight for his country" "The courage to lead Pittsburgh" "Jack Wagner Mayor."	To say the least, I was extremely lucky, or I would not be here tonight."

In the 1992 U.S. Senate race in Colorado, Ben Nighthorse Campbell ran an heroic ad that highlighted his Native American heritage and his poor background. Again, the hero stands out, because he possesses an uncommon commodity—"his dreams and his courage." Facing overwhelming odds, the leader struggles to make it to the top. Once at the top, he tries to help those who are less fortunate than he. And his quest is to heal. His life stands as a testament to the health and vigor of the American dream is still alive.

The 1992 Campbell "American Dream" Ad

Video	Audio
White letters on black: "Imagine this." Photo of Campbell as a little boy in a sailor suit. Black and white photo as a boy, smiling. Close-up of photo.	Announcer [VO]: "Imagine this: a young Native American, his mother a victim of tuberculosis, his father of chronic alcoholism. Early on the young boy learns first hand what happens when people are divided from one another. His sister and he are placed in separate orphanages. The odds are against them, but the odds themselves could not

Photo of Campbell in Korea. Photo of Campbell as athlete at Olympic games with a medal around his neck.	rob the young boy of his most valuable possessions: his dreams and his courage. At 17, he dons his country's uniform in the Korean War. In 1964, he again wears the uniform of his country. As a member of the United States Olympic team, his fellow athletes chose the young Native American to carry the flag in the closing ceremony. His name: Ben Nighthorse Campbell.
Super: "Ben Nighthorse Campbell" Campbell in cowboy attire saddles horse and rides.	Throughout his life he has known how important real jobs are. A lesson he learned early loading and hauling crates of tomatoes and pears from the fields to the markets. He taught high school during the day and rode in the back of an ambulance as a
Dusk scene. Ambulance workers. Super: "Pro-Choice"	young deputy at night. His strong pro-choice stand comes from seeing a young woman in that ambulance one night, the victim of a back alley abortion. And as a man who saw his own family broken by poverty and illness,
Black and white photo of Campbell as young boy; Close-up of face, Super: "Pro-Health Care."	Ben Nighthorse Campbell's commitment to affordable, quality health care for all Americans is real. And as a chief of the
Campbell in Native American dress on horseback.	Northern Cheyenne, his respect for the earth, the land, and the water is also real. As a husband
Black and white photo of family.	and father, as a lawmaker who has made a difference in people's
Black and white photo of Campbell talking with elderly. Color photos of Campbell with children, with young people.	lives. Ben Nighthorse Campbell knows you cannot lead unless you can heal. He has put the real lessons of an extraordinary life to work. To heal, to lead, and to bring us together. And while the politics of the past have sought to divide us. Ben Nighthorse
Black with white lettering: "Real life. Real work. Real leadership." Campbell on horse riding. Super:	Campbell has united us. Real life. Real work. Real leadership. Ben Nighthorse Campbell for Colorado's U.S. senator. The time

| "Ben Nighthorse Campbell for U.S. | is now." |
| Senate." | |

Postive Issue Spots

Argument ads, or what we term positive issue spots, link a given candidate with certain issues or political themes that are salient with the voters (see Diamond & Bates, 1988 and Payne, Marlier, & Baukus 1989). In other words, these ads attempt to tell the voters "what the candidate stands for" so that in time those issues become personified by the candidacy of the sponsor. Because different groups of voters have different salient issues, positive issue spots often target specific groups of voters. For example, an ad demonstrating a candidate's support for social security will be directed at the elderly population. It is important to remember, however, that these ads are not argumentative; they merely establish the political issues associated with a given candidate before the argumentation period of negative political advertising begins, if it begins. They are rarely specific as to what action should be taken. Joslyn (1986) and Kern (1989) have demonstrated that in most American political advertising, candidates make no concrete proposals; rather they are "against crime" or "for better education."

In Tennessee's U.S. Senate race in 1994, Fred Thompson ran a campaign based on "common-sense ideas." The following ad illustrates the approach taken by the campaign, but please note that although the ad highlights governing principles or issues, it does not provide any solutions (Johnson-Cartee & Copeland, 1991a). This is an example of what Joslyn (1986) has called "bogus policy appeals."

The 1994 Thompson "Common Sense" Ad

Video	Audio
Thompson in work shirt walks on to a porch in the country. Super: "Fred Thompson U.S. Senate."	Thompson [SOT]: "To get elected today, a politician will say just about anything. And then they get to Washington, and we find out what they really believe. I'm Fred Thompson, and I want to tell you what I believe right now. I believe you can't spend more than you got comin' [sic] in. And we can't tax ourselves into prosperity. I believe you can't pay people more not to work than

	to work. And criminals can't hurt anybody, if they're behind bars. Common sense? Maybe. But it sure isn't common in Washington right now."

In 1990 the former mayor of Charlotte, North Carolina, Democrat Harvey Gantt, ran against long-time incumbent Republican Jesse Helms in the U.S. Senate race. During the 1990 campaign, the central issue across the country was education, and so Gantt tried to pitch himself as the education candidate. Notice that Gantt basically says that he supports education. Once again the ad fails to offer a solution to the nation's educational problems, nor does Gantt promise to do anything specific if elected.

The 1990 Gantt "From the Heart" Ad

Video	Audio
White letters on black. The words scroll as the announcer reads.	Announcer [VO]: "North Carolina's SAT scores are about the worst in the nation."
Harvey Gantt talking.	Gantt [SOT]: "There are over a million children in North Carolina schools; what kind of future will they have, if we don't get to work right now?"
Footage of Gantt talking.	Announcer [VO]: "He's talking with children about what's important to North Carolina. Talking from the heart."
Harvey Gantt talking.	Gantt [SOT]: "I didn't start out with much in the world. But getting an education, for me that was the key. That was really the key to opportunity."
Gantt with kids.	Announcer [VO]: "He knows first hand that a good education is how you build a future."
Gantt talking.	Gantt [SOT]: "Few things have mattered more in my life than education. And nothing is going

	to matter more to me than education in the United States Senate."
Still of Harvey Gantt. Super: "Harvey Gantt U.S. Senate."	Announcer [VO]: "Harvey Gantt for Senate."

2

Negative Political Advertising

Negative political advertising as a field of study, as a modern campaign tactic, and as a popularized social ill is one of the most widely misunderstood concepts in the political communication arena. The controversy surrounding the use of negative political advertising is based on a set of arguments, some explicit and some implicit, that negative political advertising has an effect that is different and more harmful on the body politic than positive political advertising. These arguments may be due to the pejorative tone of the phrase "negative political advertising." There must be something bad about it since the very name includes the word "negative." And if there is something bad about negative political advertising, it must be doing something bad to the individual, to political institutions, and to society.

Indeed, negative political advertising has become synonymous with the term *mudslinging*. Stewart (1975) reported that when survey respondents were asked to define mudslinging tactics, the most popular responses were: "twists, distorts, or misleads in his charges against his opponent; attacks the personal life, or character of his opponent; presents irrelevant facts and charges against his opponent or for his own ideas." According to Stewart, the voters saw "mudslinging as a candidate bent on destroying his opponent with every means at his disposal, regardless of ethical considerations or simple honesty" (p. 281).

Journalists/political analysts, product advertisers, and even some political campaign consultants themselves have helped link negative political advertising and mudslinging in the public mind. The journalistic mindset necessitates that reporters and analysts perceive "negative advertising" as conflictual and therefore newsworthy. In this mindset, all conflict is newsworthy because it upsets the status quo. Conflict then is abnormal, and in its abnormality rests its news value. Journalists are predisposed to treat societal abnormalities as destructive, and they in turn pass on this evaluation to negative political advertising. In addition, journalism educators train journalists to view themselves as the watchdogs of the political process. As the so-called Fourth Estate, the idea that an advertising campaign might determine the outcome of an election flies in the face of the journalists' view of a reasoned democratic process where the most "qualified candidate" wins (see Johnson-Cartee & Copeland, 1991b).

Similarly, product advertisers rail against their political advertising brethren because they resent the freedom of expression that political advertisers enjoy. Indeed, product advertisers fail to see the constitutional differences between commercial speech, which can be regulated, and political speech, which is generally unfettered.

Political consultants are often squeamish about admitting to creating negative political advertising. Alternating their public pronouncements, political consultants falsely deny their use of negative advertising, creatively rename negative ads in value-positive language (which reporters and voters see through), and insipidly offer apologies for their use of negative political advertising. The end result is that some political consultants have fostered the notion that negative political advertising is in fact unethical. (For a detailed analysis of the public controversy surrounding negative political advertising, see Johnson-Cartee & Copeland, 1991a, 1991b.)

Negative political advertising, an umbrella term that encompasses a number of campaign advertising strategies and tactics, can be ethical or unethical, true or false. Negative political ads should be judged individually, succeeding or failing on their own strengths or weaknesses.

OPERATIONALIZATION

Negative political advertising is political advertising that implicitly or explicitly places the opposition in an inferior position. Negative political advertising is a manifestation of a political ad hominem argument, an argument that calls into question a given candidate's fitness for office—that is, his or her leadership ability. As research has shown, fitness for office is the crucial voter test when making the voting decision. Ad hominem arguments may be either true or false. Those that are truthful should be considered legitimate forms of argumentation, and those that are false should be considered specious forms of argumentation (see Cragan & Cutbirth, 1984, p. 230). In this use then, legitimate forms of argumentation conform to the recognized principles, standards, rules, and values of society. Thus, legitimate forms are ethical forms of ad hominem arguments.

Cragan and Cutbirth (1984) suggested a three-part criteria for evaluating the legitimacy of political ad hominem arguments, which in turn can be used to assess the legitimacy of negative political ads. The argument, they said, should be "(1) logically relevant; (2) factually supportable; and (3) artistically structured" (p. 230). If the argument is not relevant to the given political situation, then the argument is useless. The argument must be valid not in the eyes of the candidate or political consultant but in the eyes of the voters. The argument must be factually supportable in that the news media and the opposition is likely to take the sponsor to task for misleading the public. In such a case, the sponsor making the argument calls into question his or her own fitness for public office. And finally, the argument must be artistically structured or dramatized; accordingly, appropriate political symbols must be used to reach the desired target audiences.

Since the early 1980s, negative advertising has become the dominant strategy for most campaigns for high-visibility offices in the United States. Although challengers are more likely to use negative advertising because strong negative ads can make up for smaller campaign war chests, incumbents also make wide use of negative ads. In order to better understand the consultant's fascination with negative advertising, it is necessary to review the negative information literature. According to Kellermann (1984), the negativity effect is as follows: "the tendency for negative information to be weighted more heavily than positive information when forming evaluations of social stimuli. Across widely varying events, setting, and persons, positive experiences or positive aspects of stimuli have been found to be less influential in the formation of judgments than are negative experiences or negative aspects of stimuli" (p. 37; see also Anderson, 1965; Hamilton & Huffman, 1971; Hamilton & Zanna, 1972; Hodges, 1974; Jordan, 1965; Levin & Schmidt, 1969; Miller & Rowe, 1967; Warr & Jackson, 1976; Wyer, 1970). Negative information is so powerful that Richey, Koenigs, Richey, and Fortin (1975) found that one negative behavior could effectively neutralize five positive behaviors. Kellermann (1984) has suggested that negative information "exhibits a greater capacity to alter already existing impressions" (p. 38; see also, Briscoe, Woodyard, & Shaw, 1967; Cusumano & Richey, 1970, Freedman & Steinbruner, 1964; Gray-Little, 1973; Kanouse & Hanson, 1972; Leventhal & Singer, 1964; Mayo & Crockett, 1964) and that negative information is retained far longer than positive information (Winnick and Archer, 1974). The influence of negative information is strong because it is easier to retrieve than positive information during information processing (Feldman, 1966;

Reeves, Thorson, & Schleuder, 1986;   Richey, Koenigs, Richey, &
Fortin, 1975), and it is retained in long-term memory (Richey, Koenigs,
Richey, & Fortin, 1975). Richey, McClelland, and Shimkunas (1967)
found that negative first impressions are much more difficult to
change than positive first impressions.

     This negativity effect is very pronounced for presidential candi-
dates. Negative information obtained about presidential candidates
is weighted more heavily than positive information (Lau, 1980).
Kernell (1977) and Lau (1982) have provided additional
documentation of the presence of the negativity effect in political
behavior.

Having positive facts associated with one's name is not as important as not having negative facts associated with one's name. On the face of it, these results
could be interpreted to suggest that candidates might profitably spend more time
in their campaigns stressing their opponent's shortcomings than their own
strengths. (Lau, 1982, p. 373)

In the language of the political consultant, campaigns should spend
considerable time driving up their opposition's negatives.

     Lau's (1985) evidence suggests that the "dynamics of political
evaluation may be fundamentally different for different types of
political figures (e.g., presidents versus congresspersons)" (p, 119). He
identified two types of negativity effects in political behavior. The
first, the *figure ground hypothesis,* finds that negativity is "based on
the greater salience of negative information in a largely positive
world" (p. 119). In other words. "If the background or context against
which specific information about people is evaluated is more often
positive than negative, then negative stimuli will more often seem
extreme due to judgmental contrast than will positive stimuli" (p. 121).
The second,*cost orientation hypothesis,* finds negativity is "based on
the survival value of avoiding costs rather than approaching gains"
(p. 119). According to Lau, people are "more strongly motivated to
avoid costs than to approach gain. . . . The more one can win or lose,
the more one should be cost oriented" (p. 122). Moreover, "the
perception of presidential candidates is affected by both types of
negativity effects, but . . . negativity in congressional elections is based
solely on perceptual processes" (p. 119). Voters only associate risk
with their choice of a president.

     Richey, Koenig, Richey, and Fortin (1975) concluded that neg-
ative information is far more influential than positive information
when one is dealing with impressions of character.

Heavier weighting of negative information has been found in character evaluations made from mixed behavioral descriptions designed to have moral-ethical

implications (a) in various proportions of positive and negative information; (b) across a considerable range of stimulus polarity (Cusumano, & Richey, 1970); (c) with qualifications, across sexes and ages (Birmingham, 1972; Richey & Dwyer, 1970; Gray-Little, 1973); (d) across four cultures (Richey, McClelland & Shimkunas, 1967; Gaborit, 1973; Gray-Little, 1973; Moran, 1973); (e) whether the stimulus persons are hypothetical strangers or acquaintances (Rickey, McClelland, Shimkunas, 1967; Richey, Richey, & Thieman, 1972); and (f) whether the stimulus is a printed description or a videotape dramatization (Richey, McClelland, & Shimkunas, 1967; Sheehan, 1971). (p. 240)

Klein's aggregate-level analysis (1991) of National Election Study surveys from 1984 and 1988 found that "character weaknesses were more important than strengths in determining the public's evaluations of the candidate and the ultimate vote" (p. 412). However, Pfau and Burgoon (1988) report that character attacks were not as successful in changing attitudes or voting intentions during the latter stages of political campaign as were issue attack messages. They suggest that because voters evaluate a candidate's character early in the campaign, character messages are more effective before the voter attitudes on character have crystallized. In addition, it is very difficult to change a judgment concerning a candidate's character once it has been made (see also Hofstetter, Zukin, & Buss, 1978; Kinder, 1978; Patterson, 1980; Patterson & McClure, 1976; Strouse, 1975). Thus, issue appeals may have more influence during the latter stages of the campaign.

Most recently, researchers have examined the negativity effect with regard to polispots. Shapiro and Rieger (1989) demonstrated that negative polispots are more memorable than positive ads. The case that under certain circumstances, negative political advertising may be more persuasive, retained longer, and easier to retrieve than positive political advertising has sufficient merit to be considered true. However, one warning should be noted. As negative political advertising becomes more prevalent, it may well lose its power in American society. It may be that it is the discordant nature of negative information that gives it much of its strength. Lau (1985) writes: "In either case what is certain is that positive information is more important in a clearly negative ground than is a clearly positive ground, while negative information is more important in a clearly positive ground than in a clearly negative ground" (pp. 129-130). Ironically, as negative political advertising becomes more accepted by political candidates as the most efficient means to conduct a political campaign, its power may at the same time be severely diminished.

ACADEMIC DEBATE

Academicians have been slow to understand the potential usefulness of negative ads, and an examination of the history of negative ad research reveals many twists and turns. Historically, negative political advertising has been described in the political advertising literature as the "direct reference or attacking political advertisement" (Surlin & Gordon, 1977, p. 97). According to Garramone (1984), Surlin and Gordon "operationalized the genre as advertising which attacks the other candidate personally, the issues for which the other candidate stands, or the party of the other candidate" (p. 250). In the 1980s the academic literature on negative political advertising found it to be predominantly ineffective (Garramone, 1984; Hill, 1989; Lemert, Elliot, Bernstein, Rosenberg, Nestvold, 1991; Merritt, 1984; Robinson, 1981a; Shapiro & Rieger, 1989). Indeed, the academic literature suggested that not only was negative political advertising at its best ineffective, but also that it could have three possible damaging effects: boomerang, victim syndrome, and double impairment effects (see Johnson-Cartee & Copeland, 1991a). The *boomerang* or *backlash effect* is the unintended consequence of creating "more negative feelings toward the sponsor, rather than toward the target" (Garramone, 1984, p. 251; see also Hill, 1989; Shapiro & Rieger, 1989, 1992). The *victim syndrome effect* is the unintended consequence of voters perceiving an ad as being unfair or dishonest and then generating their own positive feelings toward the attacked candidate with whom they developed some empathy while attending to the ad (Garramone, 1984; Robinson, 1981a). The *double impairment effect* occurs when negative advertising is said to evoke "a negative effect toward both the targeted opponent and the sponsor" (Merritt, 1984, p. 37).

Some evidence suggests, however, that these three consequences are not inevitable. We previously reported that we could find no evidence to support a generic boomerang effect for all candidate-sponsored negative political advertising (Johnson-Cartee & Copeland, 1991). Our research indicates that researchers are far more likely to find a boomerang effect when studies use a single-point-in-time survey method, when lab experiments use home-made political ad messages as their stimuli, or when an unacceptable topic is used in the negative ad. Viewers often judge advertising by their evaluation of the production values in the ad (Garramone, 1986; Kaid & Davidson, 1986; MacKenzie & Lutz, 1989; Owen, 1991; Shyles, 1986); and, clearly, a home-made stimulus ad will not satisfy today's sophisticated voter. Moreover, while voters say they dislike negative ads, their dislike does not stop them from retaining the information contained within the ad or in finding the ad persuasive (Copeland & Johnson-Cartee, 1990; Johnson-Cartee & Copeland, 1987, 1989a, 1989b, 1990b, 1991a). A parallel experience was reported by the makers of Charmin bathroom tissue in the 1970s. While focus group members repeatedly told researchers that they hated Mr. Whipple and those obnoxious, irritating commercials, they still used the product. Charmin sales soared. The current view is that properly constructed negative ads are most effective in helping a candidate gain votes (see e.g., Lemert, Elliot, Bernstein, Rosenberg, & Nestvold, 1991).

A boomerang effect may occur when a negative ad is perceived as being unfair or dishonest or, more specifically, when the ad utilizes personal attacks such as those dealing with religion, marital history, or medical history (see Johnson & Copeland, 1987; Johnson-Cartee & Copeland, 1989b, 1991a; Kahn & Greer, 1994). In 1992, Shapiro and Rieger presented conclusive evidence of a boomerang effect resulting from an attack on a candidate's personal characteristics, which they term "image." Thus, a backlash effect is the result of the type of appeal used rather than a negative advertising strategy.

There is also some evidence that independently sponsored negative ads pose less chance of a potential boomerang effect than candidate-sponsored negative political ads. The independently sponsored ad is an ad "not directly linked with a candidate. An organization physically separated from either a political party or a candidate's campaign organization, sponsors the ad" (Johnson-Cartee & Copeland, 1991a). A common example of such an organization is a political action committee. Because of this separation, voters may perceive such ads as more trustworthy than a candidate-sponsored ad because when a message source appears to be personally involved in the topic the message is less persuasive (Harmon & Coney, 1982). Garramone (1985) argues that independently sponsored ads have "resulted in greater intended effects against the targeted candidate and in reduced backlash effects against the opponent" than candidate-sponsored negative ads (p. 157). Kaid and Boydston (1987), in their study of independently sponsored negative political advertising, found no evidence of the boomerang effect, and they reported that such advertising "reduces the image evaluation of the targeted politician. While the negative effect was greater for those in the political party opposite that of the targeted politician, respondents of the politician's own party were also affected" (p. 193).

In addition, we have found that there is no generic victim syndrome effect associated with negative political advertising strategies (Johnson-Cartee & Copeland, 1991a). Rather, the research that shows such an effect (for example, Robinson, 1981a) was conducted during the 1980 campaign, one of the most vituperative negative campaigns ever presented to the American public. The type of negative political appeal used was likely the cause of the observed effect. Indeed, the 1980 election year may be characterized by unfair, misleading, and frequently dishonest attacks made on liberal U.S. senators by the National Conservative Political Action Committee.

And as we have previously indicated, American voters dislike unfair or dishonest attacks.

We have found in our own studies no evidence to support the double impairment effect witnessed by Merritt (1984) as being an inevitable outcome of using negative political advertising. And, more significantly, we previously questioned the wisdom of over-generalizing from a one-time descriptive study of southern California residents (Johnson-Cartee and Copeland, 1991a).

While researchers' attentions have been focused primarily on the possible detrimental effects of a negative political advertising strategy, they have overwhelmingly found little, if any, empirical verification of the effectiveness of candidate-sponsored negative political advertising (Basil, Schooler, & Reeves, 1991; Garramone, 1984; Hill, 1989; Merritt, 1984; Newhagen & Reeves, 1991; Shapiro & Rieger, 1989). The overwhelming result is that most researchers believe that negative political advertising does not work and may hurt the sponsoring candidate. Perplexed by political consultants' continued use of this controversial form, other researchers have continued to investigate. Recently, empirical studies have begun to document the potential beneficial effects of negative political advertising (Garramone, Atkin, Pinkleton, & Cole, 1990; James, 1992; Johnson-Cartee & Copeland, 1991a; Kern, 1989; Pfau & Burgoon, 1989; Shapiro & Rieger, 1992). Garramone, Atkin, Pinkleton, and Cole (1990) reported that "negative commercials may lead to greater candidate image discrimination and greater attitude polarization than their positive counterparts" (p. 299). And "negative and positive commercials did not differ, however, in their effects on involvement in the election, communication behavior regarding the election, and likelihood of turning out to vote in the election" (Garramone, et al., 1990, p. 299).

In summary, negative political advertising may have been prematurely labeled as an ineffective advertising strategy owing to definitional and operational difficulties. Today both consultants and academicians are touting the power of negative political advertising. In an interview with Janet Mullins, the media director of the 1988 Bush campaign, Devlin (1989) reports that Mullins explained the phenomenon of negative political advertising in this way: "Everybody hates negative ads; then they rate them most effective in terms of decision making. There isn't any long-term effect. . . . It is kind of like birth pains. Two days later, you forget how much it hurt. The same is true for negative political advertising" (p. 407). Similarly, after that same election cycle Kathleen Hall Jamieson was quoted as saying: "There is a strong advantage to the candidate who attacks early and defines the terrain, sculpts the opponent's image and then defines himself in the shadows" (Grove, 1988, p. A1).

THREE MODES OF NEGATIVE POLITICAL ADVERTISING

Our review of the existing literature has led us to conclude that, by limiting the operationalization of negative political advertising to direct attack spots, researchers have narrowed the range of possible effects of negative polispots (see Johnson-Cartee & Copeland, 1991a). We have found that "it is a grievous reductionism to ignore the negative strategies and resulting consequences associated with ads that directly compare candidates or that indirectly imply the candidate comparison" (Johnson-Cartee & Copeland, 1991a, p. 17). Viewers regard direct comparison ads and implied comparison ads as less conflictual and potentially more fair than direct attack spots; they are also potentially as powerful or even more powerful than direct attack ads (Gronbeck, 1985; Johnson-Cartee & Copeland; 1991a). In *Negative Political Advertising* (1991a) we adopted Gronbeck's (1985) typology: direct attack ads, direct comparison ads, and implied comparison ads.

Direct Attack

Direct attack ads directly attack a specific candidate or party. According to Merritt (1984), a negative attack ad "focuses primarily on degrading perceptions of the rival, to the advantage of the sponsor" (p. 27). Direct attack ads only attack the opposition; they do not compare one candidate with another. The merits of the sponsor or other candidate(s) are never mentioned. The opponent who is attacked is either named specifically "John Doe," or euphemistically with phrases such as "my opponent," "the Republican challenger," or the "current probate judge." In some instances, the candidate who is attacked is not named but is pictured in the advertisement. Political parties may be attacked in the same way as an individual candidate, by either name, leaders associated with the party, or symbol. Direct attack ads identify the competitor "for the purpose of imputing inferiority" (Merritt, 1984, p. 27). Direct attack advertising is based on the assumption that "voters mark their ballots against rather than for certain candidates" (Hellweg, 1988, p. 14). The phrase "voting for the lesser of two evils" is common in the U.S.

Research has shown that such one-sided presentations are most effective in "converting the less educated" and are "generally more effective as a reinforcing device" (Weiss, 1966, p. 130). Direct attack ads have been shown to significantly decrease both the candidate evaluation scores and candidate preference scores of the targeted candidates (Johnson-Cartee & Copeland, 1991a). However, the observed drop was not as great as that witnessed for the direct comparison spot.

Often humor is used not to soften the blow but to make the direct attack more palatable to the viewers (see Chapter 4). In 1990 Deno Seder Productions produced a direct attack ad against David Duke who was running for the U.S. Senate in Louisiana. The ad was sponsored by the Louisiana Coalition, an independent political action committee. The ad is a take-off on an easily recognizable game show, "Jeopardy." And it gets its name from Lewis Carroll's poem, the Jabberwocky, a farcical treatment of political discourse. The ad won a first place in the American Association of Political Consultant's Poli-award competition.

The 1990 Louisiana Coalition "Jabberwocky" Ad

Video	Audio
Jabberwocky set with three contestants (Bill, Debbie and Alan). The game show host bounds onto the stage.	Game Show Host [SOT]: "Thank you and welcome to Jabberwocky. The game program all America loves to watch. Bill, Alan, and Debbie, are you ready?"
Contestants seen standing behind the contestants' podiums. Smiling host is seen.	Chorus [SOT]: "Ready!" Host [SOT]: "Debbie, you first."
Cut to shot of Debbie.	Debbie [SOT]: "I'll try false patriots for 300, will you please?"
Footage of game board. What host reads appears enlarged on screen.	Host [VO]: "He was kicked out of ROTC, lied about serving his country, and never spent a single day in the military." BUZZER SOUNDS
Debbie is on screen.	Host [VO]: "Debbie!" Debbie [SOT]: "Who is David Duke?" Host [VO]: "Correct!" Debbie [SOT]: "Good Buddies for 300."
Game Board. What the Host reads aloud.	Host [VO]: "He hired ex-Nazis to work on his political campaign."

Bill is on screen.	BUZZER SOUNDS
Bill is on screen.	Host [VO]: "Bill."
	Bill [SOT]: "Who is David Duke?"
Bill is on screen.	Host [VO]: "Yes!"
Bill is on screen.	Bill [SOT]: "Paul, I'll try tax cheats for 200."
Game Board. What host reads is enlarged.	Host [VO]: "He failed to file state income taxes from 1984 to 1987."
Alan is on screen.	BUZZER SOUNDS
	HOST [VO]: "Alan?"
Alan is on screen.	Alan [SOT]: "Who was David Duke?"
	Host [VO]: "That's right!"
Game Board.	Alan [SOT]: "Crazy ideas for 400, Paul."
	BUZZER SOUNDS
View of contestants and host.	Host [SOT]: "He has advocated that America be divided into separate race nations."
	BUZZER SOUNDS
	HOST [SOT]: "Debbie, again!"
	Debbie [SOT]: "Who is David Duke?"
	Host [SOT]: "Correct!"
Debbie is on screen.	Debbie [SOT]: "Basement book sellers for 300."
Game Board. What the host reads is enlarged on screen.	Host [VO]: "He says he's changed his ways, but just last year he was caught selling Nazi books and

	tapes from the basement of his legislative office."
	BUZZER SOUNDS
	Host [VO]: "Alan?"
Alan is on screen.	Alan [SOT]: "Who was David Duke?"
	Host [VO]: "Yes!"
	BELL RINGS
Host is on screen.	Host [SOT]: "And that's the end of round two. Stay tuned folks, we will be right back."
Super: "Who is David Duke?"	

In 1992 Ron Staskiewicz ran for the U.S. House of Representatives in Nebraska on a platform that promised he would work to reduce the national debt. However, Ron had quite a few financial skeletons in his closet, and his Democratic opponent Peter Hoagland took him to task for his hypocrisy in a direct attack spot.

The 1992 Hoagland "National Debt" Ad

Video	Audio
Ron Staskiewicz walking toward the camera, talking as he walks. Super: "Ron Staskiewicz Businessman." Map of South Dakota. Super in a flag: "Don't drink the Water." Waves on bottom of flag. Flag flips to "Don't give him credit," And flag then sinks. Footage of ten pages of legal documents, Judgment Docket on top of pages. Super: "Ten Lawsuits" in red. Super: "He still hasn't paid."	Announcer [VO]: "Businessman Ron Staskiewicz claims he'll reduce the national debt. But when Ron Staskiewicz opened a bar in Vermilion, South Dakota and named it 'Don't Drink the Water,' it should have been named: 'Don't Give Him Credit.' Because when the bar went under, ten lawsuits were filed by businesses and former employees. But Ron Staskiewicz left the state with a trail of bad debts behind him. He still hasn't paid.
White lettering on black, scrolls as announcer reads. "Sorry, Ron, but you can't run away from the national debt."	Sorry, Ron, but you can't run away from the national debt."

Direct Comparison

Direct comparison ads specifically compare one candidate with another, and, not surprisingly, the sponsor's candidate (whether the sponsor is a political party, political action committee, or an individual candidate) has the competitive edge in such a comparison. Unlike the direct attack ad, the direct comparison ad features the candidate as well as the opposition. A true comparison ad actually contrasts the records, experience, or issue positions of the candidates. A direct comparison ad identifies the competitor "for the purpose of claiming superiority" (Prasad, 1976, p. 128). Such ads focus "primarily on enhancing perceptions of the sponsor, even at the expense of the competitor" (Merritt, 1984, p. 27). According to Gronbeck (1985), the direct comparison ad works on the assumption that voters compare candidates when making a voting decision. This assumption was later supported by Choi and Becker (1987).

Many consultants believe that voters accept the comparison ad more readily than the direct attack ad in that they view the comparison ad as being fair because two sides are presented. Research has shown that such two-sided presentations are "more effective than one-sided presentation as a device for converting the highly educated, and as a safeguard against later counter-propaganda" (Weiss, 1966, p. 130). The direct comparison spot has been found to create the greatest statistically significant decrease in the targeted candidate's evaluation scores and candidate voting preference scores (when compared to implied comparison ads and direct attack ads) (Johnson-Cartee & Copeland, 1991a).

During the 1988 presidential primary season, the Democratic congressman from Missouri, Richard Gephardt, attacked the Democratic governor of Massachusetts, Michael Dukakis, for being out of touch with the farm community. Gephardt capitalized on Dukakis's own remarks in order to make Dukakis look silly. Gephardt had run a populist campaign, so the ad reinforced his overall message: "I'm one of you, and I'm for you." And as a corollary, "He's not one of you; and he isn't for you."

The 1988 Gephardt "Belgian Endive" Spot

Video	Audio
White letters on black screen that read "Compare Two Candidates." Two black and white photos show Gephardt and Dukakis. The Gephardt photo is now color and shows him walking with union	Announcer [VO]: "Compare two candidates for president. Dick Gephardt is fighting for a bill to save American jobs. Mike

workers. "Compare Two Candidates" now turns into "Trade Bill to Save Jobs." Under Gephardt photo, letters read "Yes"; under Dukakis,"No." Title changes to "Save the Family Farm Bill." Gephardt photo now shows him at a rally with a child in arms. Under Gephardt, "Yes," under Dukakis, "?" Cut to white letters on black screen, "Dukakis to farmers, Grow blueberries, flowers and Belgian endive. *Washington Post*, Feb. 15, 1987." Cut back to original screen. Gephardt color photo shows him talking to women. Under photo, "Cut Taxes," under Dukakis, "Raised Taxes."Cut to photo of Gephardt mingling with a crowd at a rally.	Dukakis is opposed to it. Gephardt is for the family farm bill. Dukakis won't take a stand. He says our farmers have to diversify and grow blueberries, flowers, and Belgian endive. Gephardt fought to cut income taxes. Dukakis is one of the biggest tax raisers in Massachusetts history. These are some of the reasons why southerners are for Gephardt, not Dukakis."

(*Source*: Payne, Marlier, & Baukus, 1989, p. 374.)

Not all direct comparison spots are paid for by the candidate. In 1988 the Democratic National Committee aired a direct comparison spot during the presidential campaign.

The 1988 DNC "Education" Ad

Video	Audio
Photo of Bush "1987 Education" (Writing appears on chalkboard, starts eating up education)	Announcer [VO]: "For seven and one-half years, George Bush supported cut backs in American education (drum cadence). He even sat by while college loans for working families were cut.
Photo of Bush "1988."	And now suddenly, George Bush says he'll be the Education President. (Upbeat Music)
Screen rolls up, flip/flop. Photo of Dukakis. Words of announcer appear on screen.	Michael Dukakis won't just give us a slogan. He's committed to a new national College Loan
"A real commitment to education."	Program to make sure that any American kid can afford to go to

> college.
> Michael Dukakis for President.
> The best America is yet to come."

Implied Comparison

The implied comparison ad is the negative ad most frequently mislabeled in academic research, because an ad cannot be determined to be an implied comparison ad apart from the totality of the advertising and public relations campaign. The implied comparison ad does not name opposition candidates either specifically or euphemistically, and in some instances, it may not feature the sponsoring candidate (party or political action committee) until the tag. "The implied comparison ads are not negative in and of themselves, but it is their public's interpretation of those ads that give them their negative character" (Johnson-Cartee & Copeland, 1991a, p. 46; see also Diamond & Bates, 1988; Jamieson, 1984; Schwartz, 1976). In essence, voters are lured into making a comparison in their own minds. In this cognitive process rests the power of implied comparison ads, for they force upon the viewer a deductive analysis that stirs an internal dialogue and leaves the residue of a learned experience. Clearly, use of the implied comparison ad may have advantages because such ads are generally not perceived as negative in and of themselves; the viewer supplies the negative interpretation.

Unlike the direct attack ads and comparison ads, the implied comparison ad uses the deductive approach as, the audience must infer the primary premise of who the opposition candidate is and how that candidate is being criticized—the use of a truncated deductive logic is called an enthymeme. Clearly, use of the implied comparison ad assumes that the viewer has knowledge of the candidate's various political positions, background, record, character, and so forth. The ad taps this political information base, and within that base, the comparison is made. As a result, the successful use of implied comparison ads dictates that they not be used until both candidates have been identified clearly in the campaign. Implied comparison ads are rarely used in low-involvement, low-visibility electoral contests, "since the voter's knowledge about the candidate is far less complete than at the presidential level" (Sabato, 1981, p. 172). However, if the race's visibility is unusually significant for the level of the election, then implied comparison ads are used.

Karl Struble, a leading Democratic consultant, claims that implied negative ads are the most effective because they are so subtle (New Campaign Techniques, 1986). We reported that the indirect comparison spot created statistically significant decreases in the targeted candidate's evaluation scores and voting preference scores, while elevating the sponsoring candidate's evaluation scores and voting preference scores (Johnson-Cartee & Copeland, 1991a). However, implied comparison spots must be preceded by supportive or reinforcing messages. Political consultants must set the stage for the implied comparison ad. In this way, viewers acquire the necessary knowledge about the issues and the candidates in order to make the comparison on their own.

Tarrance (1982) has identified the "rational cross-pressuring" advertising technique. That is, candidates work to point out the disparity between what their opposition stands for and how the people feel through advertising and the news media. Without appearing to be negative, candidates can reinforce this disparity over and over again through use of the implied comparison ad.

During the 1992 presidential campaign, President Bush and his campaign strategists hammered Bill Clinton on what came to be known as the character issue. Both in direct attack spots and in implied comparison ads, the character question was put before the American public. However, the implied comparison spots were not aired until the character issue had been dealt with in a number of ways in direct attack spots. Clinton's flip-flops on political issues, his inconsistencies in his reports about his lack of military service, and his current position statements compared to his Arkansas record permitted important direct attack messages. Notice in the next ad that there is an echo of Bush's direct attack ad's tags: "It's wrong for you. It's wrong for America." At the conclusion, Bush humbles himself by asking for your vote. The tag "President Bush, Commander-in-Chief" once again makes the point that as president, the individual must serve as the commander-in-chief of the armed services. This calls into memory, once again, Clinton's lack of military experience, as well as his inconsistencies and indecisiveness on the issues, and pits this image against Bush's own well-known heroics as a World War II navy pilot and his perceived extraordinary leadership during the Persian Gulf War.

The 1992 Bush "Plain Talk" Ad

Video	Audio
White lettering on black: "Plain Talk. On the Presidency."	Announcer [VO]: "Plain talk. On the Presidency."
Bush speaking to an audience, walking among people.	Bush [SOT]: "In a few days, you'll make your choice for president of the United States. And it's a

Close-up of elderly man. Close-up of black woman. Bush talking with group, huge American flag on back wall. The locattion appears to be a theater in the round.	serious choice. The most important democracy [*sic*] our system makes. There are many times that the president alone must make tough decisions that affect people's lives. He is the commander-in-chief. And I want you to think about that. He must have the resolve, the maturity, the moral authority to lead the nation in times of crisis. In the White House, in the Oval Office, you cannot be on both sides of every issue. You must make the call and you must lead. And that's what the American people expect from their president. Our economic future here at home depends more than ever on competing in a global economy, seizing new opportunities and opening new markets and that's how we can create more jobs and economic strength. America must have a leader who understands the world. And who is prepared to act. Leaders of other nations, people all over the world, judge America by the character of the president, and the president's word must be good. People around the world expect that of the United States. The person you choose to lead America must have certain qualities—decisiveness, honesty, integrity, consistency. All of you know that the Presidency is the most serious job in the world, and we simply cannot put America's future at risk with a person who is wrong for the job and with policies that are wrong for America. When you make your choice, choose what's right for America. I need your support, and I ask for your vote."
Close-up of man and woman.	
Bush talking to audience.	
"President Bush Commander-in-Chief"	

But Bush was having his own troubles. Ross Perot mounted an independent presidential campaign in 1992 that buzzed around Bush's head like an angry bee. Again and again, the Clinton and Perot camp ads complemented each other. While Clinton was trying to discount the importance of Bush's leadership on the international scene, Ross Perot was saying the same thing. Both Clinton and Perot were focused on the "economic crisis." In the following ad, the Perot campaign subtly discounts the importance of the international scene while building up the significance of the economy in the voter's decision-making process. In short, the ad is a reminder of what Perot has asserted all along, "the failed economic leadership of the Bush presidency."

The 1992 Perot "The Economy" Ad

Video	Audio
A huge gray clock ticking in the background. A scroll of words appears over the face of the clock. The image of the clock dissolves into darkness, and then reappears again, and again.	A soft ticking is heard. Announcer [VO]: "It is a time when the threat of unemployment is greater than the threat of war. It is a time when the national debt demands as much attention as the national security. It is a time when the barriers to a better life are rising and the barriers between nations are falling. The issue is the economy. And, it is a time that demands a candidate who is not a business as usual politician, but a business leader with the know-how to balance the budget, rebuild the job base, and restore the meaning of: 'Made in the USA.' In this election, we can choose a candidate who has made the free enterprise system work, who has created thousands of jobs by
"The election is November 3. The choice is yours."	building successful businesses. The candidate is Ross Perot."

3

Combating Negative Advertising: Proactive and Reactive Strategies

A candidate entering into a campaign must be prepared to respond to attacks and likely attacks made through the opposition's negative political advertising. We have catalogued two approaches a candidate can take. The candidate may attempt to preempt attacks that may be made in the future by using an inoculation strategy, or the candidate may respond to a negative political ad after it has aired by using a response ad.

PROACTIVE INOCULATION ADS

Inoculation is a proactive strategy that may provide rich rewards for those campaigns using it. This strategy may be particularly important in those campaigns where attacks are expected from the opposition. As Republican consultant Jim Innocenzi says, "Inoculation and pre-emption are what win campaigns" (New Campaign Techniques, 1986, p. 31).

A campaign may use inoculation to prepare a candidate's adherents to withstand the charges made by the opposition and to maintain positive attitudes toward the candidate during and after the opponent's attacks. Inoculation is a defensive measure that may be used to prepare for known or presumed charges from the opposition.

Cooper and Jahoda (1947) investigated the familiar phenomenon of how people handle information that runs counter to an existing attitude. They identified four mechanisms through which an individual may deal with contrary information while maintaining their original position: First, "Identification avoided—understanding derailed," (p. 16), that is, the receiver, seeking to avoid identifying with the uncomfortable ideas and issues that have been presented, changes the meaning. The second mechanism is "the message made invalid," (p. 19). Receivers of messages may identify with those messages, but when the information runs counter to their beliefs, they invalidate the message by citing exceptions or maintaining that the idea is not correct. The third approach is "changing the frame of reference" (p. 20). Message receivers impose their own ideology on the message, transfiguring it so that this metamorphosed message supports the previously held belief. The final identified approach is viewing "the message as too difficult" (p. 20). Messages that run counter to held beliefs may simply be dismissed as being too complicated for the receiver to interpret and so are dismissed.

The tendency to avoid or distort messages that run counter to our held attitudes puts the individual at risk of having a greater attitude change should a message penetrate the receiver's defenses. In situations where avoidance mechanisms do not function, attitudes that have generally been cognitively undefended are more susceptible to persuasion (Hovland, 1959).

Papageorgis and McGuire (1961) assert that persons who actively avoid counter-arguments are vulnerable because they have avoided practicing the defense of the held attitudes. Rather than rehearse a defense of held attitudes, such people have simply tried to avoid any conflict. This lack of counterargument rehearsal leaves the receiver without the argumentative resources to adequately cope with the counterattitudinal messages. As Anderson and McGuire (1965) express it, "What [a receiver] needs in order to develop resistance is not a reassuring defense telling him the reasons his belief is true, but a threatening defense that makes him realize the belief's vulnerability" (p. 44).

Lumsdaine and Janis (1953) were one of the first to report that exposure to a "two-sided" argument—that is, messages that include both pro and con arguments—seemed to help people develop resistance to counterattitudinal arguments. The use of the two-sided argument proved much better at retaining existing attitudes under attack than providing only additional consonant information. Researchers found that simply giving people more of the same supportive information—information that was consonant with the views already held—was not as likely to protect the views of people as exposing them to counterarguments. Although exposing of people to attitude-consonant material did show an increase in agreement with the attitude, it was an increase that could easily be switched to an opposing view.

McGuire and his associates (Anderson & McGuire, 1965; McGuire, 1961a, 1961b, 1962, 1964; McGuire & Papageorgis, 1961, 1962; Papageorgis & McGuire, 1961) view the attack of these undefended attitudes as analogous to the introduction of a disease into the body of an immune-deficient patient. The immune-deficient patient does not have the biological resources to counter the invading disease. McGuire and associates used this biological example as an analog for what occurs in an unprotected cognitive system. They formulated the inoculation theory based on the familiar biological inoculation model. As McGuire writes:

In the biological analogy, the person is typically made resistant to some attacking virus by pre-exposure to a weakened dose of the virus. This mild dose stimulates his defenses so that he will be better able to overcome any massive viral attack to which he is later exposed, but it is not so strong that this pre-exposure will itself cause the disease. (1964, p. 200)

The researchers postulated that attitudes would be strengthened by exposing individuals to a relatively weak counterattitudinal message while simultaneously providing the refutation to that counterattitudinal message. Use of the defense-building counter-attitudinal message does not demonstrate a "boomerang" effect (McGuire & Papageorgis, 1961; Papageorgis & McGuire, 1961); that is, the weak counterarguments used to generate attitudinal defenses are insufficient to cause an attitude change on the part of the receiver. However, the counterattitudinal message is sufficient to have the receiver exercise a defense of the held attitude so that the receiver is prepared for more severe counterattitudinal messages.

McGuire (1964) believed that for inoculation to function successfully three conditions must be fulfilled: a person must have sufficient knowledge to defend the preexisting attitude; a person must have the opportunity to practice the defense; and a person must be motivated to use the defense.

In addition, situational factors have been demonstrated to influence the viability of inoculation as a protective force against counterattitudinal messages. These factors are the level of perceived threat by the receiver to the currently held attitude; whether the message or the messenger violates the receiver's expectations; and the message's context (Burgoon, Cohen, Miller, & Montgomery, 1978).

McGuire and Papageorgis (1961) suggested that the continued use of reinforcing support originally discredited by Lumsdaine and Janis (1953) should be called the "paper tiger effect." They were able to replicate Lumsdaine and Janis's earlier findings that the sole use of reinforcing support showed an initial strengthening of attitudes, but when these attitudes were subjected to a counterargument, these strengthened attitudes quickly crumbled. The superiority of defense-building counter-arguments over supportive information has received strong empirical support (Anderson & McGuire, 1965; McGuire, 1961b;

McGuire & Papageorgis, 1961, 1962; Tannenbaum, McCauley, & Norris, 1966).

McGuire (1961b) found that messages with additional supporting information (for example, evidence) as an adjunct to defense-building counterarguments create a more effective message than those that just contain defense-building counterarguments. The combination of defense-building counter-argument and supporting information was the strongest for maintaining attitudes when the person was faced with a new or novel attack against a held attitude. Consonant evidence embedded with the counter-attitudinal message serves as an "inhibitor to counter-persuasion" (McCroskey, 1970, p. 194).

McGuire (1962) also discovered that the inoculation effect becomes stronger as the time between exposure to the counterargument inoculation and the attack increases. McGuire believed that people used the ensuing time to practice their defenses. The practice of defending against counterattitudinal ideas works to strengthen the resistance to subsequent nonconsonant messages.

The importance of practicing defenses to arguments has solid empirical support (Festinger & Maccoby, 1964 ; Osterhouse & Brock, 1970) which demonstrates that people are more persuadable when they are distracted and unable to practice or participate in counter arguing. The optimum inoculation effect is produced when the receiver is in a passive state. The more passive the receiver when the inoculation material is administered, the greater the resistance to change. The passive receiver is seen as being better able to understand elements of the message and to practice defending attitudes as suggested by the inoculating messages (McGuire & Papageorgis, 1961).

When an individual perceives that her or his attitudes are being threatened, the research evidence is overwhelming that this perceived threat triggers a defense of the held attitude (Burgoon, Burgoon, Riess, Butler, et al., 1976; McGuire, 1961; McGuire & Papageorgis, 1961; Miller & Burgoon, 1979; Papageorgis & McGuire, 1961; Tannenbaum, 1967). Simply warning a person that the person's ideas will be coming under attack does work to strengthen the defenses against attack (McGuire & Papageorgis, 1962).

While the certainty of attack is insufficient to protect against counterattitudinal messages, some evidence has been offered that not knowing whether the attitude will be attacked may help strengthen the attitude against change. Greater inoculation effects have been demonstrated in situations where the person is unsure whether the held attitude will be challenged than being certain there will be no attack or knowing for certain there will be an attack on a person's held viewpoint (Burgoon, Burgoon, Riess, Butler, et al., 1976). As Burgoon and his co-authors note, "the presumed uncertainty associated with lack of knowledge about the likelihood of an attack would be threatening and would therefore motivate people to prepare adequate defenses" (1976, pp. 127-128).

The original topics used in McGuire's inoculation studies were what he called "cultural truisms." McGuire's work (1964) examined culturally determined mythical constructs that society generally accepts as fact. For example, he used topics such as: it is good to brush your teeth three times a day, or people should get a yearly medical checkup. Because of his emphasis on cultural truisms, McGuire cautions that inoculation works for only those beliefs that have not previously been attacked.

Pryor and Steinfatt (1978) among others believed that McGuire was being too cautious in his interpretation of his findings. They felt that inoculation applied to attitudes other than those cultural truisms that McGuire and associates had investigated. Furthermore, they contended that the attitude does not have to be attacked in exactly the same manner as suggested in the inoculating message (see also Kiesler, Collins, & Miller, 1969). Pryor and Steinfatt demonstrate that inoculation does not require attitudes that are strongly held, but it also works with those attitudes that are best described as "mid-range" (e.g., Burgoon, Burgoon, Riess, Butler, et al., 1976; Burgoon, Cohen, Miller, & Montgomery, 1978; Pryor & Steinfatt, 1978; Ullmann & Bodaken, 1975). Pryor and Steinfatt suggested that as topic salience increases, an individual's motivation and readiness to learn defensive messages also increase (p. 228).

Inoculation During a Political Campaign

Pfau and his associates have collected two sets of data that have served as a direct test of inoculation within a political context (Pfau & Burgoon, 1988; Pfau & Kenski, 1990). Although we have some reservations about the research, it illustrates the possibilities that inoculation holds. They determined that inoculation works in three specific ways: "[1] undermining the potential influence of the source of political attacks, [2] deflecting the specific content of political attacks, and [3] reducing the likelihood that political attacks will influence receiver voting intention" (Pfau & Burgoon, 1988, pp. 105-106). In addition, it has been found that inoculation works best early in the campaign (Cundy, 1986; Pfau & Kenski, 1990).

Research showing that inoculation works best on a passive receiver suggests that television may be the ideal place for inoculation advertising. Some studies (e.g., Csikszentmihalyi & Kubey, 1981; Krugman, 1966) have long demonstrated the relaxing nature of television viewing and the passive state of most of its viewers. People who receive the inoculation messages from television advertising would be in an appropriate state to practice the counterarguing defenses that are important for the inoculation process to be effective.

Campaigns may use inoculation to prepare voters who are committed and those leaning toward the candidate for possible attacks by the opposition. In 1986 media consultants began creating inoculation spots. Political consultant Charlie Black is quoted as saying, "If you know what your negatives are, and you know where you're vulnerable, you can pre-empt it" (New Campaign Techniques, 1986, p. 31). Inoculation ads serve as a "cocoon" that protects the candidate later in the race.

Although historically challengers have been associated with the use of negative ads, in recent years, incumbents have increasingly been utilizing negative advertising strategies. Because challengers are usually less well known than incumbents, there had been some question as to whether inoculation techniques would protect challengers as well as incumbents. In fact, Phau and Kenski (1990) argue that inoculation is most effective against a lesser-known opponent.

In 1979 Kitchens and Stiteler, in a case study of a local Texas election, demonstrate that a challenger was successful in inoculating the voters against subsequent attacks. The inoculation strategy utilized both direct mail and television advertisements. Kitchens and Stiteler's research suggests that inoculation ads are useful not only for the issues covered in the advertising but also for those issues that are not specifically mentioned in the inoculating material. Because the sponsor's supporters are inoculated against attacks, late campaign attacks by the opposition should meet with cognitive resistance from the sponsor's supporters. Phau and Kenski (1990) have been more specific. Their findings generally indicate that "inoculation same pretreatments are the most effective at short time intervals and with issue attacks at long intervals, but that inoculation different pretreatment are most effective at moderate intervals and with character attacks at long intervals" (p. 122).

Previously, based on a review of the literature we had suggested (Johnson-Cartee & Copeland, 1991a) that the best approach to the structure of an inoculating ad would be for the message to contain both refutational and supportive elements. Phau and Kinski's (1990) findings from their 1988 study reveal that an inoculation only message is the preferred method for message construction. They found no advantage to the use of reinforcing supportive elements with the inoculating message. We are unsure whether the political environment is one in which inoculation plus reinforcement does not work as it has in other topic areas or whether there is something idiosyncratic to Phau's and Kinski's study.

Inoculation Ads

In 1990 Frank Belloti ran for governor in the Democratic primary in Massachusetts.   Belloti was a crusading Democratic attorney general who wanted to move up to the governor's office. He faced John R. Silber in the primary. Belloti's campaign believed that his ethnic heritage and his tough, working-class background were disadvantages. The ad team therefore prepared what appears to be a straight biographical ad but one that functions as an inoculation ad by warning voters that they would hear negative ethnic stereotypes associated with Belloti's candidacy.   The ad warns the voters to pay close attention to his opponent's advertising and not let such appeals fool them.

The 1990 Belloti "Fist" Ad

Video	Audio
Belloti walks down a city street talking to a group of men and women between the ages of 20 and 35.	Belloti [SOT]: "And this is what we used to call a mixed neighborhood. You had. . . ."
Belloti is seen continuing to talk with men and women.	Narrator [VO]: "Frank Belloti was never a member of a club, any club. He was another Italian boy who had to come out of the
Scene of lone man walking down city street.	neighborhood swinging. A dead father; an underpaid mother, an outsider."
Scene of Belloti talking with men and women.	Male Group Member [VO]: "Dad, which house was yours?"
Belloti points at house.	Belloti [SOT]: "This house right here."
Footage of house.	Belloti [VO]: "See that brick house. My mother supported our family, and she worked for $18 a week."
Belloti talking with group; shot emphasizes women in group.	Belloti [SOT]: "That's why the Equal Rights Amendment was a

	very, very important thing to me. It wasn't a feminist issue; it was a family issue, a survival issue."
A man in what appears to be a community center, with two women in background.	Elderly man [SOT]: "He's decent and compassionate. He'll do anything for the disadvantaged. And go out and work hard to even the score so to speak."
Belloti enters local grocery store, shakes hands. Talks with working people outside the store.	Narrator [VO]: "The bruises were deep. When he was elected attorney general, he took up the cause of the broken and whipped, the disadvantaged, the working people, the poor."
Middle-aged woman at table with two other women drinking coffee. Black and white photos. Photo of little boy; photo of boy with dog; photo of boys; photo of teenage athlete; photo of law school composite; photo of naval officer.	Woman [SOT]: "At every turn Frank Belloti takes, people are waiting to say: 'see he really is this awful person's [sic]—dark skinned Italian'. And I don't think you ever get over those names. He grew up in a climate which we all know isn't very kind to minorities."
Middle-aged woman.	Woman [SOT]: "People had better look long and hard. And look beyond the stereotypes, when they vote for governor."
State House.	Narrator [VO]: "He moved the attorney general's office out of the state house. Fired hacks. And recruited first-rate, full-time lawyers. His team won back-pay for women who had been cheated. Won 70 million from Exxon. Fought to keep Seabrook from being charged to our state. Saved George's Bank."
Belloti talking with black woman, footage of cars on interstate, footage of Seabrook plant, footage of river banks.	
Belloti shaking hands and talking to a group near the river bank.	Belloti [VO]: "They were going to give away almost all of George's to the oil companies. And let them drill any place they wanted, any way they wanted. That's why I

	sued them."
Belloti speaking at Campaign Rally.	Belotti [SOT]: "Our state is out of control. And the people in charge have done nothing about it. We must take back our state."
Super: "Belloti. It's worth the fight"	Narrator [VO]: "Frank Belloti. Because Massachusetts is worth the fight."

During that same primary season, former California governor Jerry Brown ran an inoculation spot that addressed the issue of character and candidate suitability for office. Brown had a reputation in middle America as being a little bit weird or flaky. Indeed, his nickname during the early 1980s was Governor Moonbeam. For middle America, Brown epitomized all the "strangeness" in California. The "Care" ad basically tells the voters: "It's O.K. to be different." And even more importantly, "Different may be better." The campaign chose a female narrator for this spot. This provided two advantages. A female voice often cuts through the clutter of other advertising which is domninated by men's voices. More importantly, females are more likely to be concerned about the "caring" issues, that is, health care, children, education, and so on. And our society approves of females talking about such issues far more than males.

The 1992 Brown "Care" Ad

Video	Audio
Close-up of man carrying the body of a very ill, starving East Indian man.	Female Announcer [VO]: "What kind of man would go to Calcutta, volunteer for Mother Teresa, work in the house of the dying, help people in pain who have lost all hope? Maybe someone who really cares about helping people. Now the question is what kind of people would vote for such a man? Maybe the folks right here in Mississippi. Jerry Brown for President, because it's okay to care."
Brown in a group of people with a Dr. King poster on the wall. The majority are black. He stands up, clapping. Brown talking with black children in city street. Super: "Jerry Brown because its okay to care. Brown for President."	

Because the 1992 campaign season was predicted to be one of the hardest on incumbents in recent years—though not as hard as the 1994 congressional elections—a number of congressional incumbents chose to run inoculation spots that were meant to effectively separate them from the incumbent pack. In other words, they portrayed themselves as maverick political leaders rather than as incumbents. Congressman Rick Santorum of Pennsylvania ran a series of ads attacking the very institution that he was a member of, and he did it in such a way that he appeared to be the virtuous Washington outsider who was on the inside.

The 1992 Santorum "Anti-Washington" Ad

Video	Audio
Capitol building.	(Teletype noises in the background as if this was a news flash.)
	Announcer [VO]: "Rick Santorum was told by the congressional leaders that a freshman
White letters on black: "Seen but not heard."	congressman should be seen but not heard. Santorum introduces
"Santorum introduces health care bill."	health care bill. Rick Santorum calls for full congressional
"Rick Santorum calls for full congressional disclosure of check overdrafts."	disclosure of check overdrafts. Santorum introduces legislation to
"Santorum introduces legislation to save taxpayers $10 billion."	save taxpayers $10 billion. Santorum calls for immediate
"Santorum calls for immediate accounting of secret congressional slush fund"	accounting of secret congressional slush fund. What the leaders in Congress didn't
Photo of Rick Santorum.	realize is that Rick Santorum doesn't listen to them. He listens to you. Join the fight for better
"Join the Fight". "Santorum for Congress."	government. Vote Santorum for Congress."

In 1992 the Russ Feingold campaign for the U.S. Senate in Wisconsin ran a very unusual inoculation spot. For the first time to our knowledge, a candidate attempted to inoculate himself against all future attacks. Feingold, who was challenging an incumbant and others in the party primary, ran a series of spots that attempted a blanket inoculation. Research has shown that inoculation on one issue tends to bleed over into other issues (Kitchens & Stiteler, 1979; Pfau & Kenski, 1990). And there is some research to suggest that inoculation is most effective on lesser known candidates, for example, usually challengers (Pfau & Kenski, 1990).

The 1992 Feingold "Elvis" Ad

Video	Audio
Feingold at desk with visual displays. Newspaper headline of story says: "Underdog Feingold tries to get closest to the people." Close-ups of news headlines, "Kasten defends tactics." "Bob Kasten's been doing dirty campaigning for a long time." (Feingold holding display) "Feingold offers national health care proposal"; "Senator Feingold challenges state on lottery & wins"; "Feingold unveils deficit plan"; Tabloid newspaper with cover photo of Elvis and Feingold with the headline: "Elvis endorses Feingold. " "For U. S. Senate, Feingold."	Feingold [SOT]: "The underdog running for the United States Senate. If things are going to change around here, this man must be defeated in November, incumbent Senator Bob Kasten. Now I like to run a positive campaign, but the senator doesn't. That's why Bob Kasten's supporters hope I lose. You see not much has been written about Russ Feingold to attack. Unlike my two opponents in the primary. So to run against me, the only option is to make something up. And you voters know better than to believe everything you read."

Sure enough Feingold was attacked. Incumbent Bob Kasten positioned Feingold as being out of touch with his own party, as being far too liberal for the new Democratic party represented by Clinton and Gore. Feingold went on the air, reminding voters of his early inoculation ads. The following ad is a reactive response ad and thus, actually belongs in the next section. It is interesting here, however, because it refers back to the inoculation spots.

The 1992 Feingold "Told You So" Ad

Video	Audio
Feingold talks to camera. Newspaper headline: "Kasten sued for defamation." Russ holds up salt shaker; shakes	Feingold [SOT]: "Hi, I'm U.S. Senate candidate Russ Feingold. A while ago, I warned you voters about my opponent's history about making things up. I figured when he started distorting the truth about me, you'd take it with a grain of salt. Well get ready.

some in hand. Starts to pour salt. Stream gets longer and wider.	Because now he's telling you I have a plan to raise thousands of dollars of taxes on the middle class. Not true. Senator Kasten knows I haven't proposed any such tax increase, period. The truth is, the senator has made up something so big that a few grains of salt wouldn't be enough—a shovelful would be more like it."
Mound of salt. Feingold with snow or coal shovel. "Feingold For U. S. Senate"	

REACTIVE RESPONSE ADVERTISING

A reactive response is a defensive posture that candidates must adopt to protect themselves against attacks (McBurney & Mills, 1964). A defensive posture is not an ideal situation. In fact, it may be a particularly dangerous one for a candidate, for a defensive posture is a clear indication that the candidate is no longer controlling the campaign debate but is instead reacting to the opponent's campaign agenda.

Because campaigns often concentrate on exploring of opponents' negatives and fail to adequately analyze their own potential vulnerabilities and liabilities, campaigns are often thrown on the defensive in answering a negative attack. In some situations, the external environment suddenly changes and creates new, unforeseen vulnerabilities. What before the campaign was a sound voting decision suddenly becomes a hot negative liability when the political environment changes. Whether the campaign is poorly prepared or is caught unawares, it must respond to the attack in order to institute damage control. Any time candidates are placed on the defensive, they are left at a disadvantage.

When candidates are aware of their liabilities and no inoculation strategy is planned, campaigns should develop neutralizing reactive responses for the anticipated attacks. Even when responses are planned, the campaign is still at a disadvantage, but still the campaign is in a far superior position than a campaign that has failed to anticipate negative attacks entirely. It is important to remember that it is far harder to neutralize a negative attack than it is to inoculate against one.

When reactive responses are made to negative attacks, it is very important that these responses be made through the same communication channel through which the original attack was made (Nesbitt, 1988). In other words, if the attack was made in a radio spot on a country music station, the response should also be on a country music station. Only in this manner may consultants safely believe they have reached the same audience that was initially exposed to the attack.

Eight Modes of Reactive Responses

In 1991 we identified eight modes of reactive responses to the opposition's negative advertising: (1) Silence; (2) Confession/Redemption; (3) Sanctimonious Admission; (4) Denial/Campaign Attack; (5) Counterattack; (6) Refutation; (7) Obfuscation; and (8) Counterimaging (Johnson-Cartee & Copeland, 1991a; cf. Baukus, Payne, & Reisler, 1985). What follows is a prescriptive and descriptive analysis of each mode. Please remember that frequently the negative attack must be combated in a variety of ways in order to most effectively neutralize the attack in the eyes of various target groups. In some instances, an ad may incorporate more than one reactive response.

Silence

Before political consultants were aware of the power of negative ads, they frequently told their candidates to ignore them. They told their clients that negative ads were ineffective, and the only candidate hurt would be the sponsor, because negative ads were certain to cause a boomerang effect (New Campaign Techniques, 1986, p. 30). This advice surely caused the defeat of a number of prominent Democratic senators and congressmen during the 1980 election. "Sens. Gaylord Nelson of Wisconsin and Herman E. Talmadge of Georgia, and Rep. Richardson Preyer of North Carolina,...[fell] victim to campaigns in which they declined to respond to challengers on the attack" (New Campaign Techniques, 1986, p. 30; Tarrance, 1982, p. 5). Today, consultants point to the now infamous 1980 defeats when advising candidates to respond to negative attacks (see Hagstrom & Guskind, 1986; Orlik, 1990). The lesson was clear: "mud sticks if it goes unanswered."

In certain situations, candidates may want to "stay above" the negative politics in a campaign. But Brummett (1980) has warned that this is a dangerous strategy in that strategic silence violates the voter's expectations. In politics, talk establishes and maintains political relationships. By refusing to talk, a political leader denies his or her relationship with the voters, and such an action leaves the candidate's behavior open to interpretation. Brummett concludes that strategic silences allow the news media to define the leader's behavior without the leader's input into the process. Such silences create a situation in which "mystery, uncertainty, passivity, and relinquishment" rule the day (p. 297). A strategic silence relinquishes the candidate's persona into the hands of the mass media. Edelman (1964) has maintained that "the basic condition for the displacement of political leadership is the leader's inability or lack of opportunity to convey the impression of coping with an opposition" (pp. 81-82). Americans have a bias in favor of activism and "admire men who get things done, men who radiate faith and confidence. Americans are not inclined toward doubt; they like to be all for or all against something, right away if possible" (Roper, 1957, pp. 219-220).

In the 1988 presidential elections, Michael Dukakis failed to respond to a number of the Bush campaign's negative attacks until late in the campaign. Ed McCabe, a national advertising consultant, wrote that the major problem with Michael Dukakis during the 1988 presidential campaign was that he never realized that "there's one thing the American people dislike more than someone who fights dirty. And that's someone who climbs into the ring and won't fight" (1988, p. 48). We explained it this way: "If a candidate ignores a negative attack, Americans give credence to the attack, because, at some level, voters believe that if the candidate does not fight back then the attack must be true" (Johnson-Cartee & Copeland, 1991a, pp. 224-225).

Confession/Redemption

Most prominent religions in the United States teach that confessional experiences are cleansing and a route to redemption. For this reason, the voters often "forgive" a candidate who publicly confesses his or her mistakes and apologizes. Sabato (1981) and Berkman and Kitch (1986) have called the confession/redemption ad an apologia, or an apology strategy. In 1969 New York mayor John Lindsay confessed that he had made numerous mistakes; he also reminded voters that he had done far more right than he had done wrong. And in this way, Lindsay was redeemed.

The 1969 Lindsay "Mistakes" Ad

Video	Audio
Fade-in to extreme close-up of Lindsay.	(Birds are faintly audible in background throughout.)
	Lindsay (SOF): "I guessed wrong on the weather before the city's biggest snowfall last winter, and that was a mistake. But I put
Slow zoom out, revealing his casual dress. He is sitting on a porch.	6,000 more cops on the street, and that was no mistake. The school strike went on too long, and we all made some mistakes. But I brought 225,000 new jobs to this

town, and that was no mistake.
And I fought for three years to put
a fourth police platoon on the
streets, and that was not a
mistake. And I reduced the
deadliest gas in the air by 50
percent, and I forced the landlords
to roll back unfair rents, and we
did not have a Detroit, or a Watts,
or a Newark in this city, and
those were no mistakes. The
things that go wrong are what
make this the second toughest job
in America. But the things that go
right are what make me want it."

Fade to black, then white Super:
"Vote for Mayor Lindsay. It's the
second toughest job in America."

(*Source*: Diamond & Bates, 1988, pp. 321-322)

Sanctimonious Admission

In some situations, candidates are able to turn the tables on their opponent by admitting that they had done whatever the opponent accused them of in the negative ad, but they present this past action as being quite virtuous rather than worthy of condemnation. The candidate appears to be saying, "Yes, I did it, and I'm damn glad I did it; and furthermore, if I had to do it all over again, I'd do the same exact thing." Such a stance plays to the American public's desire to see a leader stake a position and stand by it without caving in to political pressures. This type of response also places the opposition in the uncomfortable situation of having attacked someone on a matter that may now seem desirable by the voters.

In some circumstances, candidates when admitting that they did what the opponent has criticized them for, go on to explain why they acted as they did. They then turn the voters' attention to other actions of the candidate that the voters may find more desirable and beneficial. In other words, the ad dramatizes this idea: "Yes, I did that. I believed that I had to vote that way. And I'd do it again. But it's important to remember that I also did this and this, and they're more important to you." Smith and Hunt (1978) and Roering and Paul (1976) have demonstrated that an individual's credibility is enhanced when the person is willing to point out both perceived weaknesses and strengths.

In 1978 incumbent U. S. senator John Tower of Texas used a combination reactive response ad that first of all admitted that he had refused to shake his challenger's hand, thus violating the "gentleman" rules of political battle. Tower then goes on to imply that he would continue to refuse in the future, because his opponent was carrying on a negative campaign against not only him but his family. Notice that Tower doesn't even name his opponent. And Tower's signature appears at the tag, which implies that he personally endorsed the ad, thereby giving it more credibility.

The 1978 Tower "Handshake" Ad

Video	Audio
John Tower sits on desk. He holds up newspaper. Close-up of two newspaper photos.	Tower [SOT]: "Perhaps you've seen this picture of my refusal to shake the hand of my opponent.
John Tower sits on desk with flag behind him.	I was brought up to believe that a handshake is a symbol of friendship and respect. Not a meaningless hypocritical gesture. My opponent has slurred my wife, my daughters, and falsified my record. My kind of Texan doesn't shake hands with that kind of man. Integrity is one Texas tradition you can count on me to uphold."
Signature of John Tower. "He stands for Texas. Always has. Always will."	

Denial /Attack Campaign

The most popular response strategy to a negative ad is to deny the accusation and then to turn and attack the opposition for "dirty campaigning." Candidates who are "guilty" as charged often ignore the specific attack but respond by accusing the opposition of "mudslinging." Such a response gives the appearance of denial without actually going on the public record as denying the charge. Candidates may choose to make denial and subsequently attack the opponent's "dirty campaign" themselves (a candidate confrontation charge), or they may choose surrogates. Family members, close personal friends, or voters themselves may make the denial and "dirty campaign" charge.

In 1990 incumbant Republican Governor Guy Hunt attacked Democratic challenger Paul Hubbert in a most unsavory ad. The ad accused Dr. Hubbert, the director of the Alabama Education Association (AEA), the state's teachers association, of deliberately seeking out and hiring homosexuals for Alabama's schools. The AEA supports nondiscriminatory hiring practices as does the National Education Association. Supporting nondiscriminatory hiring practices is a far cry from deliberately recruiting homosexuals for classroom assignments. The Hubbert campaign wanted immediately to go on the air and call Hunt a liar. Because the initial ad was made by a female actress posing as an elementary schoolteacher, Hubbert wanted to ask Hunt to step out from behind his paid actresses and face Hubbert "like a man" (Letcher, 1991). But Frank Greer, Hubbert's media consultant, thought that the use of this ad by the Hunt campaign guaranteed Hubbert's win. Greer believed that the ad was so blatantly unfair that the ad would boomerang on Hunt and that it was an act of a desperate campaign.

Greer, a native Alabamian, had a bad case of what some might call "Potomac fever" or "Within the Beltway jaundice." Southern states are far more conservative on gay and lesbian issues and voters tell pollsters that they do not approve of gays and lesbians in the classroom. Alabama is one of the more conservative Southern states and its Bible-belt voters responded to the hot button that the Hunt campaign had provided. The Hubbert campaign dropped eleven points in the polls, and the ad ultimately cost the Democrats the election. Eventually, the Greer ad team did respond. The ad Greer created denied the charge and countercharged the Hunt campaign with using dirty tactics. On the surface, such an ad would be appropriate for Alabama. But in the long run, the response ad that was aired did more to hurt Hubbert than help. Greer chose Hubbert's Church of Christ minister to make the response. This calm, mild-mannered minister denied the allegations against Hubbert, defended the AEA director's honor, and shamed Hunt for his treachery. Perhaps Greer chose Hubbert's preacher to respond because Guy Hunt was himself a Baptist minister. But in Alabama, the political culture dictates that if attacked, a man defends himself and does not run to get his preacher to protect him. Hubbert's instincts to respond were correct, but he felt constrained by the advice of his paid consultants.

The 1990 Hubbert "Enough" Ad

Video	Audio
Minister speaking directly into the camera.	Minister [SOT]: "Enough is enough. I've stood by for several

Super: "Mr. Wayne Baker, Highland Church of Christ."	weeks and watched the false character assassination of a member of the church I serve. I'm Paul Hubbert's minister. Paul is a decent, moral god-fearing family man who would never condone immorality or indecency on the part of anyone. For his opponent to make such charges is ridiculous and untrue. I pray we won't let Guy Hunt's campaign tactics against Paul Hubbert rob us of the opportunity of electing a truly outstanding new leader for Alabama."

Although this surrogate denial/dirty campaign tactics response didn't work for Hubbert, such surrogate responses can be very effective. Kern (1989) has pointed out that surrogate ads using white-haired wives, mothers, or grandmothers are particularly effective. The notion is that white-haired ladies don't lie. Because our society expects women to be more emotional than men, the message they convey can be more emotion laden. In our society, women are allowed to safely express emotions of resentment and anger more than men. In the 1980 presidential election, Nancy Reagan appeared in a denial/dirty campaign tactics charge ad in which she told voters that she deeply resented Carter's accusations "as a wife, and a mother, and woman."

In the U.S. Senate race in Georgia in 1992, Republican candidate Paul Coverdell used an elderly woman, Margie Lopp from Cuthbert, Georgia, in a direct attack ad against incumbent Senator Wyche Fowler. Lopp sang a country and western jingle that told Georgia voters: "Let's put Paul Coverdell in the Senate and put Wyche Fowler out." Fowler's campaign attacked both the commercial and Ms. Lopp. To respond, the Coverdell campaign put Margie Lopp back on the air defending her jingle and attacking Fowler's campaign tactics. Notice that there is a charge of "throw[ing] mud" in this ad. "Mudslinging" accusations of opponent's advertising is a frequently used method of denial.

The 1992 Coverdell "Margie's Comeback" Ad

Video	Audio
Close-up of radio.	Radio playing in the background, [SOT]: "Let's put Paul Coverdell in the Senate and . . ."
Margie cuts off radio.	

She sits in a chair with an afghan.	Margie [SOT]: "I know some of you don't like my jingle, but I wrote it to help Paul Coverdell. Like most Georgians, Paul thinks taxes are too high and its time to put term limits on Congress. Wyche Fowler has been in Congress 16 years, and he's raised taxes and opposed term limits. Now he's using slick ads to hide his record and throw mud on Paul Coverdell. Wyche Fowler should be ashamed. I trust Paul Coverdell, and you can too."
"Margie Lopp, age 73, Cuthbert, Georgia"	
Super: "Paul Coverdell for U. S. Senate."	

Mudslinging demonstration ads were used across the country in the 1980s (Diamond & Bates, 1988,), and historically, they date back to a t least the 1960s. The format is usually the same. A campaign poster is assaulted with large globs of mud, a visual representation of "mudslinging." In the 1992 U.S. Senate Democratic primary campaign in Wisconsin, Russ Feingold used cardboard cutouts of his opponents to make his point.

The 1992 Feingold "Mudslinging" Ad

Video	Audio
Russ Feingold talking to camera. Super: "Russ Feingold"	Feingold [SOT]: "Hi, I'm Russ Feingold, the underdog running for the U. S. Senate. For the last few weeks, my opponents have been taking shots at one another."
Mud hits photos of opponents.	Sound of mud hitting photos. "Smack, Smack" with each hit.
Feingold talking.	Feingold [SOT]: "While they've been discrediting each other, I've been issuing my 82-point plan to eliminate the federal deficit. And I've been talking to you voters about the need to establish a long-term care [sic] for the elderly. Plus a National Health Care System. How have I kept clear of the
Feingold bends over two	mudslinging? Simple, I refuse to

cardboard cutouts of his opponents. Mud starts flying on boards and at Feingold; he ducks.	stoop to this level."
Super: "Wisconsin can't afford anything less." "Feingold" in blue.	Announcer [VO]: "Vote Feingold on September 8th."
	Mud hits [SOT]: "Smack, Smack, etc."
	Feingold [SOT]: "Uh, Oh. I must be gaining on them."

During the 1992 Democratic primary for president, Paul Tsongas ran a denial with a dirty campaign tactics charge ad that lambasted Bill Clinton. Tsongas played on the fears of many Democratic voters that Clinton wasn't to be trusted.

The 1992 Tsongas "Say Anything" Ad

Video	Audio
Black screen with white lettering: "I desperately want to be President"— Bill Clinton, *New York* Magazine, 1/20/92. Paul Tsongas in black and white photo at desk. Bullets: "Protect Social Security"; "Extend Medical Coverage"; "End Age Discrimination."	Announcer [VO]: "Some will say anything to be elected president. Now Bill Clinton is distorting Paul Tsongas' record on social security, trying to scare people. But Bill Clinton knows that for 10 years in the Congress, Paul Tsongas fought to protect social security, to extend medical coverage, and to end age discrimination. Isn't it time we sent a message that we've had enough negative campaigning?
Photos of Clinton and Tsongas. Super: "Tsongas, Democrat for President." Footage of Tsongas greeting supporters.	Vote for Paul Tsongas. Someone we can believe in."

Counterattack

In some situations, it is difficult or even impossible for a candidate to deny or refute a negative ad. When this occurs, the consultant usually recommends a counterattack strategy. The counterattack is an ad that responds to a negative ad by attacking the sponsor of the ad (see Baukus, Payne, & Reisler, 1985). The strategy behind the counterattack is to "fight fire with fire" (see Kern, 1989). Normally, the counterattack ad escalates the negativity in the campaign. In order to get voters' attention away from the attacking ad, the counterattack ad must be far more powerful or explosive than the original ad.

In the 1992 U.S. Senate campaign in Wisconsin, incumbent senator Bob Kasten finally counterattacked challenger Russ Feingold. Feingold had attacked Kasten's record using condemnatory newspaper headlines to back up his charges. Kasten chose not to refute or deny. He simply attacked.

The 1992 Kasten "Too Liberal" Ad

Video	Audio
Black lettering on white background: "A New Democratic Party?" Clinton and Gore in background of frame.	Announcer [VO]: "They say there's a new Democratic party? The party of Bill Clinton and Al Gore. (Cymbal crashes in background with each point made.) A party that favors a middle class tax cut, the death penalty, and reforming welfare. Russ Feingold opposes not only Bob Kasten on these issues but even his own party, Bill Clinton and Al Gore. When asked about Bill Clinton's tax proposals, Feingold said he thought Clinton could be convinced to raise taxes a little more. Now if Russ Feingold is out of step with his own party. Isn't he out of step with Wisconsin?"
Super: "Middle-Class Tax Cut"; "Death Penalty"; "Welfare Reform."	
Feingold in background. Super: "Feingold opposes." Boxes with the words: "Welfare Reform, Death Penalty, Middle-Class Tax Cuts. "Super: "Feingold to Clinton: 'Raise taxes a little more.'"—*Milwaukee Sentinel*, 10/17/92; Feingold in background using salt shaker. Super: "Out of step with Wisconsin"	

Refutation

A refutation response ad uses logical appeals that produce evidence designed to destroy the credibility of the previous negative attack. The evidence presented as refutation must be documented, irrefutable and believable (see McGuire, 1961b; McCroskey, 1969, 1970). Because voters believe refutation responses before they will other types of responses, the golden rule is: "if you can refute the charge, refute it." For this reason, refutation ads are considered to be the optimal reactive response (see Garramone, 1985a; Salmore & Salmore, 1985).

McCroskey (1970) found that the evidence provided in messages positively affected attitude change even when the evidence was delivered by sources with low credibility.   Although including evidence in messages presented by high-credibility sources did not increase the source's credibility ratings, it is important to remember that high-credibility status will itself positively impact on the degree of attitude change among the audience. McCroskey concluded: "Evidence appeared to serve as an inhibitor to counterpersuasion" (p. 194).

During the Gantt/Helms U.S. Senate race in North Carolina in 1990, Helms refuted a number of Gantt's charges by using expert testi- monials and his own voting record to support his position. In this ad Helms uses the golden rule we mentioned, "if you can refute the charge, refute it." Notice, also, the counterattack tag at the end of the spot.

The 1990 Helms "Education" Ad

Video	Audio
Gantt photo on right. Announcer's introductory words on left side of screen. White letters on black: "Look at the facts." *Congressional Record* title page.	Announcer [VO]: "Harvey Gantt is attacking Senator Helms on education. Look at the facts. . . . The official congressional record shows that Senator Helms sponsored competency tests for teachers to raise standards and quality. Increased school lunch funds by cutting foreign aid. Nine hundred million dollars to make our schools drug free. And on February 20, Senator Helms voted for the Dropout Prevention Program. The one Gantt implies that Helms didn't support. Harvey Gantt's record on Education? NONE."
Helms photo on left. Super: "Sponsored." Announcer's words displayed starting with "competency" and ending with "didn't support."	
Bill appears under writing.	
Gantt's photo on right. Announcer 's words on left.	

In 1994 the National Rifle Association's Political Victory Fund was active in a number of campaigns. They produced a number of independently sponsored ads attacking members of Congress who had voted to ban assault rifles. Charlton Heston was the public figure surrogate who made the attack. Many of the attacked candidates failed to respond, but Bob Kerrey chose to answer and refuted the Heston spot with both logical and emotional arguments.

The 1994 Kerrey "No AK47 Needed" Ad

Video	Audio
Bob Kerrey with other hunters, practicing skeet shooting. White print on blue background: "A message to Charlton Heston from Bob Kerrey."	Announcer [VO]: "This is a message to Charlton Heston from Senator Bob Kerrey."
Kerry talking.	Kerrey [SOT]: "I'm a hunter, and I believe in the constitutional right to bear arms. When it's time to hunt birds, you need a good gun like this Reuger Red Label.
Kerrey opens breech on shotgun and closes it.	
Hands gun to someone off screen. Off-screen person hands him an AK47.	Twenty-five years ago in the War in Viet Nam, people hunted me. They needed a good weapon like this AK47. But you don't need one of these to hunt birds."

Obfuscation

In appearance, the obfuscation ad resembles a refutation ad in terms of its tone and organizational structure. But the obfuscation ad does not contain any evidence. What it does present is a great deal of fancy footwork and a fair amount of sleight of hand. Dramatic assertions and protestations are presented as evidence but are merely will-o-the-wisps in the candidate's desperate attempts to avoid publicly denying the charge when the charge is true.

In 1992 the Clinton/Gore campaign successfully placed the blame for America's economic woes on the Republican political legacy of Ronald Reagan and George Bush. While Bush promised in his own ads to beat the Democratic Congress in his next term, the national Republican party ran a series of anti-Democratic-controlled Congress spots, trying to shift the blame to the Democrats. The spots exaggerated the power of the Democratically controlled House and Senate. Such spots would be accurate in a system such as Great Britain's where the party in the majority determines all policy and maverick politicians within the party are not tolerated and party reprisals are swiftly executed. But the United States has a legislative system that traditionally functions as a bipartisan process with little or no party discipline. In essence, the bills and amendments passed are usually the result of a bipartisan effort. In addition, the president himself in recent years has taken on more and more power through executive orders. The Republicans chose to use a female announcer because the ad was talking about our nation's children.

The 1992 RNC "Ghetto" Ad

Video	Audio
Ghetto children playing in the street, dilapidated buildings. Black and white children playing together. Close-up of little white girl. Close-up of black male child. Scenes of children playing in streets.	Female Announcer [VO]: "These kids are on borrowed time. In the 30 seconds it takes to watch this ad, the national debt will grow over $300,000. The Washington politicians don't care about these kids. For thirty-eight years, one party, the Democrats, have run Congress. Spending every dollar, busting every budget. The Democrats say they care about America's kids, but the national debt keeps getting bigger and bigger. And we know who is
Super: "For a new Congress Vote Republican"	going to have to pay for it. For a new Congress vote Republican.

A similar attitude is struck in this RNC ad.

The 1992 RNC "New Congress" Ad

Video	Audio
Blue photograph of Capitol. Scroll of announcer's words. The Capitol gets closer.	Announcer [VO]: "In the last few months, you've heard a lot of political rhetoric. Here are some facts you haven't heard. The Democrats have run this House for thirty-eight years. For almost four decades, chairing all the committees . . . deciding every floor vote . . . writing all the rules. Thirty-eight straight years of one party in charge. If you're unhappy with the way the Democrats have run Congress—the scandals, the
Super: "Vote Republican. For a New Congress."	abuses, the perks, vote Republican for a new Congress."

Counterimaging

Counterimaging is an attempt to reframe the attacked candidate's public persona. Without a contextual analysis of the campaign, it is very difficult for the analyst to tell them from a positive spot. The counterimaging ad lays out a counterproposition to that contained in the opponent's negative ad. Because of their subtle technique, counterimaging ads are generally used in combination with other reactive response ads. The idea is to make the other reactive response ad— whether it is a refutation or a denial-with-dirty-campaign-tactics-charge—more powerful by reframing the candidate's public persona in the electorate's mind.

In a congressional race, in Texas in 1992, incumbent Charlie Wilson had been portrayed by the media and his opposition as a party animal. The Wilson campaign chose to use an elderly woman in this voter editorial spot. As we've mentioned previously, elderly women are particularly effective in repairing damage done by negative publicity. The scene is a country western dance for the elderly. And Charlie Wilson is there, and he dances with her. Notice that the ad touches on Wilson's reputation, but then it goes on to suggest that it doesn't matter because Wilson is so good in other ways that are more important.

The 1992 Wilson "Square Dance" Ad

Video	Audio
Dance for elderly, country music, fiddles playing, flag on wall. Elderly lady talking in various positions in room.	Elderly Lady [SOT]: "These days the little things can mean a lot. Things like getting a social security check on time. Charlie Wilson always has time for you. He'll fight like a buzz saw to get a disability claim. It's a documented fact that Charlie Wilson has helped almost twice as many constituents with problems than any other congressman in the whole United States. Most folks get elected and you never hear from them until election time. They lose touch. Not Charlie Wilson. He stays in touch. He's always there when you need him. He's not a typical politician. And he remembers where he comes from. He's pure east Texas. Now they

Super: "Charlie Wilson, Taking Care of the Home Folks."

say Charlie Wilson's the life of the party wherever he is. But when it comes to our social security and VA benefits, Charlie is all business. Charlie Wilson, he takes care of the home folks, and he's not a bad dancer."

4

Storytelling in Political Advertising

Political commercials are purposeful, persuasive, symbolic constructions that use both video and audio imagery. As we have stated, modern campaign commercials are political short stories and lend themselves to narrative analysis. In this chapter, we analyze the various
narrative symbolic appeals, and in Chapter 5, we review the relevant
auditory and visual manipulations that form our political images.

MEDIATED POLITICS

Voters experience politics not at first hand but through the eyes
and ears of the mass media. From the mass media we obtain symbols,
which we then interpret, redefine, and alter through our communication with other people. What we know as our political world is not a
photocopy of the objective world but rather a created world of
symbols, often mass-mediated symbols.

We use symbols without questioning or thinking about their ori-
gin, and few of us realize their social, political, or personal ramifica-
tions. We often accept for ourselves the symbols that others have created without analyzing the merits or appropriateness of their symbolic logic.

Political rhetoric—the process of manipulating symbolic devices
by human agents to form attitudes or induce actions in other human
beings—is the key to how power is developed, held, and used in
American society (see Arnold, 1972; Burke, 1950; Hall, 1972). The
"symbolic devices" used in politics are the "words, actions, body
movements, and visual cues that stand for ideas and objects and to

which members of a culture attach similar meanings" (Perucci & Knudsen, 1983, p. 77). The symbolic construction "family values" became the linchpin in the Republican presidential campaign of 1992. Such a symbolic construction illustrates the type of symbolic device that political communication scholars are most often examining. For "family values" is an umbrella term that captures a world of issues, values, mores, norms, and folkways for a given ideological community. When politicians use the term *family values,* they are speaking to the conservative strain of American politics that glorifies the America of yesteryear, a time that may never have been, but one that is now held up as an ideal nevertheless. As a campaign platform, "family values" evoked the idea of perfect families living in houses with picket fences, with Pa gainfully employed and Ma making cookies in the family kitchen. As a background for this picture is the tableau of a small town with the little white church down the street and the neighborhood school where the children are all alike and eager to learn. Divorce, drugs, abortion, unemployment, welfare, domestic violence, racial divisiveness, and delinquency are not part of this picture.

Clearly, the symbolic construction "family values" is a rich rhetorical device that telegraphs a wealth of meaning in its simple utterance. "Family values" is an example of a condensation symbol, which is defined as "a highly condensed form of substitutive behavior for direct expression, allowing for the ready release of emotional tension in conscious or unconscious form" (Sapir, 1934, p. 493; see also Bennett, 1988; Edelman, 1964; Graber, 1976). Nimmo (1978) has argued that condensational symbols have more connotative meaning than denotative meaning. In other words, the significance of condensational symbols rests with the meanings that reside within individuals that are evoked when the words or phrases are used. Condensational symbols, which are "commonly salient across individuals" within a given political culture, are said to be *significant symbols* (Mead, 1934).

The condensational symbols used in a given political culture, which are widely understood and employed in everyday use, determine to a large extent what the world is like and what it will be like in the future. In other words, much of what we believe to be true about the world is simply an implication "of the particular terminology in terms of which the observations are made" (Burke, 1966, p. 50). In the political world, "voters develop stereotypes or implicit theories;— structures of related attributes or expectations—concerning various types of political figures" (Conover, 1981, p. 432). These stereotypes are based on past experiences and then are used to fill in information about political actors, groups, ideas or causes (see Conover, 1981; Lippmann, 1965, p. 170). When voters consider a candidate, a manner of speaking, a style of shirt, a turn of phrase, or a colorful yard sign may well trigger their preconceived political stereotypes. Such triggering devices are called *political cues*—"any characteristic or attribute of the candidate which stimulates voters to form additional evaluations and cognitions about the candidate" (Conover, 1981, p. 431) and which trigger existing stereotypes.

Professional political communicators are well aware of the significance of these political cues and their attendant political stereotypes. The use of such stereotypes "enables the communicator to frame his message with the least amount of lost motion, and it enables the receiver to comprehend what is being communicated with equal speed and facility" (O'Hara, 1961, p. 194; also see Gans, 1979; Lippmann, 1965). "Human beings are 'conditioned,' not directly to belief and behavior, but to a vocabulary of concepts that function as guides, warrants, reasons, or excuses for behavior and belief" (McGee, 1980, p. 6). Stereotypes are "highly condensed," significant symbol constructions.

THE RESONANCE STRATEGY

People make use of stereotypes because they are instrumental, functional, and efficient. According to Conover (1981):

People are motivated by their need to predict and organize their environment. Where the environment is not easily organized or does not readily provide the information necessary for predictions, individuals may impose an organization or create the necessary knowledge from their existing store of information. (pp. 431-432)

As students of the process, political consultants recognize voters' tendency to utilize stereotypes during election cycles. Therefore, the identification of and manipulation of political stereotypes are important weapons in the arsenal of the modern-day political consultant.

The advertising strategy that takes advantage of political stereotypes in order to evoke meaning in voters is called "the resonance strategy" (Schwartz, 1972, 1976)). Such a strategy selects persuasive messages that are "harmonious with the experience of the audience" (Patti & Frazer, 1988, p. 301; see also Schwartz, 1976). Campaign messages resonate "with information already stored within an individual and thereby induces the desired learning or behavioral effect. Resonance takes place when the stimuli put into our communication evoke meaning in a listener or viewer" (Schwartz, 1972, pp. 24-25).

Political consultants utilize the political/cultural stereotypes found in society in order to strike what Schwartz (1972) has called *responsive chords* within the voter (see also Combs, 1979; Nimmo & Combs, 1980). By striking these chords, consultants and candidates attempt to reach the "inner core" of the voter's psyche (Diamond & Bates, 1988). Schwartz (1976) concluded: "Commercials which attempt to tell the listener something are inherently not as affective as those which attach to something that is already in him. We are not focused on getting things across to people as much as out of people" (p. 352). Fisher (1970) wrote that:

One may hypothesize that rhetorical discourse will be persuasive to the extent that the image it creates regarding a subject corresponds with the image already held by the audience, the degree to which the image it implies of the audience corresponds with the self-images held by members of the audience, and the degree to which the image assumed in the message and its presentation by the communicator is attractive to the audience. (p. 131)

Analyzing Narrative Content

Although it may appear relatively easy to identify responsive chords and then utilize them in campaign messages, the process is far more complex than one might think. Even more importantly, as a voter analyzing political advertising, it might be suggested that it would be easy to understand the "stereotypic" content within the ads; however, this is not as easy as one might think either. The use of responsive chords is a highly complex process, and as we shall see, it is ripe for manipulation.

As we have previously mentioned, significant symbols are culturally shared condensational symbols that may ultimately form symbolic constructions called stereotypes. Significant symbols may appear in the form of both manifest and latent content (see Freud, 1952; Hale & Mansfield, 1986; Nimmo & Combs, 1983; Nimmo & Felsberg, 1986). Freud (1952) first made the distinction between what he described as *manifest content* (or that which is obvious, easily perceived, or on the surface) and what he termed *latent content* (or the underlying meaning, which is present but not obvious, that is, hidden). The Democratic presidential campaign in 1992 provides a useful example of manifest and latent symbolic strategies. Democratic candidate Bill Clinton utilized a Lincolnesque "poor boy makes good" manifest message in his campaign film *A Man from Hope*. In the campaign film, a saga unfolds of a poor boy with a dead father from a little town in a backwater state who got to meet the president of the United States, who went on to attend prestigious universities, who served his state as attorney general and governor, and who now was running for the presidency. The campaign film casts Clinton in the starring role in a Lincolnesque Horatio Algier success story. On the other hand, the Clinton campaign used a Fleetwood Mac song "Don't Stop," which came to latently signal not only his youthfulness and that of his vice presidential running mate but also his rejection of the Republican party's backpedaling on social programs. An understanding of both manifest and latent content is necessary to comprehend the totality of the dramatic message.

Political Environment

We cannot hope to understand both the manifest and latent meaning of symbols without analyzing the political, linguistic, and social environments in which they exist (see Saussure, 1966). Leymore (1975), Williamson (1978), and Nimmo and Felsberg (1986) have all emphasized the importance of analyzing advertising symbols in their contextual environment. With regard to product advertising, Nimmo and Felsberg (1986) wrote: "It is not sufficient, for instance, to analyze a single ad for a product or brand in isolation, either from other ads for that product or brand or in isolation from competing products or brands. All ads in the same product field must be included in the analysis" (p. 251). Thus, when we analyze verbal behavior in politics, we must analyze the political environment in order that we might examine the "total societal context in which communication occurred, an evaluation of each of the communicators and of their interactions, and judgments concerning the long-term and short-term objectives of the communication" (Graber, 1976, p. 101). This type of approach employs an educated "intuitive" strategy (Graber, 1976, p. 100).

By examining the thematic consistencies "displayed in concrete verbal and visual methods" (Nimmo & Felsberg 1986, pp. 253-254), and by then considering these consistencies in their environmental or situational context, researchers are able to decode political advertising—that is, transform latent content into manifest content. "The story is often made meaningful only when its manner of encoding interlocks with the perceptual process supplied by the viewer [the perceived situational context], which is itself culturally mediated" (Breen & Corcoran, 1982, p. 128). The individual's perceptual screen is the product of his or her past, present, and expectations for the future. Although each perceptual screen is unique to a given individual, differences among individual perceptual screens may be understood along fundamental demographic dimensions such as age, gender, ethnicity, religion, occupation, and race. In addition, political socialization and general life experiences produce various patterns of signification (see Cobb & Elder, 1972, p. 85).

Thus, a political environment analysis of "concrete signifiers" found in political advertising will ultimately reveal the candidate/consultant's perception of the political symbology of various target groups. Cobb and Elder (1972), through their analysis and testing of work done by Parsons and Shils (1951) and Smelser (1963), have developed the following hierarchical typology of political symbols:

"(1) symbols of the political community or core values; (2) regime symbols or symbols relating to political norms; (3) symbols associated with formal political roles and institutions; and (4) situational symbols to include (a) governmental authorities, (b) non-governmental personalities and groups, and (c) political issues" (p. 85). Those symbols "higher in the typology tend to be the most abstract and general, while those lower in the scheme tend to be more specific and concrete" (p. 86). Political scientists have long noted that there is more consensus among the general public concerning the more abstract notions of freedom, equality, and liberty than in the more specific applications of these terms, such as whether an individual would allow a communist, a homosexual, a female, or an African American to become president of the United States (for other examples, see Walker, Lindquist, Morey, & Walker, 1968). Whether the symbols used are abstract or specific, it is important to remember that both manifest and latent political symbols have a powerful impact (see Jamieson, 1992; see also Conover, 1981).

In a 1994 Circuit Court judicial race in Alabama, Republican Challenger Bill Kennedy lambasted Democratic incumbent John England for being a "civil rights leader." England, Tuscaloosa County's first African American Circuit judge since Reconstruction, had been appointed by the governor to fill a vacancy on the Court and was serving as the president of the New South Coalition, a predominantly African American political action committee. In repeated ads, Kennedy maintained that civil rights leaders should not be jurists, because they would and could not be impartial in court on "sensitive issues brought before the Court" ("Responsibility," *Tuscaloosa News*, 1994, p. 4B). The term *civil rights leader* was the key. The American Heritage Dictionary defines "civil rights" as "rights belonging to a person by virtue of his status as a citizen or as a member of civil society." Expressed within this definition and under our constitutional democracy is the concept of equal rights under the law or, more formally stated, "equal protection under the law." Certainly, as concerned citizens, all voters should want judges to be fair and impartial, treating all people equally and without prejudice. Then why would a candidate condemn leadership in civil rights? Because clearly, the ad provides voters a covert or latent message, a fear-inducing subtext. The ad is warning voters that an African American political leader will not be an impartial jurist—that is, he will favor African American defendants. Ironically, this charge was leveled at a circuit judge who has a record of being a strong law and order jurist. Ultimately, Kennedy was defeated. But his strategy had been clear. In the predominantly white Tuscaloosa County, Kennedy had hoped to appeal to latent racism in the community where George Wallace had once stood in the school house door blocking integration at the University of Alabama.

George Wallace, long-time governor of Alabama and frequent presidential candidate, was a master of the use of latent political symbols. Wallace frequently used the symbolic phrase *states' rights* in his public appearances, writings, and political advertising. However, "states' rights" meant more to Wallace and Wallace supporters than the political construct that states should maintain their individual sovereignty even when functioning as part of a federation of states (see Johnson-Cartee, Copeland, & Elebash, 1992; Johnson-Cartee, Elebash, & Copeland, 1992). "States' rights" was a euphemism for "segregation." Wallace and his supporters were fighting the federal court-mandated integration of schools, buses, neighborhoods, restaurants, and so on. According to Makay (1970) the Alabama governor "spoke in a kind of code"; that is, Wallace used latent political symbols (p. 172). Makay recounts a statement supposedly made by an Alabama state senator: Wallace "can use all other issues—law and order, running your own schools, protecting property rights—and never mention race. But people will know he is telling them a nigger's trying to move into your neighborhood'" (as quoted in Makay, 1970, p. 172).

Linguistic Environment

An analysis of the symbols used in political advertising must take into account not only the political environment of the advertising but alsoit must also the *linguistic conditioning* of the campaign communication. Political consultants use various multilayered political communication tactics to achieve campaign goals. If researchers ignore the political communication context for a political ad, they are likely to misinterpret the overall strategy behind the execution of that particular tactic. Political consultants "set the stage" for political ads, particularly negative polispots. For this reason, it is important to know the content of the ads that preceded a polispot and those that followed (see Gronbeck, 1992; Jamieson, 1989, 1992; Johnson-Cartee & Copeland, 1991a). In addition, public relations communication tactics must also be considered. An analysis of a political ad that takes into account the linguistic conditioning for the ad is called a *linguistic environment analysis*. In following tracking polls that reflect the effectiveness of various political spots, it is important to keep in mind that movement in the polls may be the product not only of the ad currently running but also of those that preceded it which "set the stage."

Gronbeck (1992) warns that researchers should examine *adversarial narratives*, which he calls the "pairings between opposing negative ads" (p. 336). In other words, we must examine the attack, the response to that attack, the second wave of attack, the response to that wave, and so on. In addition, researchers should look at the *sequel narratives* within each political ad campaign (Gronbeck, 1992). Campaigns may use a series of ads to drive home their point on particular issues. Gronbeck (1992) suggests that although each ad is a distinct narrative message, researchers should analyze ads within the larger narrative structure, which may be the entire ad campaign or a narrative subset of ads. Similarly, Smith and Golden (1988) suggest that well-constructed political advertising campaigns resemble a soap opera in that they are ongoing stories that present continuity and consistency in terms of the candidate's messages.

The 1990 Helms/Gantt Senate race is an interesting case study of adversarial narratives and sequel narratives. Helms had attacked Gantt's past business practices and his use or misuse of his position as mayor of Charlotte, North Carolina, and his minority status to gain economic advantages over others in the community. Gantt responded with an attack on Helms's position on abortion. A series of ads relating to the abortion issue appeared on both sides of the campaign.

The 1990 Helms "Betrayed" Ad

Video	Audio
White letters on black: "How did Harvey Gantt become a millionaire?"	Announcer [VO]: "How did Harvey Gantt become a millionaire? The public record: He used his position as mayor and his minority status to get himself and his friends a free TV station license from the government. Only weeks later they sold out to a white-owned corporation for three and one-half million dollars. The black community felt betrayed. But the deal made the mayor a millionaire. Harvey Gantt made government work for Harvey Gantt."
Headlines: "Gantt Profits from Government." "Influence Peddling Charged."	
A Television Station with sign, "WJZY46." "Gantt, Partners may make millions selling station"; "Group including Gantt might make $3 million by selling TV station"; "Gantt profits from government."	

The 1990 Gantt "His Views" Ad

Video	Audio
"He's at it again."	Announcer [VO]: "He's at it again. Jesse Helms' negative ads out to tear down Harvey Gantt. Why? Because he doesn't want you to
Jesse Helms' Negative Ads. Three TV sets shown with clips of ads:	

"Jesse Helms doesn't want you to know what he's been doing." know what he's been doing up in Washington.

Three joint resolution bills are shown: "Jesse Helms wants to change the Constitution to fit. . .his views." A highlighted section of bill: "To amend the Constitution of the United States." Highlighted: "Outlaw abortion even for victims of rape and incest"; "Jesse Helms wants to outlaw abortion even for victims of rape and incest."

Jesse Helms has been trying to change the Constitution of the United States to fit his views.

To outlaw abortion even for victims of rape and incest. That's right. Jesse Helms wants to outlaw abortion even for victims of rape and incest.

Gantt talking with people.

But Harvey Gantt believes we don't need our government or Jesse Helms telling us what we can do in our private lives. Harvey Gantt for Senate. This time it's

"Harvey Gantt for U. S. Senate".   time to move forward."

The 1990 Helms "Awful Things" Ad

Video	Audio
Middle-aged woman speaking directly to camera	Woman [SOT]: "It bothers me that a politician is running ads to scare women just to get votes. The truth is Harvey Gantt is avoiding some important facts. Harvey Gantt is asking you and me to approve of some pretty awful things:—aborting a child in the final weeks of pregnancy— aborting a child because it's a girl rather than a boy. That's too liberal. Harvey Gantt is asking us to approve of some pretty extreme views to vote for him."

The 1990 Gantt "Label" Ad

Video	Audio
Women in red dress in Helms' TV ad on TV, talking sound off. A sign appears: "Warning! Jesse	Announcer [VO]: "These days you need a warning label for your TV screens. Because Jesse Helms' ads

Helms' ads may be hazardous to the truth." White on black: "The facts Jesse Helms doesn't want you to know";	are hazardous to the truth. On the issue of abortion, here are the facts Jesse Helms doesn't want you to know:
Gantt photo on left. Statement on right: "Abortion should remain legal." Helms photo on right. Statement on left: "Abortion should be outlawed even for rape and incest." Gantt photo on right. Statement on left: "Trusts women to make this personal decision."	Harvey Gantt believes that abortion should remain legal. But Jesse Helms believes that abortion should be outlawed even for victims of rape and incest. Harvey Gantt trusts women to make this personal decision.
Helms photo on left. "Wants government to dictate what women can do." "Harvey Gantt for U.S. Senate" Photo of Gantt talking.	But Jesse Helms wants government to dictate what they can do. Harvey Gantt for Senate. Because the truth really matters."

The 1990 Helms "Ten Seconds" Ad

Video	Audio
White on black: "Should teenage girls be allowed to have abortions without their mothers being informed." Gantt photo on left with "Yes" under; Helms photo on right with "No" under.	Announcer [VO]: "Should teenage girls be allowed to have abortions without their mothers being informed. Harvey Gantt says yes. Jesse Helms says no; we can't undermine families."

The 1990 Helms "Sex Selection" Ad

Video	Audio
White on black: "Let's set the record straight." Photo of Gantt on right. Statement on left: "Harvey Gantt denies he would allow abortion for sex selection." Photo of Gantt on right. Statement on left: "But Harvey Gantt told the press he would allow abortion." Gantt talking.	Announcer [VO]: "Let's set the record straight. Harvey Gantt denies he would allow abortion for sex selection—when parents want a boy and not a girl. But Harvey Gantt told the press he would allow abortion." Gantt [SOT]: "Whether it's for sex selection or for whatever reason."

Picture freezes on Gantt.	Announcer [VO]: "Did he say even for sex selection?"
Gantt talking.	Gantt [SOT]: "Whether it's for sex selection or for whatever reason."
Picture freezes on Gantt.	Announcer [VO]: "Read his lips."
Slow motion of Gantt talking	Gantt [SOT]: "Whether its for sex selection or for whatever reason."
Picture freezes on Gantt.	Announcer [VO]: "Harvey Gantt denied he ever said that.
Photo of Gantt on right. Statement on left: "Harvey Gantt, Extremely Liberal with the Facts."	Harvey Gantt, extremely liberal with the facts."

An assessment of the linguistic environment is necessary in order to clearly understand both the construction of the ad and its presentation. There ia a synergism. By this we mean, the whole effect of the ads is far greater than the sum of the individual ads or 1+1=3. An analysis of the linguistic environment permits this synergism to emerge. Helms's sequel narratives and Gantt's sequel narratives highlight the need to consider the subset of issue spots within each campaign. And this mini-case study demonstrates the context established by the adversarial narrative which occurred in the process of the campaign. Indeed, the adversarial narrative highlights the function of modern political advertising as it serves as a mini-campaign debate.

Social Environment

As we have discussed, both the political and linguistic environment in which the ad is aired must be considered before a thorough analysis of an ad is made. However, an additional area must also be taken into consideration—the social environment. As a society, we share a large number of political/cultural mythologies. However, although as Americans or as Southerners or as Northerners, we may share as a community a large number of political myths, we may not always be aware of political myths and may not know that our understanding of the world is being colored by politicians triggering these hidden artifacts of American culture (see Bennett, 1980).

POLITICAL MYTHOLOGIES

Much has been written about the study of mythology in modern American life (see Barthes, 1972; Breen & Corcoran, 1982; Combs, 1991; Edelman, 1964, 1967; Gronbeck, 1989; Leymore, 1975; MacDonald, 1969; Mullins, 1972; Nimmo & Combs, 1980; Seebok, 1958; Sykes, 1965, 1966, 1970; Vatz, 1973). Myths have been studied as a national phenomenon as well as a subcultural phenomenon in various ethnic, religious or organizational groups (see Edsall & Edsall, 1991; Jamieson, 1992; Lieske, 1991; Sykes, 1965, 1966).

MacDonald (1969) and Bennett (1980) assert that the study of political mythology is most significant in understanding the political process, particularly the influence of political leaders and the mass media on the American democratic system. Edelman (1971) defines political myth as "an unquestioned belief held in common by a large group of people that gives events and actions a particular meaning" (p. 6). Similarly, Nimmo and Combs (1980) highlight the unquestioned nature of political mythologies in their definition: "A credible, dramatic, socially constructed re-presentation of perceived realities that people accept as permanent, fixed knowledge of reality while forgetting (if they were ever aware of it) its tentative, imaginative, created, and perhaps fictional qualities" (p. 16).

Whether the average voter is aware of political mythologies and their influence on everyday life is at issue, but what is not debatable is the very clear understanding that political consultants have of such influential social mythologies. And most importantly, consultants not only understand these hidden artifacts of American culture, but they also use them to manipulate voters. Myths are a powerful persuasive device. Sykes states that

Myth is used, consciously and deliberately, to arouse emotional responses; in communicating the perception of a situation it also communicates the emotions aroused by that perception. . . . In fact myth is often more concerned with communicating an emotional response to a perception than it is with communicating the perception itself. (1970, p. 20)

According to Edelman (1967), myths "make the world meaningful and rationalize conformity for those least able to assert, express, and identify themselves through innovative behavior or demonstrated political efficacy" (p. 225).

I am suggesting that political responses are frequently not based on empirical observation or rational inference from the observations; that there is a basic distinction between (1) dispassionate organization of data and (2) observation only to persuade oneself and others that preconceived worlds exist; and that the possibility of creating ardent followings through reliance upon the penchant of the anxious for organizing their perceptions in the form of these myths is a major fact of political life. (p. 225)

Types of Political Mythologies

Nimmo and Combs (1980) identified four broad categories of political myths; master myths; myths of us and them; heroic myths; and pseudo-myths. Figure 4.1 provides an outline of the types of political myths and their subcategories.

Figure 4.1
American Political Mythologies

```
┌─────────────────────────────────────────┐
│  Master Myths                            │
│      Foundation                          │
│      Sustaining                          │
│      Eschatological                      │
│          Ethnocentrism                   │
│          Altruistic Democracy            │
│          Responsible Capitalism          │
│          Small-town Pastoralism          │
│          Individualism                   │
│          Moderation                      │
│          Order                           │
│          American Dream                  │
│              Materialism                 │
│              Moralism                    │
│          Western or Frontier Myth        │
│  Us and Them Myths                       │
│  Heroic Myths                            │
│  Pseudo-Myths                            │
└─────────────────────────────────────────┘
```

Master myths

Master myths are "broad, overarching myths that constitute the collective consciousness of an entire society" (Nimmo & Combs, 1980, p. 26), and the three types of master myths are foundation, sustaining, and eschatological myths.

The *foundation myths* tell "the story of our nation's origins, its struggle for independence, and the framing of the constitution" (p. 26). The classic mythical tale of America being a "city on the hill," serving as "a beacon of light" for the rest of civilization suggests the "nobleness" of the American experiment of liberty. This particular foundation myth frequently appears in political advertising that seeks to give its sponsor a sense of stature, of vision, for he or she is able to see the light and verbalize the beacon's path for the future. A host of political leaders have used this mythical tale successfully, such as Lamar Alexander in his 1978 run for the Tennessee governorship, Richard Nixon in his 1968 and 1972 campaigns for the presidency, and Bill Clinton in his 1992 presidential bid.

In 1988 the Bush presidential campaign knew that it needed to "warm" up Bush. Bush's public image was that of a cold, patrician gentleman who entered public service because he was expected to by his family. A series of ads were produced that showed Bush talking about his own virtues as a candidate. In one spot, Bush pursues the heroic quest, and in so doing, he articulates his vision of America and satisfies the voter's need to believe in America's golden future. Americans expect their leaders to articulate the future, and they expect that articulation to be in the form of a symbolic vision. In this case, it is the restatement of the "beacon of light" and "city on a hill" myths that are so much a part of American culture. The ad uses a reassurance appeal that guarantees America that if the people just vote for Bush all will be well.

The 1988 Bush "The Mission" Ad

Video	Audio
Black with white lettering: "The Mission."	(Silence.)
Bush at convention, speaking. Flag waving. Young woman cheering at convention.	Bush [SOT]: "I'm a man who sees life in terms of missions."
Montage of faces, patriotic music, flag, cheering women crying.	Bush [VO]: "Missions defined and missions completed. I will not allow this country to be made weak again. I will keep America moving forward, always forward. For an endless enduring dream and a thousand points of light.
"George Bush Experienced Leadership for America's Future."	This is my mission and I will complete it."

The second type of master myth that Nimmo and Combs (1980) identified is a sustaining myth. *Sustaining myths* are "myths enhancing the maintenance of political relationships" (Nimmo & Combs, 1980, p. 27). Edelman (1964) identified a number of sustaining mythologies: (1) the myth of the rational voter; (2) the myth of elections determining governmental policy directions; and (3) the myth of the judicial and administrative enforcement of the law as rational and mechanical. These mythologies are frequently used in political advertising at all electoral levels. In congressional political advertising, political incumbents are shown with other powerful political figures, suggesting that underlying webs of influence tie the nation together and that these webs of informal power are easy to understand and evaluate. It is not unusual to hear arguments of seniority, clout, or power being used to dramatize the notion that a candidate should be reelected because of his or her "place" in the scheme of things (e.g., see 1986 Leahy "Moo" Ad).

Eschatological myths are master myths that "project the nation's destiny on the basis of our past and present" (Nimmo & Combs, 1980, p. 27). Gans (1979), Morreale (1991a, 1991b) and Nimmo and Combs (1980) have identified a number of eschatological myths which are frequently found not only in political advertising but also in mass mediated news reports and product advertising.

Presidential campaigns frequently use the *ethnocentrism myth* in political campaign films and in visionary appeals that are often made during the last days of the campaign (see Diamond & Bates, 1988). Ethnocentrism is the notion that America is somehow superior to other nations of the world, and political ads frequently include discussion of how much better off we are to be living in the United States than anywhere else.

Examples of the eschatological myth of an *altruistic democracy* abound. The use of an altruistic democracy concept suggests the idea that American politics should be based on the public interest and service (see Nimmo & Combs, 1980; for example, 1992 Clinton "Family" Ad). Thus, many political ads promise to end red tape, eliminate waste, fight corruption, fight fat cats, fight legislative deals, and the like (e.g., 1992 Nixon "Got The Big Guys" Ad).

Responsible capitalism "is the belief that the business community acts to increase prosperity for all without seeking unreasonable profits or exploiting workers or consumers" (Nimmo & Combs, 1980, p. 179). Ads that promise more industry, more economic growth, and therefore "greater good" for all illustrate this myth (e.g., 1992 Perot "The Economy" Ad).

Small-town pastoralism is the Jeffersonian myth that places special value on rural, pastoral America. Americans have high esteem for small towns, farmlands, and the values found there. In American political advertising, political candidates are often shown walking through towns and villages, talking and listening to the voters there. Candidates often say that they are going to the people to hear their concerns, but "the people" are the icons of rural America—farmers, general store owners, or a local postmaster.

In an ad used for a congressional race in Texas in 1994, Chet Edwards presented a collage of small-town scenes from Mound, Texas. The black and white film of the ad also evoked that old-time feeling of yesteryear.

The 1994 Edwards "Mound, Texas" Ad

Video	Audio
Black and white film of two old men dressed in overalls, sitting in front of the Mound, Texas, Post Office, a clapboard house. Shots of a school bus going down a tree-lined street. Edwards at a counter in a cafe. Woman in front of the Post Office, holding a child. Close-up of old men dressed in overalls. Flooded home. Edwards with Bulldozer and worker.	Announcer [VO]: "For most, a town like Mound, Texas, is little more than a dot on a map. But for a young man named Chet Edwards, Mound, Texas, is people and families where roots run deep and values still count. So when the families of Mound were threatened by floods, it was Chet Edwards who helped secure the new dam to protect their small town. Something the people of Mound, Texas, will not soon forget.
Edwards at his desk with flag in upper right. "Chet Edwards for Congress"	Chet Edwards, a leader who knows what counts."

Individualism is the myth of of the "rugged individual," "the self-made man," which suggests a ferocity of spirit that is associated with the lonesome, noble brow of the pioneer (see Nimmo & Combs, 1980). Political ads that dramatize this mythical appeal show the candidate standing alone, making tough decisions (e.g., 1992 Campbell "American Dream" Ad).

The myth of *moderation* is the fight for the middle-of-the-road. Successful American presidential candidates must fight for the center of the political spectrum, for it is there that victory resides. In 1992, George Bush attempted to use his reputation for moderation against Bill Clinton's leftist or liberal reputation. In a series of ads, Bush stressed his middle-of-the-road political philosophy (e.g., 1992 Bush "Plain Talk" Ad). Candidates foolish enough to believe that "extremism" in America wins elections, such as Barry Goldwater in 1964 and George McGovern in 1972, have made possible some of the greatest landslides in American history—landslides for their opponents.

The myth of *order* is one that protects the status quo in that it suggests that at all costs, "the social and political order of public, business, and professional upper-middle classes, the middle-aged, and the white-male sectors of society" should be preserved (Nimmo & Combs, 1980, p. 180). George Wallace, in his many campaigns for the American presidency, stressed order in his political ads. Wallace condemned protests, demonstrations, and so on, for they were challenges to his political order. Myths of leadership have led to the personalization of politics (see Nimmo & Combs, 1980, p. 180). People understand world events not through an analysis of economic, political, or cultural forces but through an awareness of personalities. It's the white hats against the black hats. Political advertising dramatizes the political leader as a powerful force, a force to be reckoned with by the forces of evil, however they are defined.

Morreale's (1991a) analysis of the 1984 Republican presidential campaign indicates that the eschatological myth of the *American Dream* was an important part of the Reagan symbolic strategy. The notion of the American Dream is a universal ideal or political vision that all Americans share or hold dear. "There are, however, two dichotomous versions of the myth of the American Dream—the materialistic and the moralistic—that reflect different notions of America's nature and purpose" (Morreale, 1991a, p. 58). These differences are apparent in the different interpretations of the American Dream made by the two major political parties in the United States.

The materialistic myth is associated with the traditional Republican position. It emphasizes individual initiative as the means to happiness and prosperity; it presupposes the value of competition, free enterprise, and individual freedom from governmental regulation and restraint. It promises that hard work will be rewarded, and presumes that individuals act on the basis of self-interest rather than concern for the social good. The moralistic myth, more characteristic of the Democratic view, emphasizes a need for community and society that may supersede individual needs; it is based upon a belief in equality, rights to liberty and pursuit of happiness, and the values of tolerance, charity, and compassion. (Morreale, 1991a, p. 59)

In 1982 the Democratic party presented a classic ad that demonstrated the two versions of the American Dream. The tin cup reminds us of the food lines of the Great Depression, and the champagne flutes remind us of the life-styles of the very rich.

The 1982 Democratic "Tin Cup vs. Champagne Flutes" Ad

Video	Audio
An arm is holding out a tin cup; the cup is catching trickles from above. The arm is dressed in a plaid work shirt. Suddenly champagne flute glasses appear above the tin cup. The arms are decorated with expensive jewelry and watches. The champagne is poured from one champagne flute to another and finally down to the	Narrator [VO]: "The Big Republican Tax Cut—what does it mean to the average working person? About four bucks a paycheck. Not much. But it means a lot to the wealthy. It's the Republican theory called trickle down. Give to the rich, and it will eventually trickle down to everybody else. But you've got to

tin cup.	ask yourself, just how much is trickling down to you lately?"
Finally the plaid shirt turns the tin cup upside down. One drop falls.	Sound Effects: "PLUNK!"
"It isn't Fair. It's Republican."	Narrator [VO]: That's what we thought. It isn't Fair. It's Republican."

Additional ads that demonstrate the two versions of the American Dream may be found elsewhere in this book (e.g., 1992 NRC "Ghetto" Ad; 1992 Harkin "Trickle Down" Ad).

The Reagan campaign team also utilized a closely allied eschatological myth known as the *western myth* or the *frontier thesis* (Carpenter, 1977). While this myth is understood nationally, it has a special resonance in the west. According to Morreale (1991a), this frontier thesis is the image of "quintessential 'American': cooperation, optimism, individualism, self-reliance, resiliency, steadfastness, neighborliness, confidence, wholesomeness, enthusiasm, calmness of purpose, spirit of adventure, and initiative . . . [is] the rhetorical source of the American identity" (pp. 61-62). Reagan personified this myth, as he was shown in cowboy garb on the back of a horse. His movie and television career, where he often appeared on the screen in the role of a westerner, helped further dramatize what Americans saw when they watched the Reagan campaign film, *A New Beginning*.

In a 1994 race for the U.S. Senate in Arizona, Jon Kyl clearly utilized the western or frontier spirit myth in the following campaign ad.

The 1994 Kyl "Frontier Spirit" Ad

Video	Audio
Kyl talking while driving a truck. Super in cursive: "On the road . . . with Jon Kyle." Photo of Kyl with wife and child. Photos of college campus. Scenes of desert.	Kyl [VO]: "You know Arizona is really a very special place. When Carol and I moved from Tucson, we were going to the University of Arizona. We packed up everything we owned, and we drove up to Phoenix without air conditioning. And it was so hot. It was the middle of summer time. Our radiator boiled

Kyl checks under hood. Driving again. Outside truck, standing in front of it.

over. It was great. I know when I first came here, I had concluded that I wanted to stay here for the rest of my life. People in Washington don't understand it. It's something about the land that's very enchanting."

Talking with truckers.

Scenes from desert.

Kyl sitting with large circular group of voters; they all raise hands at question.

Kyl [SOT]: "How many think reducing taxes and spending is the most important issue?"

Scenes of him driving away.

Kyl [VO]: "And it's a state where you can get out and be by yourself and just be by yourself and just think about things."

Close-up of Sign: Bee Line Cafe; Talking with man at counter.

Kyl [SOT]: "The folks that I've talked to say we want to make sure to maintain quality. . . ."

Pulls in front of a garage; shakes hands with people there.

Kyl [VO]: "People who come are willing to strike out and seek something new. They're people who are independent."

Kisses woman.

Kyl [SOT]: "Good cooking in there. Thank you."

Kyl talks to man on horse in a parade.

Kyl [VO]: "Arizona sort of embodies all that. Folks back in Washington don't seem to understand it."

Walking with woman across prairie.

Woman [VO]: "I'll tell you what Jon Kyl, you just need to go back to Washington and just keep working for Arizona."

Kyl [VO]: "All right, I'll do it (laughter)."

Close-up of Jon Kyl bumper sticker on truck.
Desert scene. Super: "Jon Kyle U.S. Senate"

Announcer [VO]: "A different kind of leader, a different kind of state. Integrity, independence. That's Arizona. That's Jon Kyle."

(Note: [VO] and [SOT] switch back and forth for two to three seconds at a time; transcript reflects major audio/video groupings.)

Us and Them Myths

The myths of us and them. "set specific social collectivities apart from others in the nation" (Nimmo & Combs, 1980, p. 27). Edelman (1967) observed that politicians use several variations on this theme:

The evocation of an outgroup, defined as "different" and as plotting to commit harmful acts. . . . A second stylized myth, consistently offered to reassure those who are frightened by the first, is the view that the political leader is benevolent and is effective in saving people from danger. . . .The third classic mythical theme like the first two, is a bulwark of followers' support for leaders. It is the belief that a group—a nation, a state, a party—can achieve victory over its enemies if it will only work, sacrifice, and obey its leaders. (pp. 223-224)

In a 1994 local referendum to increase the number of jail cells, Law Enforcement '93 used the following spot. What is interesting about the ad is that the people portraying the criminals, with one exception, are all minorties. The minorities are portrayed as ridiculing and laughing at the general public. There is only one "white" criminal in the ad and his origens are somewhat uncertain in that his eyes are not Northern European.

The 1994 Law Enforcement '93 "Jail Cells" Ad

Video	Audio
White letters on black background: "We caught them. Arrested them. And booked them. Series of mug shots, malecriminals in front of height line; two seconds each: black man, black man, hispanic man, black man, white man. Super: "We're Out of Jail Space."	Announcer [VO: "We caught them. Arrested them. And booked them. So why are these people smiling? Because they know we're out of jail space.
Two seconds each: black with back to the camera; black laughing; black acting menacing; Hispanic smirking, white laughing	If you agree that crime deserves punishment, on October 16th, you'll have a chance to say so. These people are against the Sheriff's proposition, so what does that say about how you should vote.

Super: "Crime deserves Punishment." "On October 16th Vote YES for the Sheriff's Proposition. Lock 'em Up." Please Say Yes to 444 More Jail Cells."	Please say yes to 444 more jail cells.
Jail cell doors slam on a series of seven prisoners. All are startled. New faces are all black men. Super: "We don't want anything fancy. Just a place to lock 'em up."	We don't want anything fancy. Just a place to lock 'em [sic] up."

All too frequently, myths of "us and them" are used in political ads. These ads allow candidates to channel hostility and dissatis-faction toward an individual, a group, class, object, or country and away from themselves. Such ads provide an excuse as to why things are bad or aren't as we want them. We provide a detailed analysis of the use of *us vs. them* in negative political advertising (Johnson-Cartee and Copeland, 1991a) and elsewhere (Johnson-Cartee, Copeland, and Elebash, 1992; Johnson-Cartee, Elebash, and Copeland, 1992).

Heroic Myth

Frequently, political ads attempt to link the sponsor with Amer-ican political heroes of the past or to link their opponents with the villains and fools of history. Quite frequently, heroic myths appear as themes in transfer ads, which infer either positive or negative evaluations of individuals by associating them with well-known posi-tive or negative public figures, movements, or causes (Wilcox, Ault, & Agee, 1986). In a 1992 U.S. Senate race in California, Gray Davis associated himself with the philosophies of Dr. Martin Luther King, Jr. and John F. Kennedy. And in a 1992 U. S. Senate race in Georgia, Paul Coverdell used an ad that had a Georgia voter telling other Georgians: "We've got to get rid of Wyche Fowler, he's just like Ted Kennedy."

Morreale (1991a) describes a particular type of heroic figure, which she terms the *heroic savior* or redeemer of the people:

The hero must be of obscure and mysterious origins (exemplified by the log-cabin myth of American political mythology); he embarks upon a quest and encounters evil, suffering, or death; he overcomes this challenge and is purified or trans-formed. In this way, mythic heroes can be redeemers. (p. 65)

During the 1990 race for U.S. Senate in Texas, Phil Gramm used a variety of famous individuals to tell his heroic story: Charlton Heston, Ronald Reagan, and George Bush. The ad covers the many ups and downs of Gramm's career and makes an overt reference to Gramm's ability to "bring home the bacon" (a way of complimenting Gramm's ability to get federal money and projects or, as it is often called, pork) to Texas. Most interesting of all, it also mentions Gramm's jump from the Democratic party to the Republican party—a kind of move that many politicians often choose to forget. Gramm is depicted as waging war against forces that would hurt Texas and emerging victoriously from the battle with the foes of Texas.

Similarly, Jewett and Lawrence (1977) have described what they term the *American monomyth* in popular culture:

The American monomyth begins and ends in Eden. Stories in this genre typically begin with a small community of hard-working farmers and townspeople living in harmony. A disruption of harmony occurs, and must be eliminated by the superhero, before the Edenic condition can be re-established in a happy ending. (pp. 169-170)

Jewett and Lawrence (1977) point to such movies as *Jaws, Walking Tall* or *Death Wish* and to such television series as "Little House on the Prarie" or "Star Trek" as embodiments of the American monomyth. More recent examples might include *Superman, Total Recall, Rambo, The Terminator 2, Dick Tracy. Batman,* the dark knight, provides a very interesting example of the heroic myth in that the hero has a dark side that threatens to overwhelm his good side in the struggle against evil.

Clearly then, "the American monomyth—the myth of the committed and incorruptible hero who single-handedly saves the community from evil—is deeply embedded in the American consciousness" (Nimmo & Combs, 1980, p. 153). However, although it is rare for the monomyth to appear in political forms, it is possible if the conditions are right. Frequently, the news media personify the American public as an embodiment of the monomyth when the United States faces confrontations with such "evil" world powers as Quaddafi or Saddam Hussein. A watered-down version of the American monomyth is often used by political candidates who wish to portray their courage and strength against the enemies of the people, whomever those enemies may be.

In a 1992 Democratic primary in Missouri, attorney general candidate Jay Nixon ran an ad attacking the "big guys" in Missouri. Of note is that the ad is also an example of the us versus them mythical construction.

The 1992 Nixon "Got the Big Guys" Ad

Video	Audio
"Phone Company. Big Insurance Companies" supered on screen. Photo of Jay Nixon working at desk. Southwestern Bell Bill; Nixon talking with other people in a crowd."Jay Nixon Stopped Rate Hikes." Elderly walking with Nixon; Nixon talking in courtroom. Newspaper Headlines: "Nixon Bill Targets Insurance Firms' Acts of Bad Faith."	Narrator [VO]: "These groups don't want Jay Nixon to be attorney general. Why? Because when the phone company tried to gouge customers by raising rates, Jay Nixon stood up against them. When big insurance companies tried to rip off consumers in Missouri, Jay Nixon stopped them cold.
"Protecting Consumers." Talking with consumers, elderly. Jay Nixon photo. "Missouri Senior Citizens Award." Jay Nixon at desk.	Protecting consumers. Another big reason Jay Nixon received an award from the Missouri Council of Senior Citizens for his outstanding work on the behalf of the elderly.
"Jay Nixon, Attorney General, Democrat."	In the Democratic primary, Jay Nixon for Attorney General."

Pseudo-myths

Pseudo-myths, or "myths in the making" (Nimmo & Combs, 1980, p. 27), are short-term myths used by politicians to temporarily serve instrumental functions. For example, Richard Nixon became the new and improved Nixon when he returned to American politics in 1968. Another example is that of a consummate insider running as a consummate outsider as Ronald Reagan did in 1980 (see Johnson, 1984). Bill Clinton became the "new-style Democrat" in 1992 who was going to reform the welfare state, but he quickly forgot that once he became president. Pseudo-myths are political narratives designed to achieve short-term political goals.

5

Political Advertising Appeals

A variety of narrative persuasive tactics are used in contemporary political advertising; we call such persuasive tactics *political appeals*. In our analysis, we identify three central types of persuasive appeals: (1) political issue appeals, (2) political character appeals, or (3) emotive appeals and the appeals subclassifications (see Figure 5.1). We see this tripartite division as neo-Aristotelian. Political issue appeals correspond to Aristotle's *logos*; political character appeals and personal life appeals correspond to *ethos*; and emotive appeals correspond to *pathos*. Note this list is not a typology into which a spot can be uniquely situated. Frequently, one or more persuasive appeals are used in an ad. The most commonly used appeal is emotive. Frequently, too, a single political ad will combine emotive appeals with one of the other persuasive appeals in the message structure. We provide operationalization for each of these appeals:

Political Issue Appeals: Comments or attacks concerning political beliefs, political record, political experience, political positions, voting record, political party affiliation, other political party affiliations.

Political Character Appeals: Comments or attacks concerning a candidate's credibility, honesty, trustworthiness, intelligence, work ethic, altruism, fairness, competence, charisma, vitality, strength, courage, and other personality traits. Political character appeals are also made that pertain to the candidate's personal life: Comments or attacks concerning a candidate's medical history, religion, sex life, family members, friends, marital status, current or past marriages or relationships, wealth or lack thereof and other personal life situations.

Emotive Appeals: Comments or attacks that attempt to evoke an emotional response from the audience either positively or negatively.

Figure 5.1
Political Persuasive Appeals

```
Political Issue Appeals
    Prospective Appeals
    Retrospective Appeals
Political Character Appeals
    Character Trait Appeals
    Personal Life Appeals
    Benevolent Leader Appeals
Emotional Appeals
    Negative Appeals
        Fear Appeals (Prospective & Retrospective)
        Heroes, Villains, Fools
        Transfer
        Us vs. Them
            Cowboys vs. Yankees
            Us Against Foreigners
            Class Warfare
            Anti-Washington
            Us vs. The Different
        Humorous Appeals
            Ridicule (Disparagement)
            Self-deprecation
    Positive Appeals
        Compassion Appeals
        Hope Appeals
        Reassurance Appeals
        Pride Appeals
        Empathy Appeals
```

POLITICAL ISSUE APPEALS

Political issue appeals have been considered primarily as the presentation of rational arguments or *logos,* and they are usually constructed either deductively or inductively. Deductive logic moves from the general to the specific, whereas induction argues from the specific to the general (see Johnson-Cartee & Copeland, 1991a). The key ingredient in political issue appeals is *evidence* which we mean as "Factual statements originating from a source other than the speaker, objects not created by the speaker, and opinions of persons other than the speaker that are offered in support of the speaker's claims" (McCroskey, 1969, p. 170). Perloff (1993) has identified a number of evidentary messages: public or private figure testimonials, government statistics, eyewitness reports, and other factual statements. Our concept of evidence includes visual evidence. Political advertising frequently contains pages of governmental records, tax returns, bounced checks, newspaper headlines, or news copy. Ads that resemble visual documentaries rely on the visual "evidence" to carry the primary message of the ad. Scenes of social protest and war were common during the 1968 and 1972 presidential campaigns. A caveat is in order: "factual statements" or opinions of others do not indicate that what is said is true or trustworthy; they may be presented as fact, but they may not be true. The rule is *caveat emptor*.

Moderate or low-credibility sources should use evidence in order to enhance attitude change (McCroskey, 1969). Although evidence does not enhance attitude change associated with a highly credible source in the short term, it will assist in producing a long-term attitude change (Burgoon & Burgoon, 1975). Petty and Cacioppo (1984) have found that low-involvement, low-ability receivers will be persuaded by the presentation of high levels of evidence, even when that evidence is poor or inadequate. Highly involved individuals with high-abilities are not likely to be persuaded by simple evidence presentations (Perloff, 1993).

But not all evidence presentations are the same. Evidence or other message arguments should be made at the beginning of the ad or at the end of the ad (see Calder, 1978; Chestnut, 1980; Gilkinson, Paulson, & Sikkink, 1954; Gulley & Berlo, 1956). Placing your most effective arguments in the middle is the least effective structure to use (Perloff, 1993).

Although the use of evidence has its advantages, candidates have often chosen to present vague discussions of their positions or stands on the issues. Downs (1957) first suggested that candidates have a vested interest in avoiding clear-cut policy stands. He believed that ambiguity actually maximized a candidate's support levels. In this same vein, Shepsle (1972) suggested what he terms a theory of campaign ambiguity. He suggests that candidates' policy stands are the outcome of an expected utility model of risky decision making. For Shepsle both voters and candidates approach policy decision making as they would a lottery. When voters are accepting of risk, then candidates are more willing to take policy stands. Page (1976) is critical of this "lottery" approach and suggests that an emphasis allocation approach is superior to the lottery approach in understanding a candidate's decision-making process.

As a candidate decides how to allocate emphasis among different appeals it is clear that he must consider how citizens' preferences are distributed, how strong they are, and how steeply utility functions drop off with increasing distance from the most preferred points. If, for example, all citizens prefer precisely the same thing, and feel very intensely about it, a candidate can safely take that stand and emphasize his position strongly, winning good will, and votes from everyone. If, on the other hand, preferences are intense but widely dispersed— e.g., bimodally distributed—any stand the candidate takes will offend someone. If he agrees with the left-hand mode, he will outrage voters on the right; if he switches and takes a stand on the right-hand mode, he will alienate people on the left; and if he moves to the middle, everyone is disgruntled. Obviously the candidate's best strategy is to avoid issues of a divisive sort, and place (as nearly as possible) *no* emphasis on them, but devote all his time, money and energy to matters of consensus. (p. 749)

Benjamin Page (1978) wrote that "the most striking features of candidates' rhetoric about policy is its extreme vagueness" (p. 152). Diamond and Marin (1989) and Patterson (1980) have termed these vague, umbrella consensus policy statements *diffuse issues*. A content analysis of 506 televised political commercials found that only the very rare candidate provided clear, specific, detailed policy preferences (Josyln, 1986). Phrases that say a candidate is for "the return of traditional American values," for "more jobs for those who are able to work," or for "a stronger America" are not telling us much about the candidate's specific positions on the issues. Rather, they do tell us a lot about what the candidate thinks we want to hear, for the ads are relying on the "'stored information' of the citizenry to provide a context for the appeal" (Josyln, 1986; Schwartz, 1976). Clearly, this "stored information" is heavily "value laden," so the viewers end up reading what they want to into these vague phrases Josyln (1986) writes:

What is striking about these bogus policy appeals is that they are without risk to the candidates and are a considerable distance from the types of policy alternatives that public officials face. They are more similar to consensually held values than they are to policy promises, and they are hardly the sort of appeal with which anyone could seriously disagree. Almost everyone is in favor of a strong national defense, a revitalized NATO alliance, a competitive international marketplace, consumer protection, and a better health care system. (p. 149)

The rationale for such "diffuse issues" or "bogus policy appeals" is simple: they work.

Joslyn identified two types of policy appeals: prospective policy appeals and retrospective policy appeals. *Prospective policy appeals* are discussions of future governmental policies and may be characterized as either reassurance appeals or fear appeals. Candidates may make prospective policy promises in order to reassure voters. Or candidates may attack other candidates or parties by making the opposition's proposed policies associated with fear or anxiety. While *retrospective policy appeals* are discussions of past governmental policies, they call upon voters to judge their own satisfaction level with those policies. Retrospective policy appeals may be characterized as either reassurance appeals or fear appeals. Candidates point to the achievements of the past in order to reinforce voters' satisfaction levels with the status quo. Or candidates may choose to attack the policies of the past in an attempt to persuade voters to condemn the policies of the past by voting for change.

During the 1992 presidential primary season, Democratic candidate Bob Kerrey, U.S. senator from Nebraska ran a series of positive issue spots, using a variety of proscriptive policy appeals. A former popular governor of Nebraska, Kerrey was a first-term U.S. senator making a run for the White House. He tried to position himself as the "man with a plan" or as the Democratic field's only issue oriented candidate (see Arterton, 1984).

The 1992 Kerrey "Shattered" Ad

Video	Audio
Kerrey standing in a hospital room. Super: "Bob Kerrey Democrat for President"	Kerrey [SOT]: "This is a place where lives are saved, but it's also become a place where lives are financially shattered. I'm Bob Kerrey, and I'm the only candidate with a bill in Congress that creates National Health
Super: "The Kerrey Bill makes Health Care a basic right," "Lowers family Health Care costs by $500 a year." "Guarantees coverage even if you lose your job." Kerrey talks with people (doctors and nurses, two men, and one black woman).	insurance. The Kerrey Bill establishes health care as a basic right, lowers the average family's health bill by over $500 a year, and guarantees health insurance even if you lose your job. In a country like ours, its time we made health care a fundamental right for all Americans." Announcer [VO]: "Fight back America."

During the 1992 general election presidential campaign, the Bush team found it necessary to address the currents of fear and uncertainty that had plagued the last nine months of the Bush presidency. While the following ad uses the conventional technique of the retrospective appeal in reminding voters that it was the Republican administration that brought an end to war and the conventional technique of reassurance, it also makes a decided prospective policy appeal as well.

The 1992 Bush "Bush Agenda" Ad

Video	Audio
Bush in the Oval Office looking out window. Camera looks down on parade; a giant American flag is unfurled.	Bush [VO]: "Today for the first time in half a century, America is not at war. And America's wartime economy is changing to a peacetime economy. But that change has brought fear and uncertainty."
Bush talking directly to camera.	Bush [SOT]: "The fear of losing a job, of losing a home, the uncertainty of tough economic competition from around the world. But with change comes opportunity."
Bush signs agenda for American Renewal. Kids in school room saying pledge of allegiance. Nurses working on a computer. Pregnant woman looking out window. Mother with baby in arms. Barber shop window. Black man on phone. Steel worker. Bush with wife and grandchildren.	Bush [VO]: "And my agenda for American renewal can be the bridge to the future. It provides a choice of quality schools so our children have the knowledge to compete. It provides job training so workers have the new skills to compete. It provides health care for all and controls the costs so our people can afford to compete. And my agenda strengthens small businesses that create two out of every three jobs, so we have the new jobs to compete. Today we stand at the threshold of a new era. We've changed the world around us. Together we must do the same at home."

POLITICAL CHARACTER APPEALS

Political character appeals may pertain to two distinct domains in a candidate's persona. First, they may address those character traits that impact a candidate's ability to perform in office, or second, political character appeals may refer to those personal life variables that infer candidate suitability for office. Research has shown that the majority of Americans do not approve of ads that make personal life attacks against and opponent, and in this sense, such ads may be deemed as illegitimate forms of argumentation (see Johnson-Cartee &

Copeland, 1989b, 1991a; see also Johnson & Copeland, 1987).   Recent political studies have emphasized the significance of the perception of candidate character traits in voting decisions (Glass, 1985; Miller, Wattenberg, and Malanchuk, 1986; Oft-Rose, 1989).   Arterton (1984) provides evidence to suggest that entire presidential campaigns have been orchestrated around the issue of "character" appeals.   As an example of a character campaign, he cites the 1976 Carter presidential campaign.

Joslyn (1986) identified what he termed the *benevolent leader appeal* which gives the voter a choice based not on ideological beliefs or on issue positions but on personality characteristics.   The election then gives the voter the "opportunity to select those public officials who possess the personality traits appropriate for the role to which they aspire" (pp. 161-162).   The six clusters of character attributes that are used most frequently in American political advertising are compassion, empathy, integrity, activity, strength, and knowledge (pp. 162-170).

Andersen (1989) reminds political observers that voters are constantly observing the words and deeds of modern political actors.   The voters use these observations to create the candidate's character. Andersen writes: "*Every choice, conscious or not relevant or not, provides a basis upon which an inference can be made as to the ethics and values of the individual making the choice*" (p. 482; italics in original).   As we have mentioned previously, ethos, or the candidate's character is a highly important variable in the voters' decision-making processes.   This is not a new observation.   Aristotle put it this way:

The character [ethos] of the speaker is a cause of persuasion . . . for as a rule we trust men of probity more, and more quickly, about things in general, while on points outside the realm of exact knowledge, where opinion is divided, we trust them absolutely. . . . It is not true, as some writers on the art maintain, that the probity of the speaker contributes nothing to his persuasiveness; on the contrary, we might almost affirm that his character [ethos] is the most potent of all the means to persuasion. (Cooper, 1932, p. 8, as quoted in Andersen, 1989, pp. 480-481)

The 1988 Bush presidential campaign produced a number of positive political character ads. However, one of these ads stands out, because Bush attempts the delicate task of both associating himself with the very popular Reagan and at the same time distancing himself to become a political hero in his own right.   In the ad, Bush establishes himself as a man with enough courage and self-conviction to be president.

The 1988 Bush "I Am That Man" Ad

Video	Audio
Black screen with white letters: "The Experience."	Bush [VO]: "For seven and a half years, I've worked with a great president."
Bush speaking at the Convention.	Bush [SOT]: "I've seen what crosses that big desk. I've seen the unexpected crisis that arise in a cable in a young aide's hand."
A night aerial view of the White House.	Bush [VO]: "And so I know that what it all comes down to in this election is the man at the desk. And who should sit at that desk— my friend, I am that man."
Photo of Bush. Super: "George Bush Experienced Leadership for America's Future."	

During the 1992 presidential campaign, the Bush team attacked Clinton's credibility over and over. In this direct-attack flip-flop ad, the Bush team reviews the inconsistencies in Clinton's public statements.

The 1992 Bush "Flip-Flop" Ad

Video	Audio
Split screen. A figure on each side in a suit with different color shirts and ties. Large opaque circle conceals face on each individual. The attention swings back and forth as points are made.	Announcer [VO]: "The presidential candidate on the left stood for military action in the Persian Gulf. While the candidate on the right agreed with those who opposed it. (Bill Clinton's voice, sound under, can't distinguish words, just tone). He says he wouldn't rule out term limits. While he said he's personally opposed to term limits. This candidate was called up for military service. While this one
Opaque circles are removed. Bill Clinton on both sides of screen.	claims he wasn't. One of these candidates is Bill Clinton. Unfortunately, so is the other."

> Bill Clinton [VO]: "There is a
> simple explanation for why this
> happened."

EMOTIONAL APPEALS

In 1936 Hartmann found that emotional political leaflets had a "greater impressive and retentive effect" (p. 111) than did rational political leaflets, and he concluded that "there seems to be no escape from the decision that the emotional political appeal is a better vote-getting instrument than the rational approach" (p. 113). Since that time, numerous researchers have examined the advantages and disadvantages of the use of persuasive emotional appeals. Included in that examination has been an extensive debate concerning the relationship, if any, existing between cognitions and emotions (Abelson, 1983; Breckler, 1984; Conover & Feldman, 1986; Lazarus, 1982; Roseman, Abelson, & Ewing, 1986; Roseman, 1979, 1984; Weiner, 1982; Zajonc, 1980, 1984). It would be beneficial to review the major concepts in this area of research.

This debate has become increasingly important in that researchers have determined that a voter's "feelings" about a candidate were equivalent to their voting intention (Brody & Page, 1973). Therefore, the study of emotions has become increasingly important in political science and communication research (Abelson, Kinder, Peters, & Fiske, 1982; Conover & Feldman, 1986; Marcus, 1985).

Early research failed to distinguish between different types of appeals (e.g., Hartmann, 1936). If a distinction was made, the emphasis of the research was on fear appeals. In 1986, Roseman, Abelson and Ewing identified a series of emotional appeals used in public affairs communication. The group applied these constructs to the organizational appeals of various civic and political groups.

Roseman et al. (1986) found that three types of political action messages were most often used in public affairs communication:

1. People are suffering, and we've got to help them (pity).
2. We've been treated unfairly by the bad guys, and we're going to put an end to it (anger).
3. Something terrible might happen, unless we act now to avoid it (fear-hope). (pp. 292-293)

They have identified a number of emotional appeals and the associated emotions in political communication: dangerous problem/fear; opportunity for resolution/hope; others as agents of problem/anger; others as targets of resolution/pity; self as agent of problem/guilt; self as agent of resolution/pride; those who help us achieve desired goal states/gratitude; unsatisfied goal states/discontent; and unsatisfied goal states/frustration (p. 283). All of these are easily discernible in political advertising.

In reviewing the various emotional appeals and associated emotion states, we can discern several that are most likely to be used in negative or positive political advertising.

Negative Political Appeals
    Dangerous problem/fear
    Others as agents of problem/anger
    Unsatisfied goal states, discontent or frustration
Positive Political Appeals
    Those who help us achieve desired goal states/gratitude
    Opportunity for resolution/hope
    Self as agent of resolution/pride

Roseman et al. also identified the self as agent of problem/guilt appeal, which is likely to be used in either an inoculation ad or a reactive responsive political ad.

In analyzing the persuasive effects of emotions, Roseman and colleagues warn that both the emotional content of the message and the emotional tendencies of the audience must be taken into account. Fear appeals did not follow the normal resonance theory for audiences who had already been identified as having high fear components. Roseman et al. found that fearful people did not respond to fear appeals; instead, they responded to hope appeals. This finding corresponds with early research on fear appeal which found situations in which fear appeals were ineffective (Janis, 1967) to increase the persuasiveness of fear appeals the message must contain a practical means of avoiding the feared stimulus (Beck & Lund, 1981; Lazarus, Coyne, & Folkman, 1982; Leventhal, Watts, & Pagano, 1967; Maddux & Rogers, 1983; Rogers & Mewborn, 1976; Roseman, 1984). "Perhaps the presentation of effective preventive measures generates hope, with the emotional content of successful communications . . . being fear plus hope" (Roseman et al., 1986, p. 291). Indeed, when such efficacious preventive measures were attached to high-intensity fear appeals, such message stratagems were found to be highly persuasive (Sutton & Eiser, 1984).

Conflict Resolution

People use emotional appeals not only to express emotions (Schwartz's resonance theory, 1972, 1976) but also as coping mechanisms "to feel good or better" (Roseman et al. 1986, p. 293; see also Lazarus, Coyne, & Folkman, 1982; Roseman, 1984). Clearly, these findings support the notion that political emotions are related to political cognitions. In their review of television imagery, Lanzetta, Sullivan, Masters, and McHugo (1985) concluded that "From earlier research on stereotypes and prejudice to more recent conceptualizations of 'schemas' (e.g., Leventhal, 1984), 'scripts' (e.g., Abelson, 1976, 1981) and 'networks' (e.g., Bower, 1981), it has been well recognized by psychologists that cognition can play a powerful role in emotional responses" (p. 86). Lanzetta et al. maintain that cognitive structures dealing with ideology, party identification, or attitudes will be tied to affective responses to politicians.

Like Roseman (1984), Roseman et al., (1986) found that "Emotions follow from the fate of goals. Positive emotions indicate goal attainment; negative emotions indicate goal blockage. Hopeful political appeals are preferred to fearful political appeals because they indicate successful resolution of problems" (p. 294).

Because respondents prefer optimistic political cognitions, they want problems to be either solved or resolved. This supports Kern's (1989) and our own contention (Johnson-Cartee & Copeland, 1991a) that, in order for negative political advertising to be effective, the appeal used must contain a "resolution" or a means by which the respondent's action, that is, vote, will prevent or end the negative situation. Americans are people of action; we do not respond well to political rhetoric that makes us feel small or weak. We do not like to be scolded for any shortcomings that we may have as a society. Democratic presidential candidates Walter Mondale and Michael Dukakis learned that lesson well.

USE OF EMOTIVE APPEALS IN CONTEMPORARY POLITICAL ADVERTISING.

Recently, political advertising researchers have begun to focus on *emotive spots*—those ads that appeal to the individual's emotions, often playing on cultural and universal symbols of love, family, patriotism, hope, and pride (see Kaid, Leland, & Whitney, 1992). Many political consultants believed that emotions, whether positive or negative were the key to understanding how effectively political advertising works (Diamond & Bates, 1988; Jamieson, 1984; Johnson-Cartee & Copeland, 1991a; Sabato, 1981; Schwartz, 1972; 1976). Roger Ailes, the Republican consultant who produced the "Boston Harbor" spot and the "Prison Furlough" spot for the 1988 Bush campaign, explained the effectiveness of emotions in polispots this way: "people watch TV emotionally" (Diamond & Marin, 1989, p. 385).

Lang (1991) found that "emotion may actually act to focus attention on certain aspects of the commercial and it may directly affect the way information is encoded" (p. 240). That is, emotions helped people to recall political messages.

In short, election engineering becomes a roller-coaster ride looking for the emotional hot spot or key to the voters' heart. Roberts (1986) describes the process this way:

With the use of increasingly sophisticated polling methods, videotape machines and satellite technology, political consultants . . . can now monitor the public mood on an hour-by-hour . . . basis, searching for a cresting emotion that might sway a block of marginal voters. Today's media whiz then tries to capture, and manipulate, that emotion in a new television commercial that can be put on the air overnight. (p. 38)

Kaid, Leland, and Whitney (1992) concluded in their study of 1988 presidential commercials: "Political ads that play to the elec-torate's emotions may positively influence voters. Campaigns may not be decided by the intellectual questioning of the candidate's plat-forms, issue papers, and public policy stances, but by emotional ap-peals" (p. 293). Kaid and her colleagues observed viewer responses to the 1988 presidential campaign commercials and discovered two emotional dimensions that viewers held for both Bush and Dukakis. "The first dominant factor was a hopefulness factor that contained the positive emotions of optimism, confidence, excitement, security, and patriotism. . . . The second factor was an anxiety factor comprised of the emotions of anxious, fearful, and concerned" (pp. 289-290).

Marcus (1988) also presented a two-factor model of emotional re-sponses to presidential candidates: mastery (positive emotionality) and threat (negative emotionality). He concluded that "positive emotional response is twice as influential as negative emotional re-sponse in predicting presidential candidate vote disposition to the presidential candidates" (p. 737). He also observed that the voters' reliance on emotional responses was true for all electorate strata. He concluded that "positive emotional response to the candidates is more influential than negative emotional response suggests that elections turn more on moral leadership and leadership competence and less on issues" (p. 755). He observed that because "positive emotional response to the candidates is more influential than negative emotional response suggests that elections turn more on moral leadership and leadership competence and less on issues" (p. 755).

Positive Emotive Appeals

A study of presidential campaign advertising from 1960 to 1988 found that 86 percent of all positive ads contained emotional appeals (Kaid & Johnston, 1991). Kern (1989) referred to such advertising as "*feel-good advertising*" and identified two types of thematic designs associated with it: hope appeals and reassurance appeals. According to Kern (1989), such ads are designed to build the voter's trust about the candidate. Here we will highlight a number of specific positive emotive appeals: (1) compassion; (2) hope; (3) reassurance; (4) pride; and, (5) empathy.

Compassion Appeals

In a 1990 Alabama gubernatorial campaign, Greer, Margolis, Mitchell and Associates, Inc. produced a powerful positive emotive spot for Democratic candidate Dr. Paul Hubbert. Hubbert, as director of the powerful Alabama Education Association and with his close working relationship with his assistant director and Alabama Democratic Conference president Dr. Joe Reed, was stereotyped as being the candidate for only the teachers and African Americans. Hubbert had to widen his base of support. The Heartbreak spot that follows made a powerful appeal to the heartstrings. By its very nature, the ad sent a message to all Alabamians and not just the elderly or infirm.

The 1990 Hubbert "Heartbreak" Ad

Video	Audio
An elderly man in coveralls walks with a cane across what appears to be a dilapidated farm yard. Man talks into camera while sitting on a porch in a rocking chair. He suffers from palsy. Super: Jesse Brakefield, Jasper.	Old Man [VO]: "I worked hard all my life, saved a few dollars, my wife had to go in the nursing home, and I've about used it all up. There's one candidate that cares for the old folk [sic] and that is Paul Hubbert. And I'm fer [sic] him a hundred percent."
Hubbert in suit. Talking head.	Paul Hubbert [SOT]: "I hear stories everyday that break my heart. Nothing is more important than providing quality health care for our seniors and quality education for our children. And as your governor, that's exactly what I'll do."

The Hubbert camp knew they had an advertisement that evoked positive emotions in the viewers. The spot became their most often used television ad. The best indicator of the success of a political advertisement is how do the tracking polls respond. This ad consistently created positive moves in the tracking polls.

In 1992 Buddy Darden in a congressional race ran a spot that demonstrated his appreciation and respect for hard work, tradition, and the elderly. In addition, it clearly emphasized his compassion for the common man.

The 1992 Darden "Progress" Ad

Video	Audio
City skyline at night. Farmland.	Darden [VO]: "Some people call it progress, but while skyscrapers have sprung up along the Chattahoochee time has stood still
Elderly man working the farm. Old farm buildings and farm implements. Man goes about his work.	for one man. Since 1920 J. C. Hyde has seen a lot of changes. Back then he bought this land for $10 an acre. Now land speculators and the IRS want to take it away."
Darden in a work shirt sitting on stoop with the man	Darden [SOT]: "I'm kind of old fashioned when it comes to progress."
Man doing more chores.	Darden [VO]: "So we passed a law that allows Mr. Hyde to keep his farm and preserve his way of life. It's not a big deal to most folks, but it is to J. C. Hyde and me.

Hope Appeals

Typically, hope ads utilize children and young people and highlight their everyday lives whether at work or at play (see Kern, 1989). Often the candidate's own family appears in the spot, and several generations of family members are featured together showing the continuity of family life. Kern explained the use of hope appeals in the 1984 Reagan polispots:

Continuity between generations in the campaign advertising offered hope to those of the younger generation who sought it. For the older generation the link with kids who in the visual fantasy world of the Reagan ads wear no Mohawks, help their elders and then settle down to raise families, also offers hope for the future. This intergenerational motif in advertising is bipartisan. (p. 84)

According to Kern, hope ads are used primarily by presidential candidates, and approximately 55 percent of those she coded belonged to incumbents.

In 1976 incumbent Republican president Gerald Ford ran a "Feeling Good" positive spot that utilized an upbeat song to bring home the message. Music plays an important role in hope appeals, and the theme clearly connects "the candidate with the voter's future" (p. 80).

The 1976 Ford "Feeling Good" Ad

Video	Audio
A farmhouse. Man puts an American flag in front of a rural post office. A child is pictured eating. A man in a hard hat is shown at work. Black children are pictured laughing.	Male Singing [VO]: "There's a change that's come over America. There's a change that's great to see We're living here in peace again. We're going back to work again. It's better than it used to be. I'm feeling good about America. And today is where I'm from. (The song continues to play as background while Ford speaks.) Ford [VO]: "Today America enjoys the most precious gift of all. We are at peace."
A family. Baby on father's back.	Announcer [VO]: "We are at peace with the world and peace with ourselves.
The following scenes: a baby, a man picking apples, a woman smiling, an old man, a woman nodding her head in agreement. President Ford working at his desk. Pictured with his hands folded behind his head, rocking in his desk chair. Ford is again pictured at a desk, talking and gesturing. Ford is pictured in the back seat of a car, writing on a pad of paper. Ford is pictured from behind as he speaks. A picture of an old couple, hugging and kissing, appears on screen. A picture of a smiling, young boy appears on screen.	America is smiling again, and a great many people believe the leadership of this steady, dependable man can keep America happy and smiling and secure. We know we can depend on him to work to keep us strong at home. We know we can depend on him to ease tensions among the other nations of the world. We know we can depend on him to make peace his highest priority. Peace with freedom. Is there anything more important than that?"

(*Source*: Devlin, 1986, pp.46-47)

Reassurance Appeals

Reassurance ads focus on the homeplace. The ads often use symbols that focus on national, ethnic, or local heritage (Kern, 1989) and older Americans usually have a prominent place figure in them. Again music plays a very important role, and the theme of the ad links the candidate "with the viewer's feelings about the way things are, in the place that he or she knows and loves" and how they should be (p. 80). The visual images most often associated with reassurance appeals are those of idyllic small-town America: front porches, the farm yard, a country lane, a general store, a small schoolhouse, people walking to church, and so on. The home is prominently featured both inside and out.

Incumbents most often utilize reassurance appeals: 75 percent of the reassurance appeals coded were sponsored by incumbents. This use of reassurance by incumbents is not surprising. People who are content are more likely to return their existing representatives to office than are people who are anxious about the state of the nation or of their pocketbooks. Reassurance ads were generally used more than hope appeals in that House, Senate, and presidential candidates made use of the appeal strategy (Kern, 1989).

The contemporary candidate who exemplifies reassurance is Ronald Reagan. This reassuring visage was melded with a campaign strategy. Reagan's success in 1980 and in 1984 has been attributed to his reassurance strategy (Shyles, 1988). As Shyles wrote: "But the reason the Reagan campaign style has been so successful may be that the American people have a greater desire to be reassured than to be informed about the state of the world" (p. 30).

Pride Appeals

Incumbent presidents often use pride appeals to call attention to the fact that they have maintained America's place in the world. In 1984 the Fund for a Conservative Majority produced an independent spot to support Ronald Reagan's reelection campaign. The ad was a gorgeous visual documentary that used Lee Greenwood's popular country and western song, "Proud to Be an American" in which he talks about what it means to be an American, including the willingness to defend our way of life.

Empathy Appeals

The sharing of emotions produces a state in which voters perceive that they have the same type of values or concerns as the candidate— that they are like the candidate. Empathy appeals are appeals that work to produce this emotional synchrony. They are the basis of everyman ads.

In 1986 Tom Daschle ran an empathy ad that established his shared values with the voters of South Dakota.

The 1986 Daschle "Car" Ad

Video	Audio
Outside of a Georgetown residence, BMWs, limos, and an old Pontiac drives by. Pontiac goes down the road, burning oil.	Announcer [VO]: "Among Washington's BMWs and limos is this—Since 1971, the old Pontiac has served its owner well. Sure its rusted, and it burns a little oil. But after 15 years and 238,000
Tom Daschle is driving.	miles, Tom Daschle still drives his old car to work everyday. Maybe he's sentimental or just cheap.
Daschle parks, gets out of car in front of Capitol. Super: "Tom Daschle South Dakota's Best."	Whatever the case, isn't it too bad that the rest of Washington doesn't understand that a penny saved is a penny earned."

In a 1994 Oregon referendum on Proposition 16, the so-called assisted suicide referendum, the Oregon Right to Die political action committee produced a spot that brought tears to many.

The 1994 Oregon Right to Die "Assisted Suicide" Ad

Video	Audio
A woman walking in a natural wooded area, talking to camera. Super: "Patty Rosen" "Bend." Portrait of Judy; photograph of Judy ill.	Woman [SOT]: "I'm a criminal. My 25-year-old daughter was dying of bone cancer. The pain was so great that she couldn't bear to be touched. And drugs didn't help. Judy only had a few weeks to live, and [music under]
Woman continues to walk	she decided she wanted to end her life. But it wasn't legally possible, so I broke the law and got her the pills necessary. And as she slipped peacefully away, I climbed into her bed and took her in my arms for the first time in months [crying]. When did we give up our right to run our own lives?

	Doesn't government have better things to do than make criminals of law-abiding citizens? Are we going to let one church make the rules for all of us? Measure 16 would have allowed my daughter to die with dignity. It has safeguards against abuse. I was a registered nurse. I know. Vote yes on 16. We should all have the
Super: "Yes on 26."	right to live every minute of our lives with dignity."

Use of Negative Emotional Appeals

Kern (1989) identified as "feel-bad advertising" those ads that use emotional appeals in order to make voters feel negatively about a given candidate. Such attack ads are the opposite of the reassurance appeals commonly found in positive spots. The primary negative emotional appeal is fear, and the use of fear appeals in campaign commercials has been shown to be effective (Kaid, Leland, & Whitney, 1992).

Fear Appeals

Fear appeals are political messages designed to create anxiety, uncertainty, or fear in the voters. Two fear appeals used in negative political advertising are prospective and retrospective fear appeals (Johnson-Cartee & Copeland, 1991). *Prospective fear appeals* emphasize what the candidate is likely to do or intends to do in the future based on public statements or the candidate's party's positions. Frequently, the platforms and public statements of challengers or candidates who have had no previous political experience are critically analyzed and attacked by incumbents. *Retrospective fear appeals* emphasize what a candidate or party has done in the past. This technique is often used against incumbents or candidates who have previously held political office, because they have a record that can be critically analyzed and attacked.

The literature concerning fear-appeal advertising is mixed (see Burgoon & Bettinghaus, 1980; McGuire, 1985). Little consensus exists among early researchers as to the basic effectiveness of fear appeals or of specific types or degrees of fear appeals (Colburn, 1967; Janis & Feshback, 1953; McGuire, 1968). More recently, the evidence has supported the persuasive effectiveness of high-level fear appeals over low-level fear appeals (Oskamp, 1991). To be effective a high-level fear appeal must be accompanied with specific ways to avoid what is feared (Leventhal, 1970; Leventhal, Meyers, & Nerenz, 1980; Rogers

& Mewborn, 1976).   However, fear appeals may not work on individuals who have fearful personalities. Some evidence suggests that, while fear appeals may well discourage voters from choosing a particular candidate, such appeals may also discourage these same people from voting in that they will simply try to avoid the situation in which they would be called upon to make a decision (see McGuire, 1985).

Consultants use fear appeals in order to get voters to assess the voter's "risk" in terms of their economic or political well-being if a given candidate or party should win the election. Yet research suggests that American voters evaluate political candidates in terms of risk assessment only when they are voting for the presidency (Lau, 1985).

In 1992 the Bush campaign also created a spot that utilized a prospective fear appeal coupled with a direct attack of challenger Bill Clinton during the general election campaign.   The spot specifically addresses the subject of health care under the Clinton Health Plan.

The 1992 Bush "Clinton's Health Plan" Ad

Video	Audio
Busy waiting room.	Female Announcer [VO]: "Bill Clinton's health plan puts the government in control. And that
Super: "Ration Health Care."	will ration health care and limit the doctor's ability to save your
Super: "Medicare and Medicaid Cuts."	life. His plan would require $218 billion in Medicare and Medicaid cuts over the next five years. His plan could cost 750,000 Americans their jobs. Government-run plans have been tried in Europe. Only there its
Super: "It's known as Socialized Medicine."	known as socialized medicine. You can't trust Bill Clinton's
Super: "The Clinton Health Plan. Wrong for you. Wrong for America."	health plan. The Clinton Health Plan. Wrong for you. Wrong for America."

In 1994 an independent political action committee ABEPAC produced a spot attacking Mario Cuomo's twelve-year record as governor of New York. The ad is shot in black and white, and the scenes of devastation and tragedy have a powerful impact.

The 1994 ABEPAC "Dump Cuomo" Ad

Video	Audio
Black and white photographs: "Will Work for Food" sign; "Prime Office and Retail Space Now Available" sign. A wall of wanted posters. Close-up of handgun. Lone figure at night on a city street (image turns into a negative). Chalk outline of dead body on street. Dead body on morgue gurney. Banner: "Police Line Do Not Cross;" "Going Out of Business BelowWholesale" sign. Locked, chained door. Burned out, abandoned building. "For Sale Barns & Farms" sign. Worker on high-rise platform (image turns into a negative). "Reduced" Caldwell Banker real estate sign. Old man with face in hands. Work line. Working people in subway with graffiti.	Female Announcer [VO]: "This is Mario Cuomo's New York. Cuomo coddles criminals. Day and night, we're in danger—on the street, at work, in school, even in our homes. Cuomo imposes crippling taxes. Business withers. Jobs disappear. Families suffer. Dreams die. Cuomo plays politics. Working men and women pay the bill.
People in a parking lot (image turns into a negative), Desolate area, rubbish piles. Photo of Cuomo (image turns into a negative).	Twelve years of Mario Cuomo. Can you afford four more? Dump Cuomo. Build New York."

Heroes, Villains, and Fools and the Appeals That Made Them

Frequently, emotional appeals are used to portray political candidates in the roles of heroes, villains, and fools in contemporary American politics (Combs, 1980). The heroic leader is one that embodies the fundamental themes and values of a culture. If heroes are the protagonists in political narratives, villains are the antagonists. According to Combs (1980), villains "personify evil, cunning, negative values, or other traits that the audience dislikes" (p. 94). Political campaigns often spend a great deal of resources in an attempt to cast their candidate as the hero and their opposition as the villain (see Combs, 1980; Hall, 1972). Political fools also play an important role in American politics. Frequently, candidates will take the opportunity to laugh at themselves in order to appear more human. Or a candidate may attack his opposition by portraying his opponent's actions in a foolish light.

Heroes, villains, and fools are the major characters in political mythology. The emphasis on the "who" or the individual is an important factor in understanding American political mythology. Mythical configurations of the "who" provide emotional encapsulations of political character. A demonstrated "feeling" about various characters, albeit, heroes, villains, or fools are contained within the political mythology.

Political actors create the heroes, villains, and fools of today's political arena through *transfer appeals, us against them appeals*, and *humorous appeals*. Please note that the use of these techniques does not exclude the use of other political issue appeals, political character appeals and emotional appeals, within a single commercial. Transfer appeals, Us against Them Appeals, and Humorous Appeals distinguish themselves from political character appeals by their heavy reliance on the use of emotions to achieve their ends.

Transfer Appeals

"Transfer, long a propagandistic technique, is the process of inferring either positive or negative evaluations of individuals by their association with well-known positive or negative figures, movements, or causes" (Johnson-Cartee & Copeland, 1991a, p. 100; see also Wilcox, Ault, & Agee, 1986). Thus, a candidate's political reputation may be improved or denigrated through the use of transfer appeals.

Tom Harkin, one of the contenders for the Democratic Party's nomination for president in 1992, associated himself with popular Democratic presidents in one presidential primary spot. The ad was named "Trickle Down."

The 1992 Harkin "Trickle Down" Ad

Video	Audio
Photos of Kerrey, Clinton, Tsongas. Super: "For Tax Cuts for the Rich." Tom Harkin talking to audience.	Announcer [VO]: "These three Democrats are all saying the same thing—more tax cuts for the rich and big business. Create wealth at the top, they say, and it will trickle down to us. In ten years, haven't we learned, they never, never let it trickle down. Only Tom Harkin will stop tax give aways for the rich. And do what

| Super: "Build a new nation. Tom Harkin President." | Roosevelt, Truman, and Kennedy did—invest in our people, rebuild this nation from the ground up and put America back to work." |

Sometimes candidates are evaluated negatively because of who their supporters are. In a 1990 Georgia Insurance Commission race, the following attack ad played an important role in a hotly contested campaign.

The 1990 Evans "Rules Attack 2" Ad

Video	Audio
Close-up of a screw being screwed into a wooden board. Scroll of the announcer's words.	Announcer [VO]: "The choice for Georgia Insurance Commissioner is down to this. . . . What will happen if Tim Ryles gets elected? Who pulls Ryles' strings? It's pretty clear. Over half of all his campaign contributions came from organized labor and trial lawyers. And if that's not enough, he gets $15,000 a year as a board member of a huge insurance conglomerate, Primerica Corp., the very people he wants to regulate! Now that you know, it's not hard to see what will happen to us if he wins." (Sound of screw being tightened)

In some situations, candidates are evaluated negatively because of who their political cronies are. In the 1994 gubernatorial race in New York, Mario Cuomo ran an ad ridiculing George Pataki for his association with Senator Al D'Amato. A Paul Simon song "Call me Al" runs under the finishing lines of the ad.

The 1994 Cuomo "You Can Call Me Al" Ad

Video	Audio
Photographs of George Pataki and Al D'Amato with names on the bottom of photos. Under Pataki, Super: "Handpicked by: Al	Announcer [VO]: "George Pataki, he was handpicked by Senator Al D'Amato. His campaign staff was picked by Senator Al D'Amato.

D'Amato"; "Campaign staff picked by: Al D'Amato"; "Herb London called Pataki: A puppet of Al D'Amato"; "$250,000 in bills paid by Al D'Amato"; News headlines: "Judge: Pataki campaign must return $370,000"; "Pataki told to return Al's 369G"; "D'Amato's 369G Donation to Pataki is ruled illegal"; "Refund D'Amato Cash, Pataki told"; News photo of D'Amato holding wrist of Pataki and pulling him through a crowd. Super: "Everywhere Pataki goes, Al D'Amato leads him by the hand." Close-up of hand/wrist. In yellow, Super: "George Pataki? Maybe we should call him Al?"

His own running mate called him a puppet of Al D'Amato. Nearly a quarter million dollars of Pataki's campaign bills were paid by Senator Al D'Amato. Until a judge ruled it was illegal. And made Pataki give it back. Everywhere Pataki goes, Senator Al D'Amato leads him by the hand."

Paul Simon singing [VO]: "When you call me, you can call me, Al. You can call me, Al."

Us Against Them Appeals

In recent years, researchers have paid particular attention to the undercurrents in American society which divide us (for a review, see Johnson-Cartee & Copeland, 1991a). David Bennett (1988) has suggested that these divisions are a fundamental part of the American psyche. Early in America's history, political leaders identified the American public as people who were pursuing the ideal system of government, which became the "city on the hill" myth. In conjunction with the myth that Americans were somehow chosen by God to pursue this great experiment of democracy came another version of reality—a reality based on fear. Consistently in our history, political leaders have identified the enemies from within and the enemies from without that were threatening our way of life. These so-called enemies of the people have been characterized in a variety of ways. At certain points in our history, we have feared the immigrant, the African American, the Catholic religion, the New England establishment, foreign countries, even our own governmental representatives in Washington (see Bennett, 1988; Johnson-Cartee & Copeland, 1991a).

The politics of fear often results in identifying and targeting civic hatred and contempt based on a person's race, religion, nationality, occupation, and associations (see Moore & Kalupa, 1985; Nimmo, 1978). Johnson-Cartee and Copeland (1991a) described such persuasive appeals in political advertising as the "Us Against Them" themes. And they wrote that the message is indeed simple: "We're the good guys, they're the bad guys and you and I have to fight together to hold off the bad guys" (p. 107). They identified four major strains of Us Against Them appeals in modern political advertising: (1) the Cowboys and the Yankees (populism); (2) us against the foreigners (ethnocentricism/xenophobia); (3) class warfare, and (4) the anti-Washington mentality, to which we now add a fifth, us against the different.

The Cowboys versus the Yankees. Populism has played a strong hand in American politics from the earliest days of the republic. Barrett (1988) concluded that "The clash between those who represent entrenched power and those who resent it has rivaled the tension between liberalism and conservatism in defining American campaign showdowns" (p. 16). The term Cowboys versus the Yankees was borrowed from Kirkpatrick Sale's (1975b) book *Power Shift* in which he describes a power struggle that pits different social, political, and economic cultures against one another. Specifically, it is a struggle between the Yankees, who represent the eastern establishment and typify the "world of great wealth, high culture, nurtured traditions, industrial power, and political aristocracies, the world of 'the soft heads' and 'the media,' and the 'liberal elite'" (1975a, p. 555), and the Cowboys, who represent the "aggressive, flamboyant, restless, swaggering, newfangled, open-collar, can-do Southern-rooted Baptist culture of the Southern Rim" (p. 559). Sale identifies the Southern Rim as everything outside of New England and the Great Lakes (p. 559).

In 1966 George Wallace was not eligible to run for the Alabama governor's office, because the state constitution prohibited him from succeeding himself. But Wallace's wife, Lurleen, was on the ballot, which was just about the same as having George on the ballot (see Johnson-Cartee, Elebash, & Copeland, 1992). But his campaign speeches in support of his wife sounded more like practice for his 1968 presidential bid than like speeches for Lurleen. During the campaign, Wallace practiced his Cowboy versus Yankee rhetoric on Alabama voters. Wallace's stump speeches were often filmed and recorded for use in both television and radio commercials. A transcript of one such speech shows Wallace using classic populism:

The 1968 Wallace "Hurt 'Em" Ad

I don't have no inferiority complex about runnin' for president . . . because I represent just as good and refined and cultured people as anybody else. . . . These here national politicians like Humphrey and Johnson and Nixon, they don't hang their britches on the wall and then do a flyin' jump into 'em every mornin', they put 'em on one britches leg at a time, just like the folks in Chilton County [Alabama]. . . . I promise you, we gonna stir sump'n up all over the country, from Maine to California. . . . This is the first time in yo history so many politicos been worried about us. They say we gonna hurt 'em, and I'll tell you sump'n, I wanta hurt 'em, 'cause they've hurt us long enough, and I'm tired of it! (Ayers, 1986, p. 5)

Us Against Foreigners. It is far easier for American political leaders to blame our troubles on those on the outside—those foreign countries—with whom we compete in terms of manufacturing goods and world markets than to blame ourselves, the American people or their leaders. It is easier because there is no political backlash against the attack. Americans are reassured that we are doing nothing wrong; it is just those unethical, bad people in a distant, foreign country who want to cause us harm. The 1988 presidential primary campaign saw Democratic candidate Dick Gephardt blaming the auto industry's woes on Korean imports and export practices. In the 1992 presidential primary, one of Bob Kerrey's most oft-repeated messages was: Stop unfair Japanese trade practices.

In a 1992 Texas congressional race, incumbent congressman Charlie Wilson bashed Japan for wanting to buy east Texas wood products. While Wilson is standing on the wood chip pile, an American flag appears above Wilson's head for two to three seconds to remind us that he is protecting us from the Japanese. His blustering closing rhetoric finishes his swashbuckling ad.

The 1992 Wilson "Anti-Japan" Ad

Video	Audio
Forest scene. Charlie Wilson in forest, talking.	(Fiddles playing under.) Wilson [SOT]: "Our forests are the economic heartbeat of east Texas. And these are our trees that produce 75,000 of our best
Charlie Wilson standing on a pine chip mound, American flag appears in distance for a few seconds. Logs rolling off machine.	paying jobs. Now, the Japanese want to come into east Texas so they can export our wood chips and take our jobs. And they won't even buy our paper or lumber. This is just plain crazy. It's
Charlie Wilson in forest talking, Super: "Charlie Wilson. Our Trees . . . Our Jobs."	economic suicide. They'll get our jobs over my dead body."

In 1994 the issue of illegal aliens and social services became a hot topic in California, Texas, and Florida politics. Pete Wilson, the governor of California, ran an anti-illegal alien spot that attracted national attention.

The 1994 Wilson "Enough Is Enough" Ad

Video	Audio
Black and white footage of border crossing on Interstate 5, San Diego; illegal aliens are running into the United States, unimpeded. News headline: "Wilson Sending More Guard Troops to Border"	(Depressing music under). Announcer [VO]: "They keep coming. The federal government won't stop them at the border yet requires us to pay billions to take care of them. Wilson sent the National Guard to help the Border Patrol. But that's not all."
Color tape of Wilson talking to camera; Super: "Governor Pete Wilson."	Wilson [SOT]: "I'm suing to get the federal government to control the border. And I'm working to deny state services to illegal immigrants. Enough is enough."
Black and white photo of Kathleen Brown on red background. White letters on red: Kathleen Brown supports state services to illegal immigrants. "Illegal Immigrants Wrongly Seen as Cause of Problem," Speech, Town Hall, Los Angeles, September 29, 1993.	Announcer [VO]: "Kathleen Brown thinks differently. She supports continuing state services to illegals. And says illegal immigration is not a cause of problems in California. Where do you stand?"

In 1994 we saw a resurgence in isolationist tendencies in the United States, with foreign aid an easy target. This resurgence spawned a number of political ads designed to tap into this unease with foreign involvements. In the Indiana U.S. Senate race, Jim Jontz ran a humorous ad against his opponent, Dick Lugar that plays to the feelings of "America" first.

The 1994 Jontz "Foreign Aid" Ad

Video	Audio
Jontz in a white shirt and tie, standing in front of a red truck. Trees in background.	Jontz [SOT]: "I'm Jim Jontz, candidate for United States Senate." (Country music under)
Jontz in red truck, driving by and waving.	Jontz [VO]: "When I found out that Dick Lugar helped get $3

Jontz at corn field, talking with elderly woman. Road sign: " Moscow 1."	billion for Moscow, I went to have a look."
Woman talking to Jontz.	Woman [SOT]: "No, haven't seen a cent."
Jontz driving in truck. Jontz talking to another woman in front of Lebanon town sign.	Jontz [VO]: "Then I saw that Lugar voted a quarter billion for Lebanon."
Second woman talking.	Second Woman [SOT]: "Must have been the other Lebanon."
Jontz talking to an black couple in front of a Peru town sign.	Jontz [SOT]: "It says 50 million for Peru."
Male talking.	Man [SOT]: "You must be kidding."
Jontz in front of a "Welcome to Brazil" sign with two men and a woman. Jontz scratches head. Jontz in front of Mexico sign; Scotland sign; Jontz drives through covered bridge.	Jontz [VO]: "Brazil, Mexico, Scotland. Seems like Dick Lugar took care of every place but Indiana."
Jontz talking with woman in front of Moscow sign.	Jontz [SOT]: "I'll take care of Indiana first."
Close-up of Indiana license plates: "Jontz for U. S. Senate."	Announcer [VO]: "Jim Jontz, a senator from Indiana for Indiana. And not a minute too soon."

Class Warfare. Although traditional political science literature suggests that class differences do not exist in the United States to the extent that they do in other Western democracies (Almond & Verba, 1963), class warfare appeals are present in our political advertising. Most often, they appear in ads sponsored by the Democratic national party or the Republican national party. The Republicans portray the Democrats as "irresponsible spend thrifts intent on buying votes with public money," and the Democrats portray the Republicans as "callous servants of the very rich" (Political TV Classics, 1984). Such appeals are especially prevalent during presidential election years.

During 1982, the Democratic National Committee ran an ad portraying the Republican party as a rampaging elephant.

The 1982 DNC "Elephant" Ad

Video	Audio
View through a window in a china store.	Announcer [VO]: "Two years ago, we trusted the Republicans to mind the store in Washington. They promised us they would
An elephant appears in the store and begins destroying things.	bring prosperity and respect America's heritage of fairness. Instead, they're crushing the hopes of our elderly, of workers, small business, farmers, and a generation's dreams. The Republicans have made a mess of things. Now they want to throw their weight around our state. Only thing stands between them
Super: "Vote for your state and local Democratic candidates."	and us—the Democrats. Democrats stand for fairness."

In 1982 Democratic candidate George Wallace used a series of class warfare ads to defeat Republican candidate Emory Folmer in the Alabama gubernatorial race.

The 1982 Wallace "Not for Sale" Ad

Video	Audio
Footage of State Capitol with a "For Sale" sign on the front door.	Announcer [VO]: "Some people think their money can buy anything. And this year, the rich Republicans and powerful special interest groups are spending millions of dollars trying to buy the Alabama Governor's Office for the Republicans. But one man stands in their way."
Wallace in wheelchair, tears sign up.	Wallace [SOT]: "With your help, we will show the rich Republicans on November 2nd that your governor's office is not for sale."
Super: "Wallace for Governor. For a Better Future for all Alabamians."	Announcer [VO]: "Vote for Wallace. For a better future for all Alabamians."

Class warfare spots also may be couched in the traditional liberal versus conservative debate. In 1988 the Bush presidential campaign made the term *liberal* a dirty word in American politics. Political ads that call the opponent a liberal have remained popular in every election cycle since 1988. They have become so ubiquitous that these ads may lose their power to influence. In a 1994 gubernatorial race in New York, George Pataki ran an antiliberal ad against incumbent governor Mario Cuomo. The ad strikes a powerful emotional chord with the audience.

The 1994 Pataki "Liberal on Crime" Ad

Video	Audio
A woman seated in a living room, talking. Super: "Carol McCauliff," "Red Hook, New York."	Carol McCauliff [SOT]: "Thomas was a very loving, giving, caring person."
White letters on black: "Thomas McCauliff was murdered July 10, 1994."	Carol McCauliff [VO]: "His life was tragically taken from him by a savage, career predator."
Mrs. McCauliff talking.	Carol McCauliff [SOT]: "I blame it all on Mario Cuomo and his policies, his liberal policies. Cuomo does not care about the victims of crime. He cares about the criminals."
White letters on black: "Thomas McCauliff's Killer: 6 times convicted; repeatedly paroled by Mario Cuomo's parole board."	Carol McCauliff [VO]: "He's had 12 years to do something about crime. All of a sudden now, today, he is concerned? Where's he been? Where was he when Thomas was murdered?"

(Additional class warfare ads may be found elsewhere in this book, e.g., 1990 Helms "Awful Things" Ad; 1992 NRC "Ghetto" Ad.)

The Anti-Washington Mentality. Americans resent authority in their everyday lives. In fact, as believers in the myth of rugged individualism, they dislike all authority. The farther away that authority appears in terms of both physical and social distance, the more resentment that is likely to be expressed. This resentment often takes the form of anti-Washington statements. Voters and candidates particularly lampoon "Potomac fever"—the mental disease that hits once a person's inside the interstate beltway in Washington, D.C. We believe (Johnson-Cartee and Copeland,1991a), the theme of these ads is simply this: "When political leaders go to Washington, they lose their common sense and begin legislating, appropriating, and spending money" (p. 118).

In 1992 an incumbent congressman Rick Santorum of the Eighteenth Congressional District in Pennsylvania used a series of ads that attacked his own institution (see also 1992 Santorum "Anti-Washington" Ad). In the following ad, members of Congress are portrayed as unfeeling, insensitive, loud-mouthed, gluttonous drunks.

The 1992 Santorum "Restaurant" Ad

Video	Audio
Large table of men and women in a nice restaurant. They're smoking, drinking liquor, and eating large quantities of food. They're laughing and hugging each other.	Piano music in background. Man [SOT]: "Hey! Waiter! Bring us a bottle of your very best champagne."
Waiter is seen.	Waiter [VO]: "Of course you know, sir, that it's very, very expensive."
	Man [SOT]: "Hey! Don't worry about it, if we don't have enough money, just give the bill to them."
He points to a table of children with no food or drinks. Close-ups of children's very sad expressions.	
Rick Santorum enters the room holding a child.	Santorum [SOT]: "I'm Rick Santorum. Believe it or not that's exactly what the leaders in Congress are doing. They're wasting our tax dollars, running up the deficit and then passing the bill on to your children and mine. That's simply not fair and costs Americans jobs. That's why I'll continue my fight to clean up Congress and its greedy spending practices."
Table of men and women partying. Man receives bill from the waiter.	Man [SOT]: "Hey! I'll just write a check." (Laughter)

Super: "Join the Fight!" "For our children's future vote Santorum for Congress."	Announcer [VO]: "Join the fight! For our children's future. Vote Santorum for Congress."

The Us Versus the Different. Recently, as gays and lesbians, immigrants, and other "different" groups have sought to secure their own rights, we have seen a backlash against those groups and the political leaders that are willing to represent them. Again it is a backlash based on fear; people fear anything and anyone different from themselves. In 1995 Republican candidate for the presidency, Robert Dole, returned a campaign contribution to a gay rights group after he was severely criticized by the right wing of the party for accepting it initially. In the 1992 Republican primary in Georgia, challenger Pat Buchanan used a 30-second spot to accuse George Bush of funding a governmental agency that "glorified homosexuality . . . exploited children . . . and perverted the image of Jesus Christ" (Colford, 1992, March 2, p. 32). In 1990 the incumbent Republican governor derailed a strong Democratic challenger in Alabama by accusing him of supporting the placement of homosexuals in the classroom. And in 1986 in Alabama, Republican incumbent, U. S. Senator Jeremiah Denton, accused Democratic challenger Richard Shelby of voting to use "federal funds to promote the legalization of homosexuality."

In a 1990 North Carolina Senate race, incumbent Republican Jesse Helms ran an ad attacking Democratic challenger Harvey Gantt for accepting donations from gay and lesbian organizations. Clearly, Helms is also using a transfer appeal that negatively associates Gantt with gays and lesbians, that is, "If you don't like gays or lesbians, you won't like Gantt."

The 1990 Helms "Secret Campaign" Ad

Video	Audio
Photo of Gantt on right. Scroll of announcer's opening words.	Announcer [VO]: "It seems Harvey Gantt is running two campaigns . . . a public campaign and a SECRET campaign."
Headline: "Gantt aides mum about California trip." Box that says: "won't discuss secret campaign." A gay newspaper, *The Washington Blade*, appears and then an ad invitation to a Gantt fundraiser appears. Photo of Gay Bar, The	And Gantt's friends with liberal newspapers won't discuss his secret campaign. That Gantt has run fund-raising ads in gay newspapers. That in fund-raising events in gay and lesbian bars in San Francisco, New York, and Washington, Gantt has raised

Opera. Super: "Gantt Fund Raiser, October, 5/19/90, Washington, D.C. Photo of Gay Bar, The Enoup. Super: "Gantt Fund Raiser, San Francisco, CA." News headline: "Bay Area Reporter Fundies, Queers' Clash." Box that says: "Gantt Nets $80,000 on Bay Area Trip." Photo of Gantt on right.	thousands.
News headline: "Texas Gays Supporting Harvey Gantt" with photo of Gantt. Box with: "Mandatory Law" Gay Rights.	And Harvey Gantt has promised to back mandatory gay rights laws. Including requiring local schools to hire gay teachers.
Photo of Gantt on right. Super: "Harvey Gantt is dangerously liberal. Too liberal for North Carolina."	Harvey Gantt is dangerously liberal. Too liberal for North Carolina."

Humorous Appeals. Although Nilsen (1990) has identified eleven social functions of political humor, the humor found in American political advertising is largely of two varieties: disparagement humor and self-deprecating humor. *Disparagement humor* "belittles, debases, demeans, humiliates, or otherwise victimizes" others (Zillmann, 1983, p. 85; see also, Zillmann & Cantor, 1976). From a review of the work of Zillmann and colleagues (Cantor & Zillmann, 1973; Zillmann, 1983; Zillmann, Bryant, & Cantor, 1974; Zillmann & Cantor, 1972, 1976), it appears that disparaging humor is best used in political advertising that reinforces the party faithful rather than to convert the opposition. Research shows that individuals resent humorous messages that ridicule someone they hold in high esteem (Zillmann, 1983). *Self-deprecating humor* is used by candidates to poke fun at themselves in order to disarm their critics (see Nilsen, 1990, pp. 36-37) and to prove that they have a sense of humor—the sign of an everyman. Disparagement humor is often used in negative ads while self-deprecating humor is often used in inoculation spots.

Research into the effectiveness of political humor in advertising is virtually nonexistent (Priest, 1966; Zillmann, Bryant, & Cantor, 1984). Commercial advertising research into the effectiveness of humorous appeals, though widely researched, does nothing to clarify the effectiveness and possible uses of humorous appeals. Research has had widely different results. Some researchers have found that humorous appeals improved attention, enhanced source credibility, improved the appeal of the product, and reduced irritation from being exposed to an ad. Other researchers, however, have found that humorous appeals negatively affect understanding of the ad and produce no improvement in recall and in product-related beliefs or the consumer's intention to buy (see Johnson-Cartee & Copeland, 1991a). Although there is, as yet, no clearly documented body of research to support the effectiveness of political humor, political consultants make wide use of these appeals.

Wadsworth and Kaid (1987) in their study of presidential advertising found that roughly 20 percent of all negative ads used disparagement humor. Kaid and Johnston (1991) in their study of presidential advertising from 1960 to 1988 found that humorous appeals were used in 62 percent of negative ads (p. 60).

In the attorney general's race in Alabama in 1992, Republican candidate Spencer Bachus attacked Democratic candidate Jimmy Evans with two "Hogwash" ads. Hogwash II became a statewide favorite.

The 1990 Bachus "Hogwash II" Ad

Video	Audio
A farmer in coveralls is scrubbing a white hog with a scrub brush; has a bucket.	Announcer [VO]: "Jimmy Evans claims to be a hot shot prosecutor."
Farmer stands up and points scrub brush at camera, appears angry.	Farmer [SOT]: "HOGWASH!"
Super over farmer scrubbing hog: "53 of his 200 cases were thrown out because of Evans' mistakes in the court room."	Announcer [VO]: "He's only prosecuted 200 cases and 53 of these were thrown out of court because of Evans' mistakes. Evans says he throws criminals in prison."
Farmer points to camera with his brush.	Farmer [SOT]: "HOGWASH!"
Farmer scrubs hog. Super: "Evans' record as a prosecutor isn't as ironclad as he'd have you believe. He plays fast and free with statistics." —*The Tuscaloosa News*. Super: "Evans should stop trying to mislead voters. . . ."	Announcer [VO]: "The truth is he plea-bargains more than 80 percent of all serious criminal cases. Evans' record isn't as ironclad as he claims. Fact is Evans misleads Alabama voters."

—*The Birmingham News.*

Close-up of farmer. Photo shrinks to box. Slogan reads: Vote Bachus Alabama Attorney General.	Farmer [SOT]: "Some things you just can't clean up and Jimmy Evans, your record is one of them."
The hog walks away with rear to camera.	Announcer [VO]: "Evans it's time to hit the road." (Pig snorts and grunts)

In a 1986 congressional race in North Carolina, Republican candidate Stu Epperson used a self-deprecating appeal in order to inoculate his voters against his own personal liabilities.

The 1986 Epperson "Lincoln" Ad

Video	Audio
Epperson at a make-up mirror, powdering his face.	Announcer [VO]: "A poll shows that some people won't vote for Stu Epperson because they think he's too tall and homely. So Stu decided to learn how other tall and homely candidates solved the problem."
Takes off glasses. Rubs chin in close-up; pastes on black beard. Puts on top hat. Sits down. Stands up and hits chandelier.	Stu [VO]: "Wonder what I could do. Hmm, I got an idea. This ought to work." Stu [SOT]: "Well, what do you think? Is it me? Whoops, I don't (laughs) think it's me."
Super: "Stu!" in huge letters. "Epperson U. S. Congress"	Announcer [VO]: "Stu Epperson for Congress—not just another pretty face."

6

The Power of Recorded Visual Images

Sight provides us with information both practical and aesthetic. Sighted people depend more heavily on their sense of sight than any of the other five senses; truley, it is the king of the senses.

The ability to see is the most complex of all the senses, requiring a complicated system of bio-mechanics to move the eye, adjust the iris, and change the shape of the lens within the eye. An even more complex neurophysiology is required to convert the light to electrochemical signals sent along the optic nerve to the brain which processes, constructs, and interprets what is being viewed. Nature has provided us with the ability to see images in color and in three dimensions. As such, most of us take the visual part of our world for granted.

The most popular philosophy of science, empiricism, is based on observation, despite Plato's warning that observation was not to be believed through the parable of what we now call "Plato's cave." Not even Plato's most famous student Aristotle would forgo the power of observation to discern truth. The power of observation to reveal truths would firmly grip the world, and most of the scientific advances from which we now benefit are the result of a science based on observation.

The ability to reveal truths gives suasive force to what is seen. The power to reveal truth and thus persuade are attested to by folk sayings in our culture. The persuasive power is recognized in such adages as "seeing is believing," Missouri's state motto, "Show me," or "stumbling around in the dark." Thus, the visual world is one that has persuasive power.

Those who have specialized in the visual arts, whether it be the older artists (the painters, sculptors, or stonecutters) or the newer visual artists whom Gregor Goethals (1991) labels as "publicity firms, media managers, and TV journalists" (p. 73), do so to inform, inspire, persuade, and stimulate the emotions.

RECORDED VISUAL IMAGES

This chapter examines stored visual images which in general we call recorded visual images (RVI). For our purposes RVI specifically refers to photographs, motion pictures, and video, the three most frequent visual storage media used in political advertising. These recorded visual images enable students of political advertising to review and study the manifest and latent meanings that imprint on the viewer.

RVIs also transcend time and distance, permitting the viewer to experience another time and place. As Goethals (1991) says, "Photography, film, and television . . . appear to unveil material existence and join viewers in a one-to-one relationship to it. The presence of the mediator is not so readily detected" (p. 70).

When one looks at an RVI, the people and technology necessary in creating the image are usually not considered. Thus, people who have recorded the image as well as the technology used to record, become transparent to the viewer. What the viewer experiences is what is seen, the recorded image itself. The RVI is received as if it has a contemporaneous existence; that is, that which is viewed exists as seen, now, not as a fabrication of events that took place at some other time or place. While the reality of RVI becomes less strong as people grow older (Messaris & Gross, 1977), it never completely disappears.

Lack of a clear division between recorded and contemporaneous reality can create strange relationships, resulting in what is called para-social relationships. Such relationships produce a sense of familiarity in the viewer toward the recorded subject, even though the subject may have never met or even known of the existence of the viewer. The paradox of this relationship between spectator and model, as Hudson (1990) calls it, leads to what he terms a "strange relationship" (p. 240) when "a spectral meeting of a real person, the spectator, [takes place] with another real person, the model, who has been turned into an object and turns back into a person in the mind's eye; flesh and blood that seems magically accessible, yet is out of reach" (p. 240).

RVI as a Research Tool

The use of recorded visual images to study dynamic social processes is not a new idea, but its utility in both the quantitative and qualitative study of communication has yet to be fully realized. Remarkable examples have been given of RVI's use in illuminating new findings (e.g., Bateson & Mead, 1942; Gesell, 1935; Mead & Macgregor, 1951).

The production or invention of recorded visual images is the result of many interacting forces coming into play. These forces are both internal and external to the creator of the visual record. While an RVI appears to place the viewer at a specific time and place and allows the viewer a perception of what "really" occurred, in fact, the visual image is a creation or selection from reality. Whether or not it is due to mechanical/recorder limitations, operator selection, or post-production manipulation, the RVI is only a representation of what occurred. Indeed, the introduction of RVI has been argued to have changed our way of viewing. Kouvenhaven (1975) writes of photography:

We do not yet realize, I think, how fundamentally snapshots altered the way people saw one another and the world around them by reshaping our conception of what is real and therefore important. We tend to see only what the pictorial conventions of our time are calculated to show us. From them we learn what is worth looking for and looking at. (p. 107)

In the study of nonverbal communication, researchers have relied strongly on recorded visual images to temporally freeze moments of social interaction for intensive examination of human behavior. Much of the pioneering efforts in nonverbal communication utilized RVI technologies. Hall's (1959, 1964) general studies of nonverbal communication, Birdwhistle's (1952, 1969) studies of kinesics, and Scheflen's (1972) work in body language would have been much more difficult, if not impossible, without the use of RVI.

The study of semiotics and other textual "readings" of RVIs have provided us with insights. Barthes (for example, 1972, 1977) and others (see Benson, 1980 and Benson & Anderson, 1989) have provided studies of photographs and film images, and Butler, among many others, has analyzed television shows for the use of their visuals (1985, 1986). McLuhan (1967) and Goffman (1979) have explored American ideology through its visual representations. Benson and Frandson (1976) have even proposed a rhetorically based method for the analysis of campaign posters portraying the candidate.

Techniques for using and understanding RVI have continued to develop. Examples of several systems for analyzing RVI have emerged for both still and moving images. Gesell (1935) suggested a system for the analysis of behavior from motion picture films, which he called cinemanalysis; Byers (1964) offered a system for scrutinizing behavioral data from still pictures; and Akeret (1973) detailed ways to find what he viewed as hidden meanings in family photographs. Although his was a trade book taking a loose theoretical perspective, Akeret does offer some insights into interpretation through the practical application of nonverbal displays and discussion of the orientation of objects relative to people. Archer, Kimes, and Barrios (1978) created a measurement system for use in content analysis of pictures of human figures.

Graber (1987) proposed a form of "'gestalt' coding" (p. 74) of audiovisual messages for television news which we feel offers a possible tool for use in political ads. Her approach attempts to understand both the visual and verbal elements of the story elements. This gestalt coding also takes into account the possible interpretation by the audience. The goal of this approach is to concentrate on the meanings of the story rather than on an individual element. Graber argues that her approach more closely resembles how people respond rather than the tactic normally taken by those who engage in traditional content analysis. She maintains that

Unlike most content analysts, television viewers do not see, hear, and interpret each verbal and visual cue separately. After determining the general thrust of the story, they then condense and simplify the message, fitting a limited number of suitable details into their existing cognitive structures. (p. 75)

As this very cursory review demonstrates, systematic analytical tools of RVI analysis are available, and more are constantly being developed.

Fundamentally, an RVI may be viewed as an invitation to the viewer to perceive an event that occurred in the past. The viewer engages in an active process of perception which is not passive absorption but intentional surveillance.

Recorded Visual Images and Perception

Recorded visual images are an abstraction from the environment. That which was framed for recording onto some medium was selected because of one or more of a series of converging influences. These reasons range from professional conventions (such as framing, blocking, lighting, and so on) to the future context in which the recorded visual image will be used, to the deliberate attempt to produce a persuasive image. Musello (1979) believes that a photograph—one type of recorded visual image—is an artifact of a selection process from among these influences: "The photographs that result are not simply mechanical recordings of natural events. Rather, they are the artifacts of numerous decisions which in turn are shaped by the social contexts in which they are made" (p. 117).

Arnheim (1969) contrasts the active nature of perception by comparing it to the passive process of photography, noting, that "The camera will register all detail with equal faithfulness, but vision will not" (p. 28). Thus, individuals engage in the intentional activity of perceiving rather than being passive observers, while visual recording devices capture a moment in equal detail. When a viewer examines an RVI, the action of looking is once again active and directed.

The ability of recorded visual images to communicate information about the subject of the RVI has been shown in previous studies. In the main body of social psychology literature, the use of recorded visual images has been in impression formation and attribution research. More specifically, the focus of this corpus deals with the physical attributes of the photographic subject and the impact of those attributes on the viewer. Secord (1958) has demonstrated in several studies that a viewer exposed to a photographic subject will infer personality traits of that photographed subject. Evaluations of viewer responses to wearing eyeglasses (Manz & Lueck, 1968; Thornton, 1943), eye pupil size (Hess, 1965), style of dress (Hamid, 1968), wearing lipstick (McKeachie, 1952), and smoking artifacts (Hickson, Powell, Hill, Holt, & Flick, 1979) have all used photographic stimuli and demonstrated that people will vary their judgment based on these items. Szondi (as cited in Deri, 1949) used photographs in his personality test, which asked people to describe what was happening in a situation based on what is seen in the photos. Kleinke's (1975) book on first impressions provides an excellent summary of the manner by which first impressions are built on the morphology and physical attractiveness of a perceived individual. Schneider, Hastoff, and Ellsworth (1979) caution that the type of research that Kleinke synthesizes may have reached its fruitful conclusion: "The list of physical characteristics is as endless as the list of personality traits, so perhaps nothing more is to be gained by building up a directory of relationships" (1975, p. 23).

The focus of cited attribution research is on ascribing goals, motives, or, in some of the cited research, a sociopsychological cause to the perceived acts of a viewed person. "Attribution theory deals with the rules the average individual uses in attempting to infer causes of observed behavior" (Jones, 1972, p. x). The attribution process helps to make sense of the surrounding world (Kanouse & Hanson, 1972). Heider and Simmel (1944) illustrated people's desire to ascribe causes to viewed events in a study using an animated film. In the film, two small geometric figures and one larger geometric figure were seen moving around a block that appeared to have a "door." Most people who viewed the film saw the larger geometric figure as chasing the smaller geometric figures or considered the larger geometric figure to be a bully. Clearly, this is an example of anthropormorphizing the blocks. The example illustrates that attributions are generally based on some observed behavior of the object or the environment and on the human desire to make causal inferences from the observation.

TELEVISUAL TECHNIQUES

The range of televisual production techniques easily fills entire books. Here we wish to acquaint the reader with some of the more important visual production elements (see Figure 6.1) and to review a sample of the political advertising research on some of these structural features. The coverage is not exhaustive of all the visual elements that might be examined.

Figure 6.1
Televisual Techniques

```
Motion
        Primary
                Secondary
                Tertiary
        Camera Perspectives
                Reportorial
                Objective
                Subjective
        Editing
                The Cut
                The Dissolve
                The Fade
                The Wipe
                Digital Video Effects
        Camera Angles
                Normal
                Low
                High
                Canted
        Screen Asymmetry
        Framing
```

Motion

The perception of motion is one of the strongest attractors of attention. The sensitivity of the eyes to motion stimulates the brain to adjust the eyes so that the movement within the environment may be observed. The eye is drawn to motion, as may be easily observed in the individual who is carrying on a conversation when a television is switched on in the room. You will notice that, despite the person's attempt to talk directly to another person, the speaker's eyes continually shift to the TV screen. This attraction is caused by the perceived movement in the peripheral part of the person's vision. While this sensitivity to motion along the peripheral vision is not the best behavior during a cocktail party, it proved quite handy to our ancestors in the wilds when attempting to avoid a hungry carnivore.

Zettl (1990) has proposed three categories of "motion" in television or film which are designed to account for the action viewed, whether it is created in front of the camera, by the camera, or "behind" the camera.

Primary motion is the action that occurs in front of the camera or "event motion" (Zettl, 1990, p. 272), as when an actor or, more appropriately in our case, a political candidate moves in front of the camera or something is seen entering or leaving the frame. A candidate who walks left to right across the screen is providing the primary motion.

Secondary motion is action created by the movement of the camera. For example, camera movements such as a pan (moving the lens left to right), truck (moving the entire camera to the left or the right), or zoom (changing the focal length of the lens) would all create movement on the screen. Five reasons motivate secondary motion: to follow action, to reveal action, to reveal landscape, to relate action, and to induce action (Zettl, 1990).

Tertiary movement is part of the editing or post-production process and is not physical action. It is that movement or rhythm caused by changing one visual image to another in some sequence. Tertiary movement includes the on-screen movement created by the cut or take, the wipe, matte, key effects and so on. This motion is created by switchers, videotape editors, and special effects generators.

Camera Perspectives

The camera may adopt one of three different perspectives in relation to the photographic subject: reportorial, objective, and subjective (Burrows & Woods, 1986). The *reportorial viewpoint* utilizes direct eye contact between the photographic subject and the camera lens, and the subject speaks directly to the audience. The reportorial viewpoint is most characteristic of the person-in-the-street ad, the voter editorial comment ad, the public figure testimonial ad, and the news show dramatization ad. The *objective perspective* oversees the action, while the subject(s) ignore the presence of the camera. Almost all of entertainment television adopts the objective perspective. It is most characteristic of the news interview show ad, the slice-of-life ad, and the cinema verité ad. The *subjective perspective* substitutes the camera for a person or an object in the scene. The subjective angle allows the viewer to see the action through the perspective of a participant within the scene. For example, the recent innovation of placing remote cameras in race cars allows the camera to participate in the event and by extension so, too, does the home viewer.

In political advertising, the first two perspectives (i.e., reportorial and objective) are the most common. The camera is usually addressed directly, or the camera is ignored. However, some political spots may contain both reportorial and objective perspectives. Reportorial, objective, and subjective perspectives conceptualize the relationship between subjects and the camera and by extension the audience, but they do not describe how the photographic subject is framed within the screen.

Editing

Editing is the process of "selection and assembly of shots" (Zettl, 1976, p. 510) in order to "build a screen event" (Zettl, 1973, p. 297). Editing can be used for technical reasons (continuity editing) or for aesthetic reasons (complexity editing) and is labeled tertiary motion.

Cut or Take

The *cut* or, as it is more commonly called in television, the *take* is the fundamental device for building the screen event and is the most commonly used editing technique. Zettl (1992) states that the cut is "the most common and least obtrusive" of the various transition devices available to a television director (p. 348). With this transition device one does not actually view the transition, as it takes place at the time just after the electron gun snaps off at the bottom of the screen and before it comes back on at the top.

Murray-Brown (1991) has a slightly different perspective on the cut. With regard to the fundamental nature of the cut, he observes that it is "the one that most determines the hidden message of the medium, as type does with print" (p. 23). He argues that the cut is also one of the most powerful tools for attracting attention: "Each time a cut is made a message is sent to the viewer saying, 'Look for the meaning in this cut.' On television, the cut is more potent in its ability to attract attention than the action taking place between cuts" (p. 24).

Murray-Brown (1991) makes too strong a case for the power of the cut within its normal use. Most uses of the cut are invisible to the viewer and therefore do not attract attention. However, in some instances the cut does obtrude itself. In these cases the cut can be, as Murray-Brown says, a potent force. Usually, the cut is a powerful force when it serves as the transition to make an impact, change time or place, or create rhythms. When cutting is simply designed to create continuity within a scene, we believe that it is not an important visual artifact for analysis.

In 1992 President Bush in a series of spots spoke directly to the camera. Cuts were very visible during the monologues; these obvious cuts are called jump cuts. The use of jump cuts proved to be distracting from the message, and so in this situation, the cuts were made unwisely.

Penn (1971) maintains that rapid editing creates additional energy and excitement. A style now associated with MTV. However, the use of continuous, rapid cutting may distract the viewer from the subject matter and shift attention from the message to the technique. Frequently, fast-paced editing is used in direct attack negative ads, so that it appears that layers of condemning evidence are being presented against the targeted candidate.

The Dissolve

The second most common transitional device, the *dissolve*, involves one image slowly fading out while another image slowly fades in with a temporary overlap of both fading images. The speed with which the dissolve occurs may be either slow or fast.

The Fade

The *fade* is similar to the dissolve in that the intensity of an image either increases from black to a full intensity (fade-up) or from full intensity to black (fade-out). The difference between the fade and the dissolve is that the fading images do not overlap.

The Wipe

In this transition device, the *wipe*, one image seems to wipe or push another image off the screen. The most traditional use of this device is to create a split-screen, such as seeing two people in different places speaking on the telephone. In general, these types of wipes have become passé in television, and in commercials they have become an object for self-referential humor.

Digital Video Effects

Digital video effects (DVE) are created by a conversion of the analog television signal to a binary code that a computer can manipulate. The computer then converts the massaged digital information back into an analog signal for transmission. Computer animation operates on the same principle, and this discussion of DVE includes computer-animated effects.

DVE has become very popular in production because it offers the creator of political commercials a variety of visual effects to attract the viewer's attention. An example of an advanced DVE is a computer animation process orginally developed at Industrial Light and Magic called *morphing*. This process was first seen in *Terminator 2*, in which the Terminator 2000 changes shapes, and is now viewed with regularity in music videos, television programs, and advertisements. Today it is even possible to buy software to do morphing on home computers. In 1994 morphing ads were used extensively throughout the United States. In particular, they were used to defeat incumbent Democrats in the House of Representatives and the U.S. Senate. Incumbents turned into Bill Clinton before the voters' eyes. In a congressional race in Kentucky, Ron Lewis morphed Joe Prather into Bill Clinton. In 1996, the Democrats returned the favor by having Republican opponents morph into Newt Gingrich.

The 1994 Lewis "Morphing" Ad

Video	Audio
Super white letters on black ribbon. "All professional politicians are the same." Black and white photo of Joe Prather. Super in white top left "Joe Prather." White lettering centered bottom. "Raise taxes and fees over 40 times." Prather's face changes to Clinton's while hair and glasses remain Prather's. Super in white on bottom of photograph "Awarded no-bid state contracts." Black and white photo completes change to Clinton. White super centered on bottom, "Largest tax increase in history" New super in white "Whitewater"	Announcer [VO]: "Nowdays it seems like all professional politicians are the same. In Frankfurt, Joe Prather voted to increase taxes and fees over forty times. And cuts sweetheart deals for his friend the governor and campaign contributors. Bill Clinton passes the largest tax increase in history and cuts a sweet deal with a banker friend. If you like Bill Clinton, you'll love Joe Prather.
White lettering on black bumper. "If you like Bill Clinton, " Then is added to the last line "you'll love Joe Prather." Black and White Clinton photograph. White super, "Kentucky doesn't needs another professional politician." Clinton's photo changes to Joe Prather's. White lettering on black background. "On May 24th (rest of sentence underlined in red) send a message to Bill Clinton." Red,	Kentucky doesn't need another professional politician. Kentucky doesn't need Joe Prather. Send a message to Bill Clinton. Send Ron Lewis to Congress. Ron Lewis—he's one of us.

white, and blue bumper sticker
reads "Ron Lewis for Congress."
To the right of the bumper sticker
is a color photograph of Ron
Lewis.

Camera Angles

The use of certain camera angles may influence the viewer's perception of the power or credibility of the person viewed. The viewer is
thought to adopt the relative position to the photographic subject
taken by the camera. The image from the camera becomes an extension
of the viewer's perception. Linden (1970) writes about film that "Due
to the identification of his eyes with the camera viewpoint, the film
viewer is subject to an experience of bi-sociation. Though he is liter-
ally in his seat, he negates that perspective and identifies with the
screen perspective" (p. 26). The same would be true of television.

The relationship of the camera lens to the RVI subject(s) has been
theorized to influence the viewer's perceptions of the framed individual (e.g., Arnheim, 1958). The height of the camera lens in relation to
the photographic subject may be divided into one of four types:
normal, low camera, high camera, and canted angle.

Our language illustrates the psychological importance of height
as a metaphor for inferring inferior/superior relationships. One
"looks up to" someone who is perceived as superior and respected or
"looks down on" an inferior. Through production techniques, individuals may be "elevated" in rank, that is, placed in a superior position or
denigrate by being placed in an inferior position (Zettl, 1973).

These height metaphors also translate to camera angles. The
viewer is placed into an inferior, equal, or superior height to the photographic subject, depending on the positioning of the camera lens in
relation to the subject's eyes. The first three camera angles that follow invoke the height metaphor to establish relationships between
the photographic subject and the audience.

In the *normal camera angle*, the camera lens is at the same height
from the ground as the subject's eyes; thus, the viewer sees the photographic subject eye-to-eye. Of the various camera angles, this is the
most unobtrusive for the viewer and suggests equality in terms of power
between the photographic subject and the viewer, for each is of the
same height. This is the most frequently used angle in television.

The *low camera angle* occurs when the lens is below the
photographic subject's eye level; the camera looks up at the subject.
This is the second most commonly used angle in television. Wurtzel
(1979) notes that this camera angle is frequently used in political and
automobile commercials. The effect is to place the viewer in an

inferior position in relation to the person being viewed. The photo-graphic subject is "above the viewer" and "larger than life." Such an angle helps the photographic subject take on a greater psychological importance for the viewer.

The *high camera angle* is the reverse of the low angle. The cam-era lens is placed above the eye level of the photographic subject and looks down on the subject. The effect is to place the viewer in a psy-chologically superior role in relation to the pictured individual. Viewers of sessions of the U.S. Senate and of the House of Represent-atives on C-SPAN should be familiar with this camera angle. The re-mote-controlled cameras in both houses look down on the speakers.

The *canted angle* is created by moving the camera through its hor-izontal plane. The horizon in a canted angle is no longer perpendicular to the viewer. This type of angle is supposed to suggest a sense of unre-ality or fantasy to the viewer. It was frequently used when showing villains on the "Batman" television show. It is rarely used in polit-ical commercials although it is increasingly popular in product ads.

The use of angles should be consistent within the ad. Although camera angles can add some interest, they could prove distracting to the viewer. In 1986 the media consultants for Bill McFarland, a Republican Congressional candidate in Ala-bama, created a commer-cial using very low camera angles—so low, in fact, that the viewer ap-peared to be only a foot or two from the ground. The extreme angle called more attention to itself than to the candidate. As a result, the viewer thought the ad looked "funny" or "home-made," and although viewers could recall the ad they could not remember the content. The low angle also overemphasized McFarland's girth, making him ap-pear heavier than he would have if another angle had been selected.

Zettl (1990) points out that these rules of thumb are contextually bound. This means that whether these rules of thumbs actually apply depends on the other visual and audio elements in which events occur. Thus, events or other elements within an image could negate the general psychological meanings of these angled shots.

The camera angles and their perceived meanings reported here re-flect the conventional wisdom within the television and film industry. Conventional wisdom is not always borne out when tested. For exam-ple, Tiemens (1965) found only minimal support for the theory that camera angle influenced the perceived credibility of those who ap-peared on television. On the other hand, some researchers have found differences created by camera angle (cf. Mandell & Shaw, 1973; McCain, Chilberg, & Wakshlag, 1977) McCain and White (1980) con-cluded from their literature review that "It appears that perception of a television source's potency and authority may be influenced by low angles" (p. 6).

Screen Asymmetry

Arnheim (1965) views the canvas, or in this case the television screen, as being "heavier" on the right. This asymmetry affects the amount of attention given to an object based on its placement within the screen. In television, the viewer will usually give the greatest attention to the object on the right side of the screen. Zettl (1973) writes that "the right side is more conspicuous than the left side. In fact, some magazines charge more for an ad placed on the right-hand pages than on the left-hand pages" (p. 128).

Based on his eye movement studies, Brandt (1945) concluded that the first fixation point was on the left above center. Zettl (1990) would agree that the original fixation point is on the left, but he argues that the eye naturally comes to rest on the right, thus making the right side more important. However, Metallinos and Tiemens (1977) were unable to find a clear difference between the placement of items on the left or right of the screen in an experimental setting. Their empirical results "show some evidence to suggest that retention of visual information in a newscast is enhanced when the visual elements are placed on the left side of the screen" (p. 32).

Looking at how political advertising practitioners generally use the screen, we may conclude that they prefer to use the right for the most important information. For example, in a direct comparison spot, the sponsor's photograph or text-based graphics are usually presented on the right, while his or her opponent's is placed on the left. In direct attack spots, the opponent's photograph is usually placed on the left while the condemning evidence is positioned on the right.

Framing

The framing, or field of view, of the photographic subject has been shown to have differential impact on people's perceptions of the subject. It has been argued that certain structural features mimic the cognitive process and that close-ups are equivalent to paying close attention (Hobbs, 1991; Hobbs, Frost, Dabis, & Staufferet, 1988). A close-up in televisual terms when dealing with people is of the face of the person being framed.

The face is one of two broad classes of nonverbal cue sources—the other being the body (Ekman, 1965). Of these two sources, the face is most easily manipulated when attempting to convey meaning. The centrality of the face to the expression of affect or frame of mind has been noted in many fields. In terms of evolutionary biology, Darwin (1896) discussed the face's ability to transmit emotional signals, which he attempted to demonstrate developed in the lower animals. In portraiture, the face has been of central importance. Croy (1968) counsels photographers: "Moods and feelings are depicted in special movements of facial muscles and reveal much of a person's psychological process" (p. 23). The face's ability to transmit emotions has been the subject of many empirical studies by, among others, social psychologists, political scientists, and communication researchers.

Two studies of network newscasters' expressions when presenting a story have been conducted. Friedman, Mertz, and DiMatteo (1980) analyzed whether the television network news anchors during the 1976 presidential race—Walter Cronkite (CBS), John Chancellor (NBC), and Barbara Walters, Harry Reasoner, and David Brinkley (ABC)—presented positive, neutral, or negative facial affect displays during and immediately following a story on either Ford or Carter. They concluded that all anchors except Walters had significantly higher mean positive facial expressions for Carter than for Ford. Mullen, Futrell, Stairs and others (1986) replicated the Friedman study and went on to conclude that facial expressions could affect the outcome of an election. Mullen et al. judged the three 1984 network news anchors—Tom Brokaw (NBC), Peter Jennings (ABC), and Dan Rathers (CBS)—finding that Jennings had more positive facial display for Reagan stories versus Dukakis, but that there were no perceived differences for the other two anchors. Mullen et al. (1986) concluded that "Dan Rather and Tom Brokaw did not exhibit any noticeable bias, with both newscasters appearing to be right at or above the midpoint of the 21 point scale for both candidates. However, Peter Jennings did appear to exhibit a strong positive bias in favor of Reagan" (p. 293). Mullen and colleagues also conducted a survey to determine which network anchor respondents normally viewed and for whom the respondent voted. Their conclusion was that Jennings' facial display had influenced voters to cast their ballots for Reagan. The researchers concluded that "regular viewing of a newscaster who exhibits facial expressions that are biased in favor of a particular political candidate is associated with an increased likelihood of voting for that candidate" (p. 294). While we feel uncomfortable with endorsing this conclusion, it does serve to illustrate the possible power of facial displays.

Facial displays obviously have implications for the political candidate. Sullivan and Masters (1988) propose a theoretical model that links facial displays with affect of the portrayed candidate to the viewers' emotional reaction to the pictured candidate. They believe that political support is as much affective as it is rational.

Political support depends, in part, on citizen's emotional responses after seeing or hearing leaders. The viewers' immediate impressions and emotions are integrated with other sources of information forming or modifying more generalized attitudes of support. The precise nature of the emotional response is a function of the relationship between the political leader and the viewer, the nature of the display, and the context in which the display occurs. These emotional reactions, particularly if reinforced, can become part of more enduring dispositions toward candidates or programs. (p. 346)

Programmatic research by Lanzetta, Sullivan, Masters and McHugo (1985) attempts to isolate the impact of facial displays within the political context. They summarized their results and speculation into six findings:

1. Facial displays of happiness/reassurance, anger/threat, and fear/evasiveness are perceived differently, elicit different psychophysiological responses, and interact with prior attitude message in generating self-reported emotional or attitudinal reactions.

2. Prior attitudes--although having little effect on psychophysiological responses to facial displays--interact strongly with self-reported emotional responses and cognitive assessments of the stimulus figure.

3. Partisanship predicts potency of response to display behavior. Supporters of President Reagan find his nonverbal displays of happiness/reassurance more reassuring than critics, and his displays of anger/threat, which elicit fear and hostility among critical viewers, generate a sense of strength and power among supporters.

4. Facial displays are capable of arousing and influencing viewers even when embedded in the background of a TV newscast during which the leader's voice is not heard.

5. Different candidates vary in the way they are perceived and in the emotional responses they elicit.

6. Although similar emotions are conveyed by the image, the sound, and the combined sound-plus-image presentation, these channels of communication do not seem to contribute equally to the emotional effects on viewers. (p. 112)

The researchers also correctly caution that the responses to these facial displays occur at the nonconscious level. People are not usually reflective about the facial displays presented to them. They tend, instead, to make nonconscious judgments about the individual who is exhibiting the display.

Tiemens (1978) suggests that facial displays helped Carter in his debates with Ford. Based on reaction shots taken while the other candidate was speaking, Tiemens reports that Carter was seen smiling in eleven of fifty-three reaction shots compared to three smiles in forty-one reaction shots of Ford. Reports from the contemporaneous popular press reported the facial displays with emotional attributes:

One observer notes that Carter appeared "almost casual at times, perching on his stool, jotting notes, leaning on the podium, his smiles coming close to smirks." Another observer reported that "at times Ford looked like an angry lineman glaring at a line-backer whom he was about to obliterate, though he never quite succeeded." (pp. 369-370)

The face is also the area most easily manipulated in terms of deception. Ekman and Friesen (1974) reported that respondents, when asked what types of behaviors should be managed when engaging in deception, much more often mentioned controlling the face than controlling the body. Earlier, Ekman and Friesen (1967) concluded that the face would be the area of the body that would be most congruous with the verbal deception. They also found evidence (1974) that accuracy for detecting honest and dishonest affect displays was better for body cues than facial. They concluded: "People are generally more aware of their facial behavior than their bodily activity and will therefore be more likely to disguise their face than their body" (p. 299).

Cultural nonverbal display rules suggest the type of facial expressions that are socially acceptable for a particular context. These affect display rules may vary from culture to culture and between some subcultures. As an example of a culture-bound affect display rule, in the United States women--in aggregate--tend to smile more than men--in aggregate--when interacting with adults (Rosenfeld, 1966) and with children (Bugental, Kaswan, & Gianetto, 1971; Bugental, Kaswan, & Love, 1970; Bugental, Kaswan, Love, & Fox, 1970; Frieze & Ramsey, 1976).

The importance of the face, together with the ability of the camera to provide a close-up of that face in an RVI, would suggest that people would prefer to see others in close-up. There is evidence supporting this preference for males but not for females. Just as there are affect display "smile" differences for men and women, so there are also framing preference differences.

Evidence from Europe and other cultures indicates that people evaluate close-ups more favorably than other shot lengths (Adams & Copeland, 1980; Kepplinger, 1991). A similar preference for close-ups in the United States had been demonstrated earlier (McCain & Divers, 1973; McCain & Repensky, 1972). McCain and Divers found a difference for male and female "newscasters": Females were preferred in long shots and males in medium shots and close-ups. Copeland (1989), in a content analysis of prime-time television programs, found a framing difference similar to that suggested by McCain and Divers. Male characters, when portrayed alone in the frame, are framed more tightly than females when they are portrayed alone.

This framing preference for political candidates has been demonstrated by Adams, Copeland, Fish, and Hughes (1980). Their study of registered voters showed that when the registered voter was asked to selected favored photographs clear preferences emerged. In rank ordering a preferred male and female candidate, participants preferred females in long shots and males in medium and close-up whether the registered voter was male or female.

In political advertising, the candidate is frequently framed in such a way that the audience may see the person's face and more importantly the candidate's facial expressions. Getting one's face on television is important to a politician because, as Graber (1987) testifies, "when candidates for political office are shown on the television screen, audiences tend to use the pictures to judge the candidates' personality traits such as competence, integrity, leadership, and empathy" (p. 77). Rosenberg, Bohan, McCafferty, and Harris (1986) go so far as to typify the influence of appearance on a voter's preference as "powerful," and they believe a visual depiction of a candidate "provides voters with a clear image of the candidate's character and fitness for office" (p. 119; see also Rosenberg & McCafferty, 1987). Sullivan and Masters (1988) enumerate the possible intervening forces on response to a visual representation of the candidate's face. They believe that

the effects of politicians' facial displays depend on a number of variables, including (1) the characteristics of the person being watched (e.g., leadership status and public standing, personal "style," facial conformation); (2) the nonverbal behavior observed (including paravocal cues, posture, movement, head's orientation); (3) the verbal messages accompanying the display (congruence of verbal and nonverbal affect as well as meaning); (4) the setting (partisan or nonpartisan, whether or not under the control of the leader); and (5) viewer characteristics (party identification, ideology or other relevant political opinions and "schemas," prior attitude the leader and the message content, gender). (Sullivan & Masters, 1988, p. 346)

In political advertising, the goal is to use a flattering likeness of the sponsoring candidate and, when the opponent is shown, to select an unflattering photograph. For example, in the 1986 Zschau "News Anchor" ad, a photograph showing a gaunt, open-mouthed Alan Cranston was used (see Johnson-Cartee & Copeland, 1991a). Sometimes the idea is to make the person look silly or frivolous, as happened in an ad against Fritz Hollings in which Hollings' picture was topped with different foreign hats.

Size of image may also be manipulated. For example, in direct comparison ads, the sponsoring candidate often appears in a close-up which continues to grow more prominent on-screen while the targeted candidate's photograph gets smaller through the course of the ad. Thus, leaving only a picture of the sponsoring candidate at the conclusion of the ad.

STYLISTIC ANALYSES OF POLITICAL ADS

Although many political advertising researchers discuss televisual techniques in their literature reviews, these techniques are rarely coded and reported. Rose and Fuchs (1968) studied the use of visual style elements in the 1966 California gubernatorial race between Ronald Reagan and Edward G. "Pat" Brown. While most of their article is a recounting of narratives, they do explicate some of Reagan's use of camera technique.

Devlin (1973, 1977) generally described spots and how they came to be produced for the presidential elections of 1972 and 1976, giving little analysis of visual techniques. He does discuss the use of camera perspective within the McGovern campaign commercials, but no other style elements enumerated here play an important role in his analyses. In addition, Devlin did note that the McGovern campaign used cinema verité devices to show McGovern doing things (for example, talking to voters in informal settings).

Elebash and Rosene (1982) found that in Alabama gubernatorial commercials 60-second televised ads made use of a greater number of production techniques than did 30-second ads. Techniques coded in their content analysis included the use of music, the number of announcers used, and the type of sets used.

Shyles (1983, 1986) is one of the few researchers who has used production techniques in the analysis of political advertising. Specifically, Shyles examined the political spots for various Republican and Democratic presidential contenders in the 1980 election and found that a candidate's image was positively related to high transition rates (editing), candidates oriented indirectly into the camera, and other variables.

In 1986 Kaid and Davidson identified two distinct candidate videostyles: the incumbent videostyle and the challenger videostyle. Videostyle may be defined as the "methods of self-portrayal" in political advertising (p. 185). The researchers operationalized videostyle as combining verbal content, nonverbal content, and film/video techniques. The coding choices used were cinema verité, slides with print, candidate, or someone else head on, animation/special production and combination. Fifty-five political commercials from three U.S. Senate races in 1982 were analyzed. The study revealed that incumbent ads were 90 percent positive, while challenger ads were more evenly divided, with 54 percent positive and 46 percent negative. The incumbent videostyle and the challenger videostyle are described as follows.

Incumbent videostyle. In general, the incumbent (1) uses longer commercials; (2) uses more [voter editorial comments]; (3) uses more candidate-positive focus; (4) uses more slides with print; (5) dresses more formally; 6) is represented by an announcer or other voice [neutral reporter, proselytizing reporter, visual documentary]; (7) verbally and visually stresses "competence."

    Challenger videostyle. In general, the challenger (1) uses more opposition-negative focus in ads; (2) uses cinema verité style; (3) uses ads where candidate appears "head-on" [public figure testimonials]; (4) uses more frequent eye contact with camera and audience; (5) dresses more casually; (6) speaks for self more frequently—is not represented by surrogates [candidate confrontation ads, candidate interaction ads]. (p. 199)

These videostyles complement the work of Trent and Friedenberg (1983), who identified incumbent and challenger campaign styles and strategies (see also Johnston, 1991; Kaid & Johnston, 1991; Kitchens & Stiteler, 1979).

7

Style: Composition of Polispots

In order to understand the composition of polispots, we must examine the stylistic devices used. *Style* is the way the narrative is told. It can be defined as the "way in which audio, visual, and narrative techniques are used" (Johnson-Cartee & Copeland, 1991a, p. 127) in the construction of political advertising.

Consultants make a wide variety of stylistic choices when constructing political advertising. Making the right choices usually produces memorable, and more importantly, effective political ads. Making the wrong choice often produces ineffective political advertising that wastes the candidate's resources. In this chapter, we focus on the narrative stylistic decisions that must be made in order to create a successful ad.

THE ROLE OF THE CANDIDATE IN THE AD

Perhaps the most obvious stylistic device in candidate-sponsored ads is the role of the candidate in the ad. Three types of candidate presentation styles have been identified: candidate presentation ads, candidate interactional ads, and surrogate ads (see Johnson-Cartee & Copeland, 1991a).

Candidate Presentation Ads

Today, it is not unusual to see a political candidate appear in his or her own political advertising, but this is a relatively recent change in our political culture. Until the end of the 1800s, presidential candidates refused to campaign for public office, believing that it was undignified. Instead, their supporters spoke for them. Campaign lore said that successful candidates should stay above the political fray of the campaign. Jamieson (1984) notes that it was not until the presidential election of 1912 that the modern model of an activist presidential candidate became accepted. Carroll (1980) and Diamond and Bates (1988) report that by the time of the first presidential television campaign in 1952, the candidate was expected to appear in his own political advertising (see also Jamieson, 1984).

Candidate presentation ads are ads in which the candidate appears in the spot and personally delivers the political messages or appeals. Johnston (1991) calls such ads *introspection ads,* which she describes as "those where the candidate speaks for him- or herself, reflecting on issue positions or personal feelings in the ad" (p. 61). During the last two presidential election years, we have seen an increase in the use of candidate presentation ads. Perhaps this is a response to the increased attention given to the importance of communication styles and candidate characteristics in media coverage and the voter's decision-making processes.

During the 1992 presidential campaign, Democratic candidate Bill Clinton suffered from a credibility problem that resulted from a number of missteps and misstatements during the course of the campaign. From negative publicity concerning possible extramarital affairs to a series of misstatements concerning how he avoided the Viet Nam draft, Clinton's credibility quotient was in trouble. In addition, the incumbent president, George Bush, was taking advantage of that credibility problem by consistently hammering at the "trust" factor. For this reason, the Clinton campaign decided to use a number of candidate presentation ads. Clearly, the strategy was to improve Clinton's credibility by having him deliver his own messages; ads are deemed more believable if the candidates themselves make the pitch. By having Clinton on the air, it was an opportunity to portray him as a likable and personable individual, and the campaign hoped that such positive evaluations might boost his credibility. Clinton's campaign went so far as to have Clinton personally narrate one of his own political biography spots. While a candidate may appear in a biographical ad or even have one or two speaking parts within the ad, it is unusual for a candidate to deliver his own biography.

The 1992 Clinton "Personal Bio" Ad

Video	Audio
Black and white scenes of Hope, Arkansas train station. Photo of Clinton as a boy.	Clinton [VO]: "I was born in a little town called Hope, Arkansas, three months after my father died."

Clinton in color talking.	Clinton [SOT]: "I remember that old two-story house where I lived with my grandparents."
President Kennedy approaching podium.	Clinton [VO]: "They had a very limited income."
Clinton talking again.	Clinton [SOT]: "It was in 1963 that I went to Washington and met President Kennedy at the Boys' Nation Program."
Black and white of Clinton meeting Kennedy.	Clinton [VO]: "And I remember just thinking what an incredible country this was that someone"
Clinton talking.	Clinton [SOT]: "like me who had no money or anything would be given the opportunity to meet the president. That's how I"
Photo of Clinton studying.	Clinton [VO]: "decided that I could really do public service, cause I cared so much about people."
Clinton talking.	Clinton [SOT]: "I worked my way through law school with part time jobs, anything I could find."
Footage of old houses; Clinton sworn in as governor. Clinton with child at a computer station. Clinton with elderly woman. Clinton working late at desk. Clinton shaking hands. Clinton with little girl.	Clinton [VO]: "And after I graduated I really didn't care about making a lot of money, I just wanted to go home and see if I could make a difference. We've worked hard in education and health care, to create jobs and we've made real progress. Now it's exhilarating to me to think that as president that I could change all of our peoples' lives for the better. And bring hope back to the American Dream."

Until the 1990 election campaign cycle, it was also highly un-usual for candidates to appear in negative spots attacking their oppo-nents. Consultants knew that when the candidate did appear the credibility of the ad went way up, but many political leaders were re-luctant to utilize this technique. Using surrogates to deliver the nega-tive appeals provides the fiction that the attacks are not from the sponsoring candidate. The surrogate offers the appearance of the can-didate being above such political tactics. By 1990, however, candi-dates began appearing in their own negative polispots, particularly when the races were tight. Incumbent Republican Senator Jesse Helms of North Carolina serves as an excellent example of this relatively recent phenomenon. Helms, fighting for his political survival in the 1990 race, went to the airwaves in a series of direct comparison negative ads that clearly left his opponent, Democratic candidate Harvey Gantt, at a disadvantage. The Helms ad used latent political symbology to tap racial stereotypes and underlying white resentments. The phrase "something for nothing" taps the racial stereotype that African Americans expect something for nothing, that is, money for no work, and Helms' warning that there is "no such thing as a free lunch" harks back to the individualist creed that diametrically opposes the community or social welfare creed, which is stereotypically viewed as being supported by political liberals.

The 1990 Helms "Free Lunch" Ad

Video	Audio
Helms in an office. Super: "Senator Jesse Helms"	Helms [SOT]: "This is Jesse Helms, and I'll never try to get your vote by promising something for nothing. There's no such thing as a free lunch. Now Harvey Gantt is a liberal. He's promised everything to everybody with you paying the bill. The question is who will cast your vote in the United States Senate, a liberal Harvey Gantt or a conservative Jesse Helms. I hope you'll help me Tuesday."

Candidate Interactional Ads

Candidate interactional ads are spots, in which the candidate appears conversing with ordinary people. The information contained in the spot is presented as an interaction between or among people. The presence of a camera is ignored by those within the ad. Candidate interactional spots are not used as often today as they were in the 1960s. Frequently voters see *pseudo-candidate interactional spots*, in which candidates are walking through an audience delivering scripted lines. Close-ups of the audience give the appearance that they are participating, but in reality it is a candidate presentation spot. The Bush campaign in 1992 made extensive use of these pseudo-candidate interactional spots often giving the appearance that Bush was appearing in a theater-in-the-round. Candidate interactional ads used today frequently take a humorous approach.

During the 1992 gubernatorial race in Washington State, Joe King ran a humorous candidate interactional ad in which the "interaction" is none too successful.

The 1992 King "Plan" Ad

Video	Audio
Man in suit on a city street handing out booklets. People scurrying by.	King [VO]: "Hi there, I'm Joe King. This is a copy of the King Plan. I'd like you to just. . . ."
Joe King directly addresses the camera. Super: "Joe King."	King [SOT]: "I'm Joe King. When I first started running for governor, I was frustrated by sound bites and TV ads."
King starts trying to hand booklet out again; people avoid him. Background footage of him trying to give the plan away, unsuccessful attempts.	King [VO]: "plan for the future of this state. The King Plan. As governor. . . . So I wrote this plan on how I'm going to govern Washington. Then I tried giving it away. And then I got a polite suggestion from a constituent."
A Fish Salesperson yelling.	Fish Salesperson (yelling) [SOT]: "Hah, Joe, why don't you mail it?"
King continues to hand them out.	King [VO]: "So I have. And in a few days, you'll be getting it."
Super: "Joe King Governor."	Announcer [VO]: "Joe King and his Plan because real issues take longer than 30 seconds."

During the 1986 Senate race in Vermont, incumbent Democratic senator Patrick Leahy ran a humorous candidate interaction ad that has Leahy saying very little but the farmers and, yes, even, the cows saying a lot.

The 1986 Leahy "Moo" Ad

Video	Audio
Two farmers and Patrick Leahy standing in a pasture. The farmers behind a fence. The senator in front of the fence. Cows in the background.	Farmer I [SOT]: "Hi, I think you all know this bald fellow." Leahy [SOT]: *"Tall* fellow."
Farmer II talking.	Farmer II [SOT]: "You know whenever we need a hard working senator, Leahy is always there to help."
Farmer I talking.	Farmer I [SOT]: "Yeah, and now he's awful close to being chairman of the U.S. Senate Agricultural Committee. And if you and your family have any idea what this means to Vermont. You'll know what to do."
Farmers run to put Leahy bumper stickers on cows. Super: "Call now for your free cow stickers. 1-800-Leahy-86."	(Fiddle Music) Cows [SOT]: "Moo, Moo."

Surrogate Ads

In surrogate ads, the candidate does not appear in the spot; instead, surrogates are chosen to make the political appeal on behalf of the candidate. There are two types of surrogates: public figure and private citizen.

Public Figure Testimonials

Public figure testimonials use well-known public figures especially entertainment personalities, political figures, and business or corporate executives. In 1990 Governor Jim Martin of North Carolina endorsed Jesse Helms for U.S. senator. And in 1992, Paul Hubbert, the Democratic candidate for governor in Alabama, called upon a prominent former chairman and chief executive officer of one of the state's largest banks to tell Alabama voters that Hubbert was indeed a friend of business and industry. Public figure testimonials rely on the theory of credibility transfer. As well-known, respected individuals, they lend their own credibility to the candidate they are endorsing.

In 1994 Charlton Heston appeared in a series of public figure testimonials for the National Rifle Association. Heston attacked congressmen and senators who had supported the ban on assault rifles.

The 1994 NRAPVF "Shame On You" Ad

Video	Audio
Charlton Heston in a suit talking.	Heston [SOT]: "Jim Sasser, Tennessee gun owners trusted you when you said that you'd oppose any legislation that interferes with the right to keep and bear arms. And when you said Congress should do nothing to infringe on that right. That's fine. Except you went to Congress and voted for the first Federal gun ban in American history. So Jim— don't blame Tennessee voters for
White letters on black: "Bill Frist For U.S. Senate"	protecting freedom and voting Bill Frist for U.S. Senate."

Private Citizen Surrogates

Private citizen surrogates appear more frequently in political advertising than do public figures. Everyday voters often participate because they support the candidate. Paid professional actors who are unknown to the general public may appear in political advertising portraying citizens who support the candidate. The person-in-the-street, voter editorial comment, neutral reporter, proselytizing reporter, and slice-of-life spots are examples of political ads that use private rather than public surrogates.

In 1994 Massachusetts incumbent U.S. senator Edward Kennedy went to Indiana to find private citizen surrogates to attack his opponent Mitt Romney. A series of Marion, Indiana citizens let Romney have it.

The 1994 Kennedy "You Don't Want Romney" Ad

Video	Audio
White letters on black: "Former SCM Employees Talk about Mitt	(Music under)

Romney's Record in Business"

Woman in blue/black sweater, talking to camera.	First Woman [SOT]: "I would like to say to Mitt Romney, 'if you think you'd make such a good senator, come out here to Marion, Indiana and see what your company has done to these people.'"
Auburn-haired woman, talking.	Second Woman [SOT]: "We had no rights anymore."
Young man, talking.	Man [SOT]: "They cut the wages."
Large woman in blue sweater, talking.	Third Woman: "We no longer had insurance."
Long-haired woman, talking.	Fourth Woman: "Basically cut our throats."
Woman in blue/black sweater, talking.	First Woman: "I'd like to say to the people of Massachusetts, that [if] you think it can't happen to you, think again. Because we thought it wouldn't happen here either."

NEWS-STYLE NARRATIVES

Narrative techniques establish the "pattern of events" that place order on the "*characters* performing actions in incidents that interrelate to comprise a 'single, whole, and complete' action" (Holman, 1972, pp. 397-398). Political advertising has long been recognized as adopting the style and format of television news (Jamieson, 1992; Jamieson & Campbell, 1983; Johnson-Cartee & Copeland, 1991a). Jamieson (1992) suggests that this trend began with the 1968 Humphry versus Nixon presidential race.

With the de-stabilization of political parties and the corresponding increase in voters who split their votes between Republicans and Democrats, modern media consultants attempted to imitate the very news shows that ticket-splitters used to make their voting decisions (see Devries & Tarrance, 1972). No longer could political consultants hope to win November victories based on party identification alone. Advertising had to do more than sell to the party faithful; modern political advertising had to reach those who were not persuaded by party linkages—those who have come to be known as political independents. Hard-sell party ads were out, and a modern news style genre that primarily focused on the candidate or the candidate's opponent was in (see Jamieson, 1992; Johnson-Cartee & Copeland, 1991a).

News style genre ads resemble broadcast news packages in that they attempt to imitate the same form and style of a news story. We have earlier described these ads. We wrote "The spots are brief and conversational. They have a beginning, a middle, and an end. There are protagonists and antagonists. There is conflict. They are fast-paced, colorful, and dramatic. They are thematic; and, they tell a story (Johnson-Cartee & Copeland, 1991a, p. 140; see also Garvey & Rivers, 1982). The news-style genre was chosen for two reasons. First because, television news is far more credible than television advertising; and second, because television news is the primary source of political information for the majority of independents. As an added benefit, the political consultant can place the ads around newscasts, which increases the likelihood that voters will mistake political spots as real news pieces (DeVries, 1971; Diamond & Bates, 1988; Jamieson, 1992; Johnson-Cartee & Copeland, 1991a; Kelly, 1984; Wilson, 1987). Accordingly, the most frequent and preferred position for political ad placement is around or within news programming (Wilson, 1987).

Jamieson (1992) writes that news has become "the grammar of political spots" (p. 150). Today, a consultant's measure is often based on how well the political spots produced resemble broadcast news packages. In 1984, James Kelly wrote that the Reagan campaign's "managers . . . [had] done such a seamless job of presenting their candidate . . . that viewers often had trouble telling the paid political announcements from the evening news" (p. 36).

Although consultants have contrived to have ads resemble broadcast packages, this may not be difficult to accomplish. Jamieson (1992) maintains that news and advertising already share a number of similarities that work to blur the distinctions between news packages and political spot ads:

Political spots are brief, usually either thirty or sixty second; they assert but do not argue; when they offer evidence it often assumes the form of the example, although not necessarily the representative example; they both personalize and visualize abstract concepts; because they are brief assertions based in dramatic narrative and/or example and rely on what can be shown, they also favor the simple over the complex. (p. 150)

News style narratives are very popular. We have identified eleven negative dramatic narratives used in the news-style genre (see

Figure 7.1) that can easily be adapted to all forms of political advertising.

Figure 7.1
News-Style Narratives

The Person-in-the-Street Ad.
The Voter Editorial Comment Ad.
The Public Figure Testimonial Ad.
The Neutral Reporter Package Ad.
The Proselytizing Reporter Package Ad.
The News Interview Show Ad.
The News Show Dramatization Ad.
The Visual Documentary Ad.
The Slice-of-Life Ad.
The Cinema Verité Ad.
The "Saturday Night Live" News Segment Ad.

Researchers have used similar terms to mean widely different styles; for this reason, we define the terms as we use them here. Our definition of a particular term may not be the same as that of others using the same term. However, our typology and terms are consistent within this book and in our other writings, and offer a means to unify the discussion of political advertising stylistic devices (Johnson-Cartee & Copeland, 1991a).

The Person-in-the-Street Ad

On slow news days, assignment editors may send broadcast journalists out to stop passersby on America's public streets and ask their opinions on various issues of the day. Such a technique resembles a haphazard sample of the public's opinion. During the presidential elections of 1976 and 1980, person-in-the-street ads were used extensively (see Jamieson, 1984).

Consultants seek out people who visually represent the important targeted groups of the campaign to appear in the ads. In this way, the campaign is providing the voters the opportunity to identify with someone like themselves who supports the candidate. For this reason, some consultants report that person-in-the-street ads are far better at reinforcing those already identifying with the candidate than they are at persuading voters to support the candidate (Devlin, 1981). Berkman and Kitch (1986) and Sabato (1981) report that person-in-the-street ads are particularly effective with liberals. Person-in-the-street ads have been known to generate the highest audience recall of all political advertising formats (Sabato, 1981). In some situations, the people seen are real voters, and in other situations, they are paid professional actors chosen to represent certain desirable demographic characteristics.

In 1992 the Bush campaign made extensive use of people-in-the-street ads prior to the presidential debates and immediately afterward. Notice that the ad uses a combination of fear appeals and character credibility attacks.

The 1992 Bush "October 1992" Ad

Video	Audio
White letters on black: "October 1992."	(Crowd noises in background.)
Working man talking.	Working man [SOT]: "I don't believe him. I don't believe him one bit."
Elderly woman talking.	Elderly woman [SOT]: "I don't believe him."
Young woman talking.	Young woman [SOT]: "Trust."
Elderly woman, Super: "Where will Bill Clinton get the money for his big promises?"	Elderly woman in suit [SOT]: "I don't know much about Clinton except promises."
Young businessman in suit, talking.	Young businessman in suit [SOT]: "He tells everybody what they want to hear."
Man in suit outdoors, talking.	Man in suit outdoors [SOT]: "Well, he wants to spend more money and the only place he can get it is from the taxpayers."
Man with dark mustache, talking.	Man with dark mustache [SOT]: "Higher taxes."
Young woman with headband, talking.	Young woman with headband [SOT]: "Less food on the table."
Man with dark mustache, talking.	Man with dark mustache [SOT]: "Broken promises."
Young woman with headband, talking.	Young woman with headband [SOT]: "Less clothes on the kids' back [sic]."

Blond man with blond mustache, talking.	Blond man [SOT]: "I don't know how we can take anymore taxes."
Young woman with headband, talking.	Young woman with headband [SOT]: "Less money to go to the doctors."
Working man talking.	Working man [SOT]: "He's [sic] raised taxes in Arkansas, and he'll raise taxes here."
Young woman with headband, talking.	Young woman with headband [SOT]: "Just less of everything."
Super, white letters on black: To be continued "tomorrow."	

In addition to the person-in-the-street ad, consultants often use voters or public figures in a number of situations. A single voter may speak directly into the camera, or a well known politician or entertainment figure may be the lone figure in an ad. Researchers frequently group voter editorial spots and public figure testimonial ads into what they call "the talking head" spots (see Devlin, 1986, 1987; Johnston, 1991). We prefer to make a distinction between the two. Voter editorial comment spots base their persuasive premise on homophily—that is, on establishing the similarity between the person presented in the ad and the viewer at home. In contrast, public figure testimonial ads base their persuasive premise on credibility transfer (lending the personality's credibility to the sponsoring candidate), heterophily (differences between the person presented in the ad and the viewer), or homophily.

The Voter Editorial Comment Ad

While the person-in-the-street ad gives the appearance of a television news person stopping voters as they go about their daily lives, the voter editorial comment spot uses actual voters or paid professional actors to make a more formal presentation. These presentations have the voter speaking directly into the camera from a studio or other staged setting. They often resemble guest editorials that many television stations run in order to give the appearance that television stations are attending to and are responsive to public opinion in the community.

Voter editorial comment spots frequently recount tragic circumstances. In 1990 Democratic Congressman Tim Wirth was running for a

U.S. Senate seat in Colorado. A private citizen, Ed Shields, appeared in and narrated the television spot.

The 1990 Wirth "Testimonial" Ad

Video	Audio
Man in kitchen with a typewriter on kitchen table. He is typing a letter, reading aloud as he types.	Man [VO]: "The day after Christmas, we discovered our two-year-old, Danny, dead beneath a collapsed bed."
Color photo of young boy in a picture frame.	Announcer [VO]: "From a letter to the *Rocky Mountain News*:"
Close-up of man typing. Close-up of typewriter keys and letter.	Man [SOT]: "Fearing that the same tragedy that befell us could reoccur at any time, I contacted a long list of politicians. The *only* legitimate response came from Tim Wirth."
Tim Wirth talking to staff.	Wirth [SOT]: "I think these are the beds we want to check out."
Wirth and his staff testing beds in stores; demonstrated small model test and model collapses.	Man [VO]: "Wirth and his staff spent an enormous amount of time on this matter. They did their own testing of these beds in department stores. And reviewed the official testing by the Consumer Products Safety Division."
Wirth to a CPSD official.	Wirth [SOT]: "We think that is exactly what happened."
Wirth, official, and staff continue to talk.	Man [VO]: "As a result, I have seen safety guidelines implemented throughout the bedding industry."
Man is typing.	Man [VO]: "I am proud that Wirth is a national leader. But I'm prouder still that my congressman cares deeply about individuals."
Man removes paper from typewriter and looks up.	Sincerely, Ed Shields. Urbana."

In 1992 the Tom Daschle campaign for a U.S. Senate seat in South Dakota ran two private figure testimonial spots. Both related tragic circumstances. One featured a mother telling the voters that her son's insurance company had refused to pay for a bone marrow transplant, after her son was diagnosed as having leukemia. The second featured a Viet Nam veteran describing his experiences dealing with the government bureaucracy, after he had been exposed to Agent Orange. In both circumstances, Tom Daschle intervened and put things right. These ads are very powerful because the voters empathize with these real-life people and their sorrows.

The 1992 Daschle "Viet Nam Vet" Ad

Video	Audio
A veteran in camouflage gear, seated at a kitchen table. Military decorations on shirt front. Old photo of soldier in combat uniform. Aircraft flying over jungle.	Vet [SOT]: "Viet Nam . . . was pure hell. Day after day after day. (Dramatic military music under) Aircraft would fly over and just open the spray up. All of the sudden, we'd feel the Agent Orange coming down through the trees like a fog. Saturating us. You could feel it burning the skin. It would get on your hands and through your hair, in your bloodstream."
Looking at a war monument.	Announcer [VO]: "Today, Bud Hill with wife and daughter suffers from a soft tissue sarcoma cancer as a result of his exposure to the defoliant Agent Orange."
Vet talking.	Vet [SOT]: "I was having problems with the V.A., and I called Tom Daschle."
Daschle working in Congress, walking through doors, talking on phone.	Announcer [VO]: "Angered by Washington's inaction. Tom Daschle took on the Veterans' Administration. And won."
Vet talking.	Vet [SOT]: "Tom Daschle got the legislation passed to compensate Viet Nam veterans for disability caused by Agent Orange. Tom

	fought the Congress and the Senate all by himself. Tom cares for the veteran. He cares for the families of the veterans. Tom Daschle was
Photo of Daschle talking with others. Super: "Daschle '92."	right there with us. Because he is one of us. Tom is a vet."

In 1992 Milton Marks ran against former San Francisco district attorney Joe Freitas, Jr., for a California State Senate seat. Marks used a private citizen testimonial to remind people how poorly Freitas had performed as district attorney.

The 1992 Marks "Remember Dan White" Ad

Video	Audio
A black female speaks directly to camera.	Woman speaking [SOT]: "Remember Dan White—took a revolver went to city hall. Shot both Harvey Milk and George Mascone, dead. Grizzly. Remember Joe Freitas the D. A. whose prosecution was so bungled White got off. White said he was driven to murder because he had eaten too many candy bars. The Twinkie Defense. Joe Freitas is back. Says the murders of Harvey Milk and George
Super: "Milton Marks for Senate."	Mascone were a long time ago."

Public Figure Testimonial Ad

Public figure testimonials may either have the candidate speaking directly to the audience or public figure surrogates addressing the audience. Thus, they may be classified as either candidate presentation ads or public figure surrogate ads, depending on the construction of the ad. In 1984 and 1986 President Ronald Reagan made a number of public figure testimonial spots for Republican congressional and senatorial candidates. In 1984 Reagan told North Carolina voters that Jesse Helms was on the right track: "For years, Jesse Helms has been telling the truth. Government can only spend what it borrows or taxes away. And, working Americans who pay this nation's bills need higher taxes like they need a plague of locusts. . . . Jesse, Helms, working for all of us in the United States Senate" (Payne & Baukus, 1988, p. 167). In 1986 Reagan told Alabama voters that Jeremiah Denton represented the same traditional values that Alabama voters and President Reagan supported. Denton had been attacked by Democratic challenger Richard Shelby for using campaign contributions to pay for country club dues and for sending misleading campaign contribution solicitation letters to elderly Alabama voters who thought they were bills. Reagan's mention of "godliness" and "decency" was an attempt to bolster Denton's sagging credibility factor.

The 1986 Denton "Reagan" Ad

Video	Audio
Reagan at podium.	(Applause)
	Announcer [VO]: "President Reagan on our senator, Jeremiah Denton."
Reagan speaking.	Reagan [SOT]: "Jeremiah and I have shared many a platform, and I just have to tell you that it always does something to stand here with a hero." (Applause)
Shot of crowd and sign that says: "God Bless America."	
Reagan talking	Reagan [SOT]: "Now that you are in the Senate, I want all the good people here in Dothan to know that courage and patriotism continue to distinguish all that you do. Indeed in the years since we were both elected, you've become one of the most persuasive leaders on Capitol Hill and an effective spokesman for the great state of Alabama. You've led the way in rebuilding America's defenses, spoken out for godliness and decency in our national life and stood up for freedom again and again around the world. . . ."
Denton stands, acknowledges applause.	(Applause)
Reagan speaking.	Reagan [SOT]: "For bravery, for keeping faith, for love of country, I think you've just heard, we all thank you."

Photo of Denton. Super: "Tested. Proven. Denton for Alabama."	Announcer [VO]: "Tested. Proven. Denton for Alabama."

The candidates themselves may appear in public figure testimonial spots. In 1960 Richard Nixon appeared in a television ad designed to attract the more liberal voters away from the Kennedy campaign. In an attempt to neutralize Kennedy's positive "new ideas, courageous leadership" image, Nixon sought to dramatize himself in this counterimaging spot as a man who had already proven his progressive leadership. Again, because he is making the appeal himself, the message has more credibility.

The 1960 Nixon "Civil Rights" Ad

Video	Audio
Nixon sits at a desk.	Announcer [SOT]: "Ladies and Gentlemen, the vice president of the United States, Richard M. Nixon."
Camera begins to zoom in slowly.	Nixon [SOT]: "I want to talk to you for a moment about civil rights for all our citizens. Why must we vigorously defend them? First, because it is right and just. Second, because we cannot compete successfully with communism if we fail to utilize completely the minds and energies of all of our citizens. And third, the whole world is watching us. When we fail to grant equality to all that makes news, bad news for America all over the world. Now the record shows there has been more progress in the past eight years than in the preceding eighty years because this administration has insisted on making progress. And I want to continue and speed up that progress. I want to help build a better America for all Americans."
Picture of Nixon and Lodge flashes on screen.	

(*Source*: Devlin, 1986, pp. 35-36)

In both 1988 and in 1992, George Bush was plagued by a public image that portrayed him as a cold, aristocratic individual who was out of touch with the common man. In 1988 Barbara Bush appeared in a spot describing her husband, telling the American people that she wished that they could only see "George" as she saw him. Mrs. Bush shares the spotlight with Charleston Heston who serves as the narrator at the end.

The 1988 Bush "Barbara" Ad

Video	Audio
Little girl running. Bush and Barbara with grandkids.	(Happy, upbeat piano music under)
Shots of a picnic with family.	Mrs. Bush [VO]: "I wish people could see him as I see him. As thousands of people see him."
Barbara talking.	Mrs. Bush [SOT]: "But you know, uh, I always loved the time someone said to George, 'how can you run for president, you don't have any constituency?'"
Bush playing with kids. Cooking in kitchen.	Mrs. Bush [VO]: "And George said, 'Well, you know I've got a great big family and thousands of friends.' And uh, that's what he has."
Photo of Bush on flight deck. Photo of Bush at U.N. Bush being sworn in as vice president. Bush with Thatcher. Bush with poor Slavic woman. Bush with Walenski. Footage of Bush lifting granddaughter in air and kissing her. Super: "George Bush, Experienced Leadership for America's Future."	Heston [VO]: "For more than 40 years, George Bush has met every challenge, his country and the world have offered up to him. The truth is the more you learn about George Bush, the more you realize that perhaps that no one in this century is better prepared to be president of the United States."

During the 1992 Republican primary, President George Bush was forced to go negative against Republican challenger Pat Buchanan. Bush was only the second incumbent president ever to air ads during the primary phase, and although many Bush insiders predicted that the campaign would never go negative during the primary, that is exactly what the campaign did (Colford, 1992, January 13, January 27).

The 1992 Bush "PX" Ad

Video	Audio
General Kelley speaking directly into camera. Super: "General P. X. Kelley, Commandant, U.S. Marine Corps, Ret."	General Kelley [SOT]: "When Pat Buchanan opposed Desert Storm, it was a disappointment to all military people. A disappointment to all Americans who supported the Gulf War. And I took it personally, I served with many of the marines who fought in Desert Storm. The last thing we need in the White House is an isolationist like Pat Buchanan. If he does not think that America should lead the world, how can we trust him to lead America?"
White letters on black: "Pat Buchanan . . .Wrong on Desert Storm. Wrong for America. "	

The Neutral Reporter Package Ad

"A neutral reporter ad sets forth a series of factual statements and then invites a judgment. These are rational political ads that offer factual data, invite or stipulate a conclusion, and warrant that conclusion" (Jamieson, 1986, pp. 18-19). Such ads were very popular during the 1976 and 1980 campaign seasons (Jamieson, 1984, 1986). By 1990 however, they had fallen into disfavor. As negative ads became more commonplace and as voters became more accustomed to them, negative ads had to become more and more strident to attract the same amount of attention. For this reason, even the appearance of neutrality became a liability. The more flamboyant the ad the greater the impact.

In Richard Nixon's second attempt at the White House, in 1968, his campaign used a neutral reporter ad about the nation's crime rate.

The 1968 Nixon "Crime" Ad

Video	Audio
White letters over black background: "A Political	(Sound of footsteps.)

Broadcast." Dissolve to city
street, night. Reflection of shoes
appears on the pavement, tilt up to
reveal middle-aged woman
walking along empty street. She
holds her hands together
apparently clasping her purse.

Announcer [VO]]: "Crimes of
violence in the United States have
almost doubled in recent years.
Today a violent crime is committed
almost every 60 seconds. A
robbery every two-and-a-half
minutes. A mugging every six
minutes. A murder every 43
minutes. And it will get worse
unless we take the offensive.
Freedom from fear is a basic right
of every American. We must
restore it."

Camera follows woman as she
passes several barred storefronts.
Then she passes the camera; it
follows her from the rear. She is
completely alone throughout the
sequence. No other pedestrians or
vehicles. Dissolve to blue
background, with white letters:
"THIS TIME VOTE LIKE YOUR
WHOLE WORLD DEPENDS ON
IT."

The Proselytizing Reporter Package Ad

The proselytizing reporter package ad is very different from the
neutral reporter package ad in that its persuasive premise is based on
an emotion-laden appeal rather than on a rational appeal. The ex-
hortative-didactic flavor of the ads brings to mind the news reporters
on Pat Robertson's "The 700 Club." Underlying the proselytizing reporter package ad is a strong moral tone.

The proselytizing reporter package ad is much more argumentative than the neutral reporter package ad in that it is highly charged
emotionally and displays a highly persuasive vocal presentation.
While the neutral reporter spot had its heyday in the late 1970s and
early 1980s, the proselytizing reporter package ad has now eclipsed it
in popularity, getting far more use in both 1990 and 1992. As our society has gotten used to a more argumentative or "hot" style of advertis-

ing, the consultants have deemed it necessary to turn the persuasion temperature up.

In other words, the proselytizing reporter makes use of what researchers call *language intensity*—that is, "the quality of language which indicates the degree to which the speaker's attitude toward a concept deviates from neutrality" (Bowers, 1964, p. 416). According to Street and Brady (1982), people have an idea of what a competent speaker sounds like, and listeners compare speakers to their "ideal speaker" image in order to arrive at credibility judgments (Ray, 1986). Perloff (1993) suggests that after careful reading of the speaker credibility literature, one may arrive at a "prototypically competent communicator" who performs in the following ways:

Speaks at a moderately fast rate of speech,
Uses powerful, forceful language,
Varies pitch levels,
Speaks loudly,
Uses a conversational style of speech, and
Speaks in a mainstream American dialect rather than in an ethnic dialect. (p. 178)

According to Perloff (1993), people who speak in this manner are considered competent or credible, and those who do not speak this way are considered to be not competent.

In 1994 Americans for Limited Terms independently sponsored a negative ad against Washington state congressman Tom Foley. Clearly, the tone of the message implies what the voters are to conclude.

The 1994 Americans for Limited Terms "Insult to Injury" Ad

Video	Audio
Black and white photo of U.S. Capitol Building. Super: "Something has Gone Terribly Wrong with the Support of Congressman Foley." Photo of "Foley; Super under: Congressman Foley's Salary: $170,000 plus"; "40% Pay Raise. "Scenes of House in session. Dark blue letters on gray: "Voters Pass Term Limits." Photo of Capitol with Foley in block upper right. A lawsuit document falls on scene; a second legal document falls.	Announcer [VO]: "Congress is in trouble. (Bell dongs) The people's house has serious problems. Under the cloak of darkness and with the help of our congressman Tom Foley, the House voted themselves a 40 percent pay raise. (Bell dongs) Then voters of this state passed term limits for career politicians. Congressman Foley doesn't like it. He sues his own voters. Then to add insult to injury, he asked the Court to have his personal legal bills paid by the

	taxpayers. And the politicians
Super: "Call Congressman Foley and ask him to <u>change his mind</u>." (underlining in yellow)	wonder why the people support term limits for career congressmen?"

During the 1992 Republican primary, the Bush campaign ran a proselytizing reporter spot that positioned Bush as the consummate "leader" of the nation.

The 1992 Bush "Leadership" Ad

Video	Audio
Bush with Boris Yeltsin.	Announcer [VO]: "Perhaps no president in our history has
Bush walks down the verandah at the White House. Bush talking to someone in Oval Office, at desk.	shown the world such strong leadership. The fear of nuclear war diminished, terrorists on notice, dictators in check. At home he stood up to an undisciplined
White letters on black: "The Bush Agenda "(stays in frame): " Strengthen Our Economy"; "Make America More Competitive." "Change Welfare: Make Able-Bodied Work." Education Reform: Responsibility and Results.	Congress, exercising twenty-six vetoes and making them stick. Now he has a plan to revitalize our economy and make America more competitive in the world. The Bush Agenda: Change the welfare system by requiring the able-bodied to work. Demand responsibility and results from our schools. And get more
Court Reform: End Exaggerated Lawsuits.	education for our money. Court reform to eliminate exaggerated lawsuits that drive up insurance
Change Washington: Term Limits and Budget Reform.	and drive out business. Change Washington by requiring term limits for Congress and deficit reduction for taxpayers. The lawyers, lobbyists, and
Bush at desk in Oval Office.	Democratic leaders will fight this president every step of the way. But this man who has changed the world, will change America. President Bush.
Super: "President Bush. The Future of America in the Hands of Experience."	The future of America in the hands of experience."

The News Interview Show Ad

The news interview show ad resembles talk/interview shows such as "Larry King," "Donahue," or "Sally Jesse Raphael." Or the ad may appear as a panel interview situation (a controlled public debate, for example) which is an important ingredient of both party and voter education movements in election campaigns. This style was heavily used during the 1952 and 1956 campaigns.

In a 1992 congressional race, two incumbent congressmen faced each other in the general election—a complication caused by redistricting. The Huckaby campaign ran an ad that simulated the standard candidate party screening panel arrangement in which candidates are interviewed prior to running in the primary or caucus. These screenings are in a question and answer interview format. This Huckaby ad is unusual because news interview show spots are usually positive ads. However, the Huckaby campaign used a dramatized internal party screening panel to sharply criticize how poor his opponent's record actually was. The opponent is never seen, is never called by his full name, and is never heard responding.

The 1992 Huckaby "Jim?" Ad

Video	Audio
Three people sit at a table. It appears to be a panel interview. A black man in a suit, a white man in shirt and tie, and a lady in a dress.	White man in tie [SOT]: "Now Jim we sent you to Congress to get things done and to vote right. But you haven't even passed one bill."
Medium close-up of woman talking.	Woman [SOT]: "Huckaby passed sixteen."
Medium close-up of white man talking.	White man [SOT]: "You voted for a 135 billion dollar tax increase."
Medium close-up of black man talking.	Black man [SOT]: "You voted against Medicare. Against the middle-income tax reduction. Against unemployment benefits."
Medium close-up of woman talking.	Woman [SOT]: "Huckaby voted yes."
Medium close-up of white man talking.	White man [SOT]: "And in the middle of a recession, you voted yourself a 35 thousand dollar pay

	raise."
Medium close-up of black man talking.	Black man [SOT]: "Huckaby voted against it."
Medium close-up of white man talking.	White man [SOT]: "What's the matter with you, Jim? Jim? Hello?"

The News Show Dramatization Ad

The news show dramatization ad actually resembles a nightly newscast or a nightly newscast story, which in the trade is called a news package. Rather than a reporter or talk show host engaging the candidate in conversation, the narrator appears to be an anchorperson or a news reporter. In 1986 Republican challenger Ed Zschau ran a direct comparison news show dramatization ad against Democratic Senator Alan Cranston in the U.S. Senate race in California. A gray-haired "anchor-person," who resembled one of the most popular news anchors in southern California, sat behind a news desk and spoke directly into the camera while the sound of a teletype machine could be heard under the voice and a matte photo appears behind the anchor's head. Because many California television stations were concerned that voters would be misled into believing that the ad was in fact a television news show, the stations added their own public disclaimer (Hagstrom & Guskind, 1986; see Johnson-Cartee & Copeland, 1991a).

In a 1992 race for U.S. Senate in Indiana, Republican Dan Coates used a humorous news show dramatization spot against Democratic candidate Joe Hogsett.

The 1992 Coates "Looking for Joe Hogsett" Ad

Video	Audio
News reporter outside of Capitol holding microphone. Super: "The search for Joe Hogsett begins, Part One."	News reporter [SOT]: "The search for Joe Hogsett begins, Part One. This morning we're at the Secretary of State's Office looking for Joe Hogsett."
A clock appears on right side of screen.	Announcer [VO]: "Day Two."
Reporter with three large	News reporter [SOT]: "Joe

reproductions of news articles uses a pointer to illustrate key points.	promised not to run for the U.S. Senate. And as these newspapers tell us—this is not complicated. Joe gave his word. Now he's going back on it. Joe's hard to find at work, because he's always campaigning."
Reporter holds hands up.	
Clock on right goes wild.	Announcer [VO]: "Day Three, Day Four."
Reporter rubs neck with handkerchief.	News reporter [SOT]: "That's our Joe, just another politician."
Clock continues to go wild.	Announcer [VO]: "Day Five, Day Six."
Clock runs wild.	Announcer [VO]: "Why did Joe Hogsett break his promise? And will Joe ever show up for work?"
News reporter talking.	News Reporter [SOT]: "He'll show up some day. I know he will. He gets paid to be here."
Super: "To be continued."	

The Visual Documentary Ad

The visual documentary ad is unusual in that the visual elements rather than the audio elements are of primary importance in presenting the message. A string of events, people, places, and things are woven together to form a strong image mosaic (Johnson-Cartee & Copeland, 1991a). In the 1968 presidential campaign, Richard Nixon ran an implied comparison visual documentary ad highlighting the horrid pictures and mistakes associated with the Viet Nam War. Underneath Nixon's own speech is a synchronized drum roll that further dramatizes the visuals.

The 1968 Nixon "Viet Nam" Ad

Video	Audio
The following pictures are flashed on screen intermittently in synchronization with the drum roll on the audio: a helicopter, soldiers firing weapons, soldiers	(A drum roll plays intermittently in synchronization with the changing pictures.) Nixon [VO]: "Never has so much military, economic, and diplomatic

running, wounded soldiers, houses ablaze, bombed houses, a weary-looking soldier, crying Asian women, a medic aiding the wounded, a distraught looking Asian man, faces of American soldiers. More close-ups of the faces of American soldiers appear on screen. Faces of Asian people flash on the screen. A picture of a helmet with "LOVE" painted on it appears on screen, followed by the words, "This Time Vote Like Your World Depended On It," and "NIXON."

power been used so ineffectively as in Viet Nam. If after all this time and all of this sacrifice and all of this support, there is still no end in sight. . . . And I say the time has come for the American people to turn to new leadership—not tied to the mistakes and the policies of the past. I pledge to you we shall have an honorable end to the war in Viet Nam."

(Source: Devlin, 1986, pp. 40-41)

During the 1992 presidential election, the Bush campaign captured a desolate mood on film. The ad was a very powerful attack on Clinton's record in Arkansas.

The 1992 Bush "Gray" Ad

Video	Audio
[Pictures are black and white emphasizing the grayness]. A lonely country road with barren trees wind blowing. Super: "Doubled State's Debt" a blowing wind bends wheat in a wheat field. Super: "Doubled Government Spending. Dark black clouds blow into picture Super: "Largest State Increase in State's History." Lightening bolts across a very dark sky.	Female Announcer [VO]: "In his twelve years as governor, Bill Clinton has doubled his state's debt, doubled government spending, and signed the largest tax increase in his state's history.
"Super: "45th worst in which to work.*" *The Corporation for Enterprise Development" One lone tree in a flat landscape the tree is bent by wind to the right. Angry storm clouds swirling.	Yet his state remains the 45th worst in which to work.
Super: "45th worst for children." " Source the Center for the Study of Social Policy."	The 45th worst for children.

Super: "Worst Environmental Policy." Source: the Institute for Southern Studies." Dark, angry clouds continue swirling,	The worst environmental policy.
Super: "Biggest Increase in Serious Crime." "Source: the FBI" Trees with scrub bushes. Windmill in far background. A buzzard on a leafless tree. Dark clouds continue to swirl angrily. Sun going down with one small bare tree in landscape with the buzzard sitting on the top branch	And the FBI says Arkansas had America's biggest increase in serious crimes. [Howling wind]And now Bill Clinton wants to do for America what he's done for Arkansas.
Super: "America can't take that risk."	America can't take that risk."

The Slice-of-Life Ad

A slice-of-life ad "calls for paid actors in 'natural' conversation during a scene from everyday life" (Sabato, 1981, p. 176; see also Devlin, 1986). Early slice-of-life ads did not meet with much success in political advertising circles because their melodramatic nature invited ridicule. In 1976 Gerald Ford aired three slice-of-life commercials in his race for the presidency and the ads brought universal criticism to the campaign. Such ads resembled toothpaste, dish washing detergent, or floor wax commercial spots with a hard sell. Recently, slice-of-life spots have been revitalized into mini-dramatizations that resemble contemporary movie or television exchanges; however, this does not always guarantee that they will be well received.

During the 1988 presidential campaign the Democratic National Committee produced about a dozen slice-of-life spots uniformly called "The Packaging of George Bush" (McCabe, 1988). The ads placed Republican consultants in a strategy room discussing possible ad and public relations appeals. Unfortunately for the Dukakis campaign, voters couldn't tell whether the spots supported or opposed Bush (Bernard, 1988; Devlin, 1989), and the ad campaign found itself facing some of the harshest criticism of any series made (Battaglio, 1988). Dan Payne, a Dukakis media producer, explained to Devlin (1989) that the packaging ads "may have only been 6% of the budget, but they accounted for 100% of the campaign's credibility. . . . People looked at them and decided Dukakis' media was incompetent" (p. 401). Perhaps what should be most remembered about slice-of-life spots is this: they can't be so simplistic that it insults the voters' intelligence, and they can't be so complex that the voters can't comprehend them in 30 seconds.

The 1988 DNC "Noriega" Ad

Video	Audio
White letters on black, "The Packaging of George Bush	
Consultant I talking." White super; "Monday 9:17 am." Camera pans left revealing other consultants sitting around table.	Consultant I [SOT]: "Ah, Geez. They're gonna kill us on this Noriega thing. Look at that headline: 'The Panamanian Drug Lord.'"
Consultant II talking.	Consultant II [SOT]: "Yeah, it's a picture of Bush with Noriega."
Consultant III talking.	Consultant III [SOT]: "Just won't let it go, will they?"
Camera moves back to consultant I talking.	Consultant I [SOT]: "Well, we need a lot better answer."
Camera moves back to frame all consultants. Consultant II talking.	Consultant II [SOT]: "Something better than 'I don't remember.'" (Group laughter)
Consultant I talking.	Consultant I [SOT]: "Well?"
Consultant II talking.	Consultant II [SOT]: "I'm working on it. I'm working on it."
Consultant III talking.	Consultant III [SOT]: "Maybe we should just stick with 'I don't remember.' (Chuckle)."
White super on black background: "They'd like to sell you a package."	Announcer [VO]: "They'd like to sell you a package.
New frame appears "Wouldn't you rather choose a president?"	Wouldn't you rather choose a president?"
Dukakis Photo.	

The Cinema Verité Ad

Cinema verité ads resemble television documentaries. "The camera is looking in on unstaged conversations" (Diamond & Bates, 1988, p. 193; see also Jamieson & Campbell, 1983). Natural lighting and natural sound are frequently used to make the ad appear more authentic. "These commercials walk the viewer through part of the candidate's day, permitting voters to eavesdrop on exchanges with important people, overhear warm human exchanges with constituents or would-be supporters, and see the candidate with family" (Jamieson & Campbell, 1983, p. 237). Charles Guggenheim, McGovern's advertising consultant in 1972, is famous for perfecting this distinctive visual style. Cinema verité was a product of the late 1960s and early 1970s, and just like love beads and Nehru jackets, cinema verité passed out of favor as an anachronism.

The Dark Humor Ad

"Saturday Night Live" began its successful television run with what has become a commercial favorite, "Weekend Update." Chevy Chase appeared as a crazed news anchor using disparagement humor to ridicule the prominent and the powerful. Humorous news packages cut in and out with Chase usually making snide asides. Political consultants have imitated the rather zany, creative, free, and dark, form of this entertainment segment when they have created their humorous spots. We have previously described these as "Saturday Night Live News Segments" but after further thought we have decided to call these dark humor ads. We described these ads in this way:

The formats run from bizarre slice-of-life segments to edited segments of spaghetti westerns. Modern, digital effects are used to mat images on and around candidates with humorous results. In some situations, the ads bring to mind such cultural icons as silent pictures and classic cartoons. Silent picture techniques reminiscent of the old Buster Keaton and Keystone Cops movies have been used: story cards, highly dramatic music compositions, and improbable settings and scenarios. Slapstick forms of comedy with actors using broadly exaggerated characterizations are common. The advertisements frequently are shot in black and white. Often cartoons and music reminiscent of cartoon classics are used. The drama that is staged is highly exaggerated, even preposterous in its presentation. And the comedic music when used serves to accentuate the highly stylized dramas. (Johnson-Cartee & Copeland, 1991a, p. 157)

J. S. White and Associates won a first place in the American Association of Political Consultants' poli-award contest for a humorous negative spot produced for challenger Richard Notte who was running for the Michigan state legislature. The ad focuses on a piece of legislation that the incumbent state senator Doug Carl had supported.

The 1990 Notte "Bingo" Ad

Video	Audio
White lettering on black background, scroll effect. Announcer's words appear. Filmed in black and white. Elderly lady in a police lineup; she poses for mug shot.	Announcer [VO]: "On March 26th, 1987 State Senator Doug Carl struck a blow against a dangerous class of criminals. . . .
A light blip occurs to imitate the flashbulb going off. Super: "BINGO?" Mug shot of lady, front side.	Doug Carl voted to keep Bingo games for seniors a crime. . . . BINGO? That ought to make us all sleep better tonight.
White lettering on black, scroll effect: "In times like these, our families need serious, hard working leadership." Super: "Richard Notte State Senator." Notte Photo.	In times like these, our families need serious, hard-working leadership. We need a new state senator. Richard Notte fighting for us."

During the 1992 campaign season, a number of incumbent congressmen faced harsh criticism of their involvement in the House bad check scandal. The controversy fueled negative ads sponsored by challengers across the country during that campaign cycle. In one 1992 race, two incumbent congressmen opposed each other in the general election because of redistricting; one had a record of bad checks, and the other did not.

The 1992 Stagger "Rubber Man" Ad

Video	Audio
Slow motion of Mollahan talking.	(Country music under) Male Singer [VO]: "Mollahan, the rubber man. He's got nothing in common with the common man.
A blue check bounces around. Super: "with no interest no penalty."	Bouncing checks for Uncle Sam, with no interest, no penalty. Mollahan, the rubber man. He's got nothing in common with the working man. He votes himself a
"He votes himself a pay raise	

worth 37,000. But he won't get a vote from me!" Man's coat with a reelect Stagger Congress button.	pay raise worth 37 thousand grand. But he won't get a vote from me!"

In 1992 Congressman Newt Gingrich, launched a tough reelection bid in Georgia, which was made even more difficult by the fact that he had bounced twenty-two checks.   Because of redistricting, Gingerich faced an unfamiliar constituency. Gingerich was reelected to the House of Representatives by a narrow margin. His opponent, Herman Clark, had given him a run for his money.

The 1992 Clark "Bouncing Check" Ad

Video	Audio
Photo of Newt Gingerich. Super: "Follow the bouncing check."	Announcer singing [VO]: "Come on along and sing along with Congressman Newt Gingerich. Congressman Newt Gingerich
"Bounced twenty-two checks." A check bouncing, marked insufficient funds in red "For more than 26,000." Newt holds check "With a bounced check here and a pay raise there. Here a check. There a check. Everywhere a bounced check.	bounced twenty-two checks. For more than 26 grand. With a bounced check here, and a bounced check there. Here a check, there a check, everywhere a bounced check.
Newt Gingerich wrote a rubber check to the IRS." A check marked IRS bounces, marked insufficient funds $9,000."	Newt Gingerich wrote a rubber check to the IRS. That check bounced like all the rest. This time for 9 grand.
"With a bounced check here and a pay raise there. Here a check. There a check. Everywhere a bounced check."	With a bounced check here, and a pay raise there. Here a check. There a check. Everywhere a bounced check. Because bouncing checks is such hard work, Newt raised his pay 40,000 a year. With a bounced check here, and a pay raise there. Here a check. There a check. Everywhere a bounced check.
22 bounced checks and a "$130,000 a year. I bet you all thought that was all. But don't	Twenty-two bounced checks and a 130 grand. I bet you all thought that was all. But don't look now;

| look now; here comes Newt Gingerich in his $67,000 chauffeured limousine. (Limousine drives across screen and piles of money appear.) | here comes Newt Gingerich in his $67,000 chauffeured Limousine. With a bounced check here and a pay raise there. Here a check, there a check. Everywhere a bounced check. With a bounced check here, and a pay raise there." (Sound goes under the last two sentences.) |

NEWSADS: UNINTENDED CONSEQUENCES

Although consultants intended political commercials to resemble news packages, this practice has led to an unexpected consequence. Jamieson (1992) has suggested that, as television news has become more interested in presenting the horse race and strategic aspects of the campaign than in presenting issues and policy preferences, the news packages have come to more closely resemble political spots. Indeed, the news emphasis on meta-campaign analysis, or what Jamieson has called the "unmasking strategy," has created a new internal dynamic in television news (p. 150). In this new dynamic, political ads are themselves news, and they are presented as such. Thus, a well-designed political campaign, through the use of impression management strategies, may expect pseudoevents or information flow control to stimulate what Jamieson has called "newsads." These *newsads* are actual news stories that examine the political advertising or public relations strategies and techniques used in the campaign. Jamieson states that such newsads are often "indistinguishable" from political commercials. Which campaign is better able to exploit "newsads" is the result of "which campaign better manipulates the press" (p. 151): "Newsads will shower down upon (1) the candidate with pseudoevents tied to sound and adbites; (2) the candidate ahead in the polls; (3) the candidate who metacommunicates more effectively than his or her opponent; and (4) the candidate who exercises the most control over interviews" (Jamieson, 1992, p. 151). A candidate who is fortunate enough to have her or his advertisement featured in a newscast has acquired a free showing of the ad.

POLITICAL TAGS

The tag is the optional closing line(s) that either summarizes the ad, directs the voter to do something, or asks a rhetorical question. Tags that summarize the appeals in the ad are called *thematic tags,* tags that direct the voters to do something, for example, "Vote on election day" are called *directive tags;* and *rhetorical question tags* call on the voter to make a personal decision about an issue or controversy. The tag is an important element in the political commercial because, as research has shown, the beginning and ending of a commercial have the greatest impact on the viewers (Calder, 1978; Chestnut, 1980). Political spot tags are strategically designed. Many campaigns use more than one tag depending on the type of ad being used, the persuasive goal of the ad, the audience targeted, and its placement during the campaign season. It is important to note that some ads do not use any form of tags.

Thematic tags

Thematic tags may be either implicit or explicit in stating their conclusions. *Implicit thematic tags* draw the ad to a close but leave the conclusion open for the audience to arrive at independently. Such statements should be used when attempting to persuade those who are highly informed politically. Such endings indicate to the viewer that the sponsor respects the targeted audience (see Sawyer, 1988). During the 1984 presidential campaign, Reagan polispots often ended with the tag: "President Reagan; doing what he was elected to do." During the 1986 U.S. Senate campaign in Alabama, Jeremiah Denton ended his polispots with: "Alabama's own Jeremiah Denton, more than just a senator." Harvey Gantt ended his negative attacks on Jesse Helms in the 1990 U.S. Senate race in North Carolina with the comment: "That's the real Jesse Helms." In 1994 populism became a major theme in many campaigns, and challengers distanced themselves from Washington as much as possible by closing their ads with "He's one of us."

On the other hand, the *explicit thematic tag* overtly states the theme of the ad. Such tags should be used when the political ad is targeted to groups that might have difficulty understanding the message or when the viewer is not motivated to arrive at the appropriate conclusion (see Fine, 1957; Hovland & Mandell, 1952). Harvey Gantt's 1990 U.S. Senate campaign in North Carolina used a three-line tag: "Harvey Gantt for Senate. He'll work for North Carolina. He'll work for you." In contrast, his opponent Republican incumbent Jesse Helms used an explicitly negative thematic tag in his campaign's refutation spots: "Harvey Gantt extremely liberal with the facts." Notice Helm's use of the double entendre. During the 1992 presidential campaign, Clinton used a series of negative ads that closed with the tag: "We can't afford four more years." In ads refuting the negative ads that the Bush campaign was running against Clinton, the Clinton campaign used a *compound* tag, which summarizes the ad but also recalls the refrain from other Clinton spots: "George Bush is trying to scare you about Bill Clinton. Nothing could be more

frightening than four more years." The Bush campaign also summarized their negative attacks on Clinton's positions in their ads in
this manner: "You can't trust Clinton Economics. It's wrong for you. It's
wrong for America."

Directive tags

Directive tags, which are frequently used in political advertising, are "an imperative force"requesting action (Sanford & Roach,
1987, p. 1; Searle, 1976). In 1992 Republican National Committee ads
ended with the tag: "For a new Congress vote Republican." Bob
Kerrey ended his presidential primary spots in 1992 with the
directive: "Fight back America!" We believe that tag lines that
direct voters to do something to be far more persuasive than those tags
that fail to call for action. Persuasion research has shown that
persuasive appeals are more likely to succeed if they say directly
what it is that they want the audience to do (Cutlip, Center, &
Broom, 1985, p. 179). In research dealing with fear appeals, it is clear
that in order for the fear appeals to be successful ads that use such
appeals must use tag lines that direct the voter to do something that
will help the voter effectively avoid the described undesirable
situation (Maddux & Rogers, 1983; Rogers, 1975; Rogers & Mewborn,
1976).

Rhetorical Question Tags

Rhetorical question tags call upon the voter to make a personal
decision at the viewing of the ad; they call for the voter to answer
the question. The research on rhetorical questions is mixed. Petty,
Cacioppo, and Heesacker (1981) found that when a message had low
personal relevance "a message with strong arguments became more persuasive, and a message with weak arguments became less persuasive
with rhetoricals [questions]" (p. 432). On the other hand, when a message had high personal relevance "a message with strong arguments
became less persuasive, and a message with weak arguments became
more persuasive with rhetoricals" (Petty, Cacioppo, & Heesacker,
1981, p. 431). In a U.S. Senate race in Illinois in 1980, Republican candidate Dave O'Neal closed an ad with the following words: "I'm
Dave O'Neal. And I say we can. Who says we can't?" Bob Kasten
used a direct attack ad against Russ Feingold in the Wisconsin U.S.
Senate race in 1992; the ad closed with: "Russ Feingold is out of step
with his own party. Isn't he out of step with Wisconsin?"
    In a 1990 ad produced for Pro-Choice, Inc., the ad takes the
viewer through a number of oppressive government actions and then
asks the unanswered question.

The 1990 Pro-Choice, Inc. "41" Ad

Video	Audio
Footage of burning books.	Announcer [VO]: "If the leaders of the country tried to tell you what you could and could not read, you'd defy them. . . . If they said you could no longer practice your
Footage of church being destroyed.	religion, you'd fight them. If they tried to control whether you
Woman in paddy wagon, door closes, truck drives away. Man and child left in street, looking longingly at truck.	should or shouldn't have children, you'd do whatever was necessary to stop them. Or would you?"
Super: "Strict anti-abortion laws are pending in 41 states." A Box appears that reads: "It's Pro Choice or No Choice."	

SPONSORSHIP

A sponsor is a person or group that pays a mass communication channel (television, radio, newspaper, magazine) to disseminate a political advertisement. In some situations, the sponsor may not have actually paid for the production of the advertisement, but the sponsor is paying for the dissemination. In our analysis, the actual producer of the spot is not as important as the person or group who pays for the dissemination of the advertising, for only the sponsor is identified within the political advertising content (see the upcoming Political Advertising Disclosure Requirement Section in this chapter). And it is only the sponsor, then, that is known to the voters who have seen the advertisement. The three primary political advertising sponsors in American politics are the candidates and their campaign committees; the political parties; and the political action committees.

Political action committees (PACs) deserve special attention here, because frequently, voters are not familiar with their campaign practices. PACs are an important source of both direct contributions and independent expenditures in modern elections. In 1992 PACs spent nearly $189 million on federal elections (Markerson & Goldstein, 1994, p. 10). The Federal Election Committee reported that independent spending in the 1988 presidential election amounted to $20.4 million (Sorauf, 1992, p. 108).

Ads sponsored by PACs are said to be *independently sponsored ads*. "The independently sponsored ad is an ad that is not directly linked with a candidate. An organization physically separated from either a political party or a candidate's campaign organization sponsors the ad" (Johnson-Cartee & Copeland, 1991, pp. 13-14). Garramone and Smith (1984) and Garramone (1985) report that independently sponsored ads have greater credibility and are more persuasive than candidate sponsored ads (see also Kaid & Boydston, 1987). Clearly, then, the sponsorship of the ad necessarily impacts the narrative style of the political ad. What is said, how it is said, and how it is visualized are all affected by the identity of the sponsor. Tarrance (1982) demonstrated that voters often give independent political action committees greater operating latitude in terms of the types of appeals made than an individual candidate (see also Johnson-Cartee & Copeland, 1991a).

Any analysis of the sponsorship of political advertisements must include a discussion of money. Political advertising is an expensive big business. According to *Advertising Age*, over $470 million went to pay for all political advertising in the 1990 congressional races (Colford, 1991). Campaigns involving prominent congressional leaders, independently wealthy candidates, or those occurring in large metropolitan areas with expensive media costs frequently spend a great deal more on advertising than do campaigns for the average candidate. In 1992 an independently wealthy Republican candidate in California, Michael Huffington, spent $5.43 million to win California's Twenty-second Congressional Seat (Markerson & Goldstein, 1994). The average cost of a U.S. House of Representative campaign in 1992 was $390,387 (Morris & Gamache, 1994, p. 5).

DISCLOSURE REQUIREMENTS FOR POLITICAL ADVERTISING

The sponsors of all political advertising which "expressly advocates the election or defeat of a clearly identified candidate, or that solicits any contribution, through any broadcasting station, newspaper, magazine, outdoor advertising facility, poster, yard sign, direct mailing, or any other form of general public political advertising" (11 CFR sec. 110.11 (a) (1) (1986)) must be fully disclosed. The sponsor must be clearly identified in a conspicuous place telling "who paid for the ad and whether it is authorized by the candidate" (Middleton & Chamberlin, 1988, p. 280; see 11 CFR sec. 110.11 (a) (2)).

The *disclaimer* is a statement telling who paid for the ad and whether it was authorized by the candidate. "The intent of the disclaimer is to frame the spot as a paid, partisan message. The problem for a media specialist is to minimize the negative effects of the label" (Schwartz, 1976, p. 349). Political consultants have found clever ways

of obfuscating the sponsor disclosure requirements for political advertising. In a 1992 U.S. Senate race, Ben Nighthorse Campbell used the
uplifting "Paid for by the Campbell Victory Fund." But an even better
use of the disclaimer comes from the 1992 Tom Daschle campaign:
"Paid for by a lot of people supporting Tom Daschle." The use of such
innocuous tags increases the likelihood that political advertisements
will be mistaken for other programming such as news (see Jamieson &
Campbell, 1983).

Disclosure statements may occur at the beginning or the end of political ads, although the most common position is at the end. Highly
controversial ads will usually have the disclaimer at the beginning of
the commercial in the hope that the actual sponsorship will not be
noted by the audience. The image of the sponsoring candidate or the
candidate's voice must be heard in order for the spot to qualify under
"fair use" provisions of the FCC. And who paid for the spot may be
either visually displayed or orally presented.   Sometimes the
disclaimers are so small or appear for such a short time that they are
virtually unreadable.

References

Abelson, R. (1976). Script processing in attitude formation and decision making. In J. S. Carroll and J. W. Payne (Eds.), *Cognition and social behavior.* Hillsdale, NJ: Lawrence Erlbaum Associates.

Abelson, R. (1981). Psychological status of the script concept. *American Psychologist, 36,* 715-729.

Abelson, R. (1983). Whatever became of consistency theory? *Personality and Social Psychology Bulletin, 9,* 37-54.

Abelson, R., Kinder, D., Peters, M., & Fiske, S. (1972). Affective and semantic components in political person perception. *Journal of Personality and Social Psychology, 42,* 619-630.

Adams, R. C., & Copeland, G. A. (1980, November). An investigation of mediated person perception comparing Jungian archetypes to perception of nonverbal cues. Paper presented at the annual meeting of the Speech Communication Association, New York.

Adams, R. C., Copeland, G. A., Fish, M., & Hughes, M. (1980). The effect of framing on selection of photographs of men and woman. *Journalism Quarterly, 57,* 463-467.

Akeret, R. U. (1973). *Photoanalysis: How to interpret the hidden psychological meaning of personal and public photographs.* New York: Wyden.

Almond, G., & Verba, S. (1963). *The civic culture.* Princeton, NJ: Princeton University Press.

Andersen, K. E. (1989). The politics of ethics and the ethics of politics. *American Behavioral Scientist, 32,* 479-492.

Anderson, L. R., & McGuire, W. J. (1965). Prior reassurance of group concensus as a factor in producing resistance to persuasion. *Sociometry, 28,* 44-56.

Anderson, N. H. (1965). Averaging vs. adding as a stimulus-combination rule in impression formation. *Journal of Experimental Psychology, 70,* 394-400.

Archer, D., Kimes, D. D., & Barrios, M. (1978, September). Face-ism. *Psychology Today,* 65-66.

Arnheim, R. (1958). *Film as art.* Berkeley, CA: University of California Press.

Arnheim, R. (1965). *Art and visual perception: A psychology of the creative eye.* Berkeley, CA: University of California Press.

Arnheim, R. (1969). *Visual thinking.* Berkeley, CA: University of California Press, 1969.

Arnold, C. C. (1972, April). *Invention and pronuntiatio in a new rhetoric..* Paper presented at the Central States Speech Communication Convention, Chicago.

Arterton, F. C. (1984). *Media politics.* Lexington, MA: Lexington Books.

Ayers, B. (1986, January. 13). Alabama's political detour coming to an end. *The Birmingham Post Herald,* p. 5.

Barrett, L. (1988, February 1). Playing populist chords. *Time,* p. 16.

Barthes, R. (1972). *Mythologies* (A. Lavers, trans). New York: Hill and Wang.

Barthes, R. (1977). *Image music text* (S. Heath, trans). New York: Hill and Wang.

Basil, M., Schooler, C., & Reeves, B. (1991). Positive and negative political advertising: Effectiveness of ads and perceptions of candidates. In F. Biocca (Ed.), *Television and political advertising,* Vol. 1 (pp. 245-262). Hillsdale, NJ: Lawrence Erlbaum Associates.

Bateson, G., & Mead, M. (1942). *Balinese character: A photographic analysis.* New York: New York Academy of Science Special Publication.

Battaglio, S. (1988, November 7). Campaign '88: Faint hearts, bloodied noses. *Adweek,* pp. 22-23.

Baukus, R. A., Payne, J. G., & Reisler, M. S. (1985). Negative polispots: Mediated arguments in the political arena. In J. R. Cox, M. O. Sillars, & G. B. Walker (Eds.), *Argument and social practice: Proceedings of the fourth SCA/AFA Conference on Argumentation* (pp. 236-252). Annandale, VA: Speech Communication Association.

Beck, K. H., & Lund, A. L. (1981). The effects of health seriousness and personal efficacy upon intentions and behavior. *Journal of Applied Social Psychology, 11,* 401-415.

Bennett, D. H. (1988). *The party of fear: From nativist movements to the new right in American history.* Chapel Hill, NC: The University of North Carolina Press.

Bennett, W. L. (1980). Myth, ritual, and political control. *Journal of Communication, 30,* 166-179.

Bennett, W. L. (1988). *News: The politics of illusion.* (2nd. ed.) New York: Longman.

Benson, T. (1980). The rhetorical structure of Frederick Wiseman's high school. *Communication Monographs, 47,* 233-261.

Benson, T. W., & Anderson, C. (1989) *Reality fictions: The films of Frederick Wiseman.* Carbondale, IL: Southern Illinois University.

Benson, T. W., & Frandson, K. D. (1976). *An orientation to nonverbal communication.* Chicago: Science Research Associates.

Berkman, R., & Kitch, L. W. (1986). *Politics in the media age.* New York: McGraw-Hill.

Bernard, S. (1988, October). Report on "NBC Nightly News."

Biocca, F. (1991). The analysis of discourse within the political ad. In F. Biocca (Ed.), *Television and political advertising,* Vol. 2 (pp. 45-59). Hillsdale, NJ: Lawrence Erlbaum Associates.

Birdwhistle, R. L. (1952). *Introduction to kinesics.* Louisville, KY: University of Louisville Press.

Birdwhistle, R. L. (Producer) (1969). *Microcultural incidents in ten zoos.* Philadelphia, PA: Eastern Pennsylvania Institute of Psychology (Film).

Birmingham, D. L. (1972). Age differences and negative salience. Unpublished Master's thesis, St. Louis, MO: St. Louis University.

Bower, G. H. (1981). Mood and memory. *American Psychologist, 36,* 129-148.

Bowers, J. W. (1964). Some correlates of language intensity. *Quarterly Journal of Speech, 50,* 415-420.

Brandt, H. F. (1945). *The psychology of seeing.* New York: The Philosophical Library.

Breckler, S. J. (1984). Empirical validation of affect, behavior, and cognition as distinct components of attitude. *Journal of Personality and Social Psychology, 47,* 1191-1205.

Breen, M., & Corcoran, F. (1982). Myth in the television discourse. *Communication Monographs, 49,* 127-136.

Briscoe, M. E., Woodyard, H. D., & Shaw, M. E. (1967). Personality impression change as a function of the favorableness of first impressions. *Journal of Personality, 35,* 343-357.

Brody, R., & Page, B. (1973). Indifference, alienation, and rational decisions: The effects of candidate evaluations on turnout and vote. *Public Choice, 15,* 1-17.

Brummett. B. (1980). Towards a theory of silence as a political strategy. *Quarterly Journal of Speech, 66,* 289-303.

Brummett, B. (1988). The homology hypothesis: Pornography on the VCR. *Critical Studies in Mass Communication, 5,* 202-216.

Bugental, D., Kaswan, J. W., & Gianetto, R. M. (1971). Perfidious feminine faces. *Journal of Personality and Social Psychology, 17,* 314-318.

Bugental, D., Kaswan, J. W., & Love, L. R. (1970). Perceptions of contradictory meanings conveyed by verbal and nonverbal channels. *Journal of Personality and Social Psychology, 16,* 647-655.

Bugental, D., Kaswan, J. W., Love, L. R., & Fox, M. N. (1970). Child versus adult perception of the evaluative messages in verbal, vocal, and visual channels. *Developmental Psychology, 2,* 367-375.

Burgoon, M., & Bettinghaus, E. P. (1980). Persuasive message strategies. In M. E. Roloff & G. R. Miller (Eds.), *Persuasion: New directions in theory and research* (pp. 141-169). Beverly Hills, CA: Sage.

Burgoon, M., & Burgoon, J. K. (1975). Message strategies in influence attempts. In G. J. Hanneman & W. J. McEwen (Eds.), *Communication and behavior* (pp. 149-165). Reading, MA: Addison-Wesley.

Burgoon, M., Burgoon, J. K., Riess, M., Butler, J., Montomery, C. L., Stinnett, W. D., Miller, M., Long, M., Vaughn, D., & Caine, B. (1976). Propensity of persuasive attack and intensity of pretreatment messages as predictors of resistance to persuasion. *Journal of Psychology, 92,* 123-129.

Burgoon, M., Cohen, M., Miller, M. D., Montgomery, C. L. (1978). An empirical test of resistance to persuasion. *Human Communication Research, 5,* 27-39.

Burke, K. (1950). *A rhetoric of motives.* New York: Prentice-Hall.

Burke, K. (1966). *Language as symbolic action.* Los Angeles: University of California Press.

Burke, K. (1969). *A grammar of motives.* Berkeley CA: University of California Press.

Burrows, T. D., & Woods, D. N. (1986). *Television production: Disciplines and techniques*. Dubuque, IA: Brown.

Butler, J. (1985). Miami Vice: The legacy of film noir. *Journal of Popular Film and Television*, 126-138.

Butler, J. (1986). Notes on the soap opera apparatus: Televisual style and "As the World Turns". *Cinema Journal,*

Butterfield, F. (1990, April 22). Dukakis says race was harmed by TV. *New York Times*, Section 1, p. 2.

Byers, P. (1964). Still photography in the systematic recording and analysis of behavioral data. *Human Organization, 23*, 78-84.

Calder, B. J. (1978). Cognitive responses, imagery, and scripts: What is the cognitive bases of attitudes? *Advances in Consumer Research, 5*, 630-634.

Cantor, J. R., & Zillmann, D. (1973). Resentment toward victimized protagonists and severity of misfortunes they suffer as factors in humor appreciation. *Journal of Experimental Research in Personality, 6*, 321-329.

Carpenter, R. H. (1977). Frederick Jackson Turner and the rhetorical impact of the frontier thesis. *Quarterly Journal of Speech, 63*, 117-129.

Carroll, R. (1980). The 1948 Truman campaign: The threshold of the modern era. *Journal of Broadcasting, 24*, 173-188.

Chestnut, R. W. (1980). Persuasive effects in marketing: Consumer information processing research. In M. E. Roloff & G. R. Miller (Eds.), *Persuasion: New directions in theory and research* (pp. 267-283). Beverly Hills, CA: Sage.

Choi, H. C., & Becker, S. L. (1987). Media use, issue/image discriminations, and voting. *Communication Research, 14*, 267-291.

Clark, E. C. (1993). *The schoolhouse door: Segregation's last stand at the University of Alabama*. New York: Oxford.

Cobb, R. W., & Elder, C. D. (1972). Individual orientations in the study of political symbolism. *Social Science Quarterly, 42*, 143-160.

Colburn, C. (1967). An experimental study of the relationship between fear appeal and topic importance in persuasion. (Doctoral Dissertation, University of Indiana, 1967). *Dissertation Abstracts International, 28*, 2364A-2365A.

Colford, S. (1991, July 22). Politics '92 seen as local ad bonanza. *Advertising Age*, pp. 1, 39.

Colford, S. (1991, November 11). Healthcare tops pols' ad agenda. *Advertising Age*, pp. 3, 79.

Colford, S. (1992, January 13). Bush may launch ads vs. Buchanan. *Advertising Age*, pp. 1, 42.

Colford, S. (1992, January 27). Buchanan takes off the gloves in N. H. *Advertising Age*, p. 3.

Colford, S. (1992, March 2). Campaign ads get down and dirty. *Advertising Age*, p. 32.

Combs, J. (1973). The dramaturgical image of political man: A modernist approach to political inquiry. Unpublished Dissertation, University of Missouri.

Combs, J. (1979). Political advertising as a popular mythmaking form. *Journal of American Culture, 2*, 331-340.

Combs, J. (1980). *Dimensions of political drama*. Santa Monica, CA: Goodyear.

Combs, J. (1991). *Polpop 2: Politics and popular culture in America today*. Bowling Green, OH: Bowling Green University Press.

Combs, J., & Nimmo, D. (1993). *The new propaganda: The dictatorship of palaver in contemporary politics*. New York: Longman.

Condon, W. S. (1984). Communication and empathy. In J. Lichtenberg, M. Bornstein, & D. Silver (Eds.), *Empathy II* (pp. 35-58). Hillsdale, NJ: Lawrence Erlbaum Associates.

Conover, P. J. (1981). Political cues and the perception of candidates. *American Politics Quarterly, 9*, 427-448.

Conover, P. J., & Feldman, S. (1986). Emotional reactions to the economy: I'm mad as hell and I'm not going to take it any more. *American Journal of Political Science, 30*, 50–78.

Cooper, E., & Jahoda, M. (1947). The evasion of propaganda: How prejudiced people respond to anti-prejudice propaganda. *Journal of Psychology, 23*, 15-25.

Cooper, L. (1932). *The rhetoric of Aristotle.* New York: Appleton-Century-Crofts.

Copeland, G. A. (1989). Face-ism and primetime television. *Journal of Broadcasting and Electronic Media, 33*, 209-214.

Copeland G. A., & Johnson-Cartee, K. S. (1990). Southerners' acceptance of negative political advertising and political efficacy and activity levels. *Southeastern Political Review, 18*, 86-102.

Cragan, J. F., & Cutbirth, C. W. (1984). A revisionist perspective on political ad hominem argument: A case study. *Central States Speech Journal, 35*, 228-237.

Croy, O. R. (1968). *The photographic portrait* (F. L. Dask, trans.). Philadelphia, PA: Focal Press.

Csikszentmihalyi, M., & Kubey, R. (1981). Televison and the rest of life: A systematic comparison of subjective experience. *Public Opinion Quarterly, 45*, 317-328.

Cundy, D. T. (1986). Political commercials and candidate image: The effect can be substantial. In L. L. Kaid, D. Nimmo, & K. Sanders (Eds.), *New perspectives on political advertising* (pp. 210-234). Carbondale, IL: Southern Illinois University Press.

Cushman, D.P. (1977). The rules perspective as a theoretical basis for the study of human communication. *Communication Quarterly, 25*, 30-45.

Cusumano, D., & Richey, M. (1970). Negative salience in impressions of character: Effects of extremeness of salient information. *Psychonomic Science, 20*, 81-83.

Cutlip, S. M., Center, A. H., & Broom, G. M. (1985). *Effective public relations,* 6th ed., Englewood Cliffs, NJ: Prentice-Hall.

Dalrymple, C. (1988, November 5). Selling presidents: Ads that subtract, *West 57th* (trans. pp. 5-7). New York: CBS News.

Darwin, C. (1896). *The expression of the emotions in man and animal.* New York: D. Appleton. (Orig-inally published, 1872.)

Deri, S. (1949). *Introduction to the Szondi test: Theory and practice.* New York: Grune and Stratton.

Devlin, L. P. (1973). Contrasts in presidential campaign commercials of 1972. *Journal of Broadcasting, 35*, 17-26.

Devlin, L. P. (1977). Contrasts in presidential campaign commercials of 1976. *Central State Speech Journal, 28*, 238-249.

Devlin, L. P. (1981). Reagan's and Carter's ad men review the 1980 television campaigns. *Communication Quarterly, 30*, 3-12.

Devlin, L. P. (1986). An analysis of presidential television commercials, 1952-1984. In L. L. Kaid, D. Nimmo, & K. R. Sanders (Eds.), *New perspectives on political advertising* (pp. 21-54). Carbondale, IL: Southern Illinois University Press.

Devlin, L. P. (1987). Campaign commercials. In L. P. Devlin (Ed.), *Political persuasion in presidential campaigns* (pp. 205-216). New Brunswick, NJ: Transaction Books.

Devlin, L. P. (1989). Contrasts in presidential campaign commercials of 1988. *American Behavioral Scientist, 32,* 389-414.

DeVries, W. (1971). Taking the voter's pulse. In R. Hiebert, R. Jones, E. Lotito, & J. Lorenz (Eds.), *The political image merchants: Strategies in the new politics* (pp. 62-81). Washington, DC: Acropolis Books.

DeVries, W., & Tarrance, V. (1972). *The ticket splitters.* Grand Rapids, MI: Eerdmans.

Diamond, E., & Bates, S. (1988). *The spot: The rise of political advertising on television* (rev. ed.). Cambridge, MA: MIT Press.

Diamond, E., & Marin, A. (1989). Spots. *American Behavioral Scientist, 32,* 382-388.

Downs, A. (1957). *An economic theory of democracy.* New York: Harper and Row.

Edelman, M. (1964). *The symbolic uses of politics.* Urbana, IL: University of Illinois Press.

Edelman, M. (1967). Myths, metaphors, and political conformity. *Psychiatry, 30,* 217-228.

Edelman, M. (1971). *Politics as symbolic action.* Chicago: Markham.

Edsall, T. B., & Edsall, M. D. (1991, May). Race. *Atlantic Monthly,* 53-86.

Ekman, P. (1965). Differential communication of affect by head and body cues. *Journal of Personality and Social Psychology, 2,* 724-726.

Ekman, P., & Friesen, W. V. (1967). Head and body cues in the judgment of emotion: A reformulation. *Perceptual and Motor Skills, 24,* 711-724.

Ekman, P., & Friesen, W. V. (1974). Detecting deception from the body and the face. *Journal of Personality and Social Psychology, 29,* 288-298.

Elebash, C., & Rosene, J. (1982). Issues in political advertising in a Deep South gubernatorial race. *Journalism Quarterly, 59,* 420-423.

Feldman, S. (1966). Motivational aspects of attitudinal elements and their place in cognitive interaction. In S. Feldman (Ed.), *Cognitive consistency: Motivational antecedents and behavioral consequences* (pp. 75-108). New York: Academic Press.

Festinger, L., & Maccoby, N. (1964). On resistance to persuasive communications. *Journal of Abnormal and Social Psychology, 68,* 359-366.

Fine, B. J. (1957). Conclusion-drawing, communicator credibility, and anxiety as factors in opinion change. *Journal of Abnormal and Social Psychology, 54,* 369-374.

Fiorina, M. P., & Shepsle, K. A. (1990). A positive theory of negative voting. In J. A. Ferejohn & J. H. Kuklinski (Eds.), *Information and democratic processes* (pp. 220-239). Urbana, IL: University of Illinois Press.

Fisher, W. R. (1970). A motive view of communication. *Quarterly Journal of Speech, 56,* 131-139.

Fisher, W. (1984). Narration as a human communication paradigm: The case of public moral argument. *Communication Monographs, 51,* 1-22.

Fisher, W. R. (1985). The narrative paradigm: An elaboration. *Communication Monographs, 52,* 347-367.

Freedman, J. L., & Steinbruner, J. D. (1964). Perceived choice and resistance to persuasion. *Journal of Abnormal and Social Psychology, 68,* 678-681.

Frentz, T. S., & Farrell, T. B. (1976). Language-action: A paradigm for communication. *Quarterly Journal of Speech, 62,* 333-349.

Freud, S. (1952). *On dreams.* New York: W. W. Norton.

Friedman, H. S., Mertz, T. I., & DiMatteo, M. R. (1980). Perceived bias in the facial expressions of television news broadcasters. *Journal of Communication, 30* (4), 103-111.

Frieze, I. H., & Ramsey, S. J. (1976). Nonverbal maintenance of tradional sex roles. *Journal of Social Issues, 32*, 133-141.

Gaborit, M. (1973). A cross-cultural comparison of negative salience in character impression. Unpublished Master's thesis. St. Louis, MO: St. Louis University.

Gans, H. (1979). *Deciding what's news.* New York: Vintage Books.

Garramone, G. M. (1984). Voter responses to negative political ads. *Journalism Quarterly, 61*, 250-259.

Garramone, G. M. (1985a). Effects of negative political advertising: The roles of sponsor and rebuttal. *Journal of Broadcasting and Electronic Media, 29*, 147-159.

Garramone, G. M. (1985b). Motivation and political information processing: Extending the gratifications approach. In S. Kraus & R. M. Perloff (Eds.), *Mass media and political thought: An information processing approach* (pp. 201-219). Beverly Hills, CA: Sage.

Garramone, G. M. (1986). Candidate image formation: The role of information processing. In L. L. Kaid, D. Nimmo, & K. R. Sanders (Eds.), *New perspectives on political advertising* (pp. 235-247). Carbondale, IL: Southern Illinois University Press.

Garramone, G. M., Atkin, C. K., Pinkleton, B. E., & Cole, R. T. (1990). Effects of negative political advertising on the political process. *Journal of Broadcasting & Electronic Media, 34*, 299-311.

Garramone, G. M., & Smith, S. J. (1984). Reactions to political advertising: The roles of sponsor and rebuttal. *Journalism Quarterly, 61*, 771-775.

Garvey, D. E., & Rivers, W. L. (1982). *Newswriting for the electronic media.* Belmont, CA: Wadsworth.

Gesell, A. (1935). Cinemanalysis: A method of behavior study. *Journal of Genetic Psychology, 47*, 3-16.

Gilkinson, H., Paulson, S. F., & Sikkink, D. E. (1954). Effects of order and authority in an argumentative speech. *Quarterly Journal of Speech, 40*, 183-192.

Glass, D. P. (1985). Evaluating presidential candidates: Who focuses on their personal attributes. *Public Opinion Quarterly, 49*, 517-534.

Goethals, G. (1991) The electronic golden calf. In A. M. Olson, C. Parr, & D. Parr (Eds.), *Video icons & values* (pp. 63-80). Albany, NY: State University of New York Press.

Goffman, E. (1979). *Gender advertisements.* Cambridge, MA: Harvard University Press.

Goodman, R. (1961). *Drama on stage.* San Francisco: Rinehart Press.

Graber, D. (1976). *Verbal behavior and politics.* Urbana, IL: University of Illinois Press.

Graber, D. A. (1987). Television news without pictures? *Critical studies in mass communicaion, 4*, 74-78.

Gray-Little, B. (1973). The salience of negative information in impression formation among two Danish samples. *Journal of Cross-Cultural Psychology, 4*, 193-206.

Gronbeck, B. (1985, November). The rhetoric of negative political advertising: Thoughts on the senatorial race ads in 1984. Paper presented at the annual meeting of the Speech Communication Association, Denver, CO.

Gronbeck, B. (1989). Mythic portraiture in the 1988 Iowa presidential caucus bio-ads. *American Behavioral Scientist, 32*, 351-364.

Gronbeck, B. (1992). Negative narratives in 1988 presidential campaign ads. *Quarterly Journal of Speech, 78,* 333-346.

Grove, L. (1988, November 13). Attack ads trickled up from state races. *The Washington Post,* A1, 18-19.

Gulley, H. E., & Berlo, D. K. (1956). Effect of intercellular and intracellular speech structure on attitude change and learning. *Speech Monographs, 23,* 288-297.

Hagstrom, J., & Guskind, R. (1986). Selling the candidates. *National Journal, 18,* 2619-2626.

Hale, K., & Mansfield, M. (1986, March). Politics: Tastes great or less filling? Paper presented at the annual meeting of the Southwestern Political Science Association, San Antonio, TX.

Hall, E. T. (1959). *The silent language.* Greenwich, CN: Premier Books.

Hall, E. T. (1964). Silent assumptions in social communication. *Disorders of Communication, 42,* 41-55.

Hall, P. (1972). A symbolic interactionist analysis of politics. *Sociological Inquiry, 42,* 35-75.

Hamid, P. N. (1968). Style of dress as a perceptual cue in impression formation. *Perceptual Motor Skills, 26,* 904-906.

Hamilton, D. L., & Huffman, L. F. (1971). Generality of impression-formation processes for evaluative and non-evaluative judgments. *Journal of Personality and Social Psychology, 20,* 200-207.

Hamilton, D. L., & Zanna, M. P. (1972). Differential weighting of favorable and unfavorable attributes in impression formation. *Journal of Experimental Research in Personality, 6,* 204-212.

Harmon, R. R., & Coney, K. A. (1982). The persuasive effects of source credibility in buy and lease situations. *Journal of Marketing Research, 19,* 255-260.

Hart, J. C. (1956). They all were born in log cabins. *American Heritage, 7,* 32-33, 102-105.

Hartmann, G. W. (1936). A field experiment on the comparative effectiveness of "emotional" and "rational"political leaflets in determining election results. *Journal of Abnormal Psychology, 31,* 99-114.

Heider, F., & Simmel, M. (1944). An experimental study of apparent behavior. *American Journal of Psychology, 57,* 243-259.

Hellweg, S. A. (1988, May). Political candidate campaign advertising: A selected review of the literature. Paper presented at the annual meeting of the International Communication Association, New Orleans, LA.

Hess, E. H. (1965). Attitude and pupil size. *Scientific American, 212,* 46-54.

Hickson, M., III, Powell, L., Hill, S. R., Jr., Holt, G. B., & Flick, H. (1979). Smoking artifacts as indicators of homophilly, attraction, and credibility. *Southern States Communication Journal, 44,* 191-200.

Hill, R. P. (1989). An exploration of voter responses to political advertisements. *Journal of Advertising, 18,* 14-22.

Hobbs, R. (1991). Television and the Shaping of Cognitive Skills. In A. M. Olson, C. Parr, & D. Parr (Eds.), *Video icons & values* (pp. 33-44). Albany, NY: State University of New York Press.

Hobbs, R., Frost, R., Dabis, A., & Stauffer, J. (1988). How first-time viewers comprehend editing conventions. *Journal of Communication, 38*(4), 50-60.

Hodges, B. H. (1974). Effect of valence on relative weighting in impression formation. *Journal of Personality and Social Psychology, 30,* 378-381.

Hofstetter, C. R., Zukin, C., & Buss, T. F. (1978). Political imagery and information in an age of television. *Journalism Quarterly, 55,* 562-569.

Holman, C. H. (1972). *A handbook to literature.* (3rd ed.) New York: Odyssey Press.

Hovland, C. I. (1959). Reconciling conflicting results derived from experimental and survey studies of attitude change. *American Psychologist, 14,* 8-17.

Hovland, C. I., & Mandell, W. (1952). An experimental comparison of conclusion-drawing by the communicator and by the audience. *Journal of Abnormal and Social Psychology, 47,* 581-588.

Hudson, L. (1990). The photographic image. In P. J. Hampson, D. F. Marks, & J.T.E. Richardson (Eds.), *Imagery: Current developments* (pp. 223-246). London: Routledge.

James, J. (1992, August). An experimental study on the effect of negative political advertising. Paper presented at the annual meeting of the Association for Education in Journalism and Mass Communication, Montreal, Canada.

Jamieson, K. H. (1984). *Packaging the presidency: A history and criticism of presidential campaign advertising.* (2nd pr.) New York: Oxford University Press.

Jamieson, K. H. (1986). The evolution of political advertising in America. In L. L. Kaid, D. Nimmo, & K. R. Sanders (Eds.), *New perspectives on political advertising* (pp. 1-20). Carbondale, IL: Southern Illinois University Press.

Jamieson, K. H. (1988). *Eloquence in an electronic age: The transformation of political speechmaking.* New York: Oxford University Press.

Jamieson, K. H. (1992). *Dirty politics: Deception, distraction, and democracy.* New York: Oxford University Press.

Jamieson, K. H., & Campbell, K. K. (1983). *The interplay of influence: Mass media and their publics in news, advertising, politics.* Belmont, CA: Wadsworth.

Janis, I. L. (1967). Effects of fear arousal on attitude change: Recent developments in theory and experimental research. In L. Berkowitz (Ed.), *Advances in experimental social psychology* (Vol. 3, pp. 167-224). New York: Academic Press.

Janis, I. L., & Feshback, S. (1953). Effects of fear-arousing communication. *Journal of Abnormal and Social Psychology, 48,* 78-92.

Jewett, R., & Lawrence, J. S. (1977). *The American Monomyth.* Garden City, NJ: Anchor Press.

Johnson, K. S. (1984). Impression management during the presidential transitions of Nixon, Carter, and Reagan: A quantitative content analysis and thematic analysis. Unpublished doctoral dissertation, University of Tennessee, Knoxville, TN.

Johnson, K. S., & Copeland, G. A. (1987, May). Setting the parameters of good taste: Negative political advertising. Paper presented at the annual meeting of the International Communication Association, Montreal, Canada.

Johnson, K. S., & Elebash, C. (1986). The contagion from the right: The Americanization of British political advertising. In L. L. Kaid, D. Nimmo, & K. Sanders (Eds.), *New perspectives on political advertising* (pp. 293-313). Carbondale, IL: Southern Illinois University Press.

Johnson-Cartee, K. S., & Copeland, G. A. (1989a, May). Alabama voters and the acceptance of negative political advertising in the 1986 elections: An historical anomaly. Paper presented at the annual meeting of the International Communication Association, San Francisco.

Johnson-Cartee, K. S., & Copeland, G. A. (1989b). Southern voters' reaction to negative political ads in the 1986 election. *Journalism Quarterly, 66,* 888-893, 986.

Johnson-Cartee, K. S., & Copeland, G. A. (1991a). *Negative political advertising: Coming of age.* Hillsdale, NJ: Lawrence Erlbaum Associates.

Johnson-Cartee, K. S., & Copeland, G. A. (1991b, March). Positivizing negative political advertising. Presentation at the Conference on Professional Responsibility and Ethics in the Political Process, American Association of Political Consultants, Colonial Williamsburg, VA.

Johnson-Cartee, K., Copeland, G.A., & Elebash, C. (1992). *Us versus them: George C. Wallace's negative political advertising,* Paper presented at the annual meeting of the Tennessee Speech Communication Association, Natchez Trace State Park.

Johnson-Cartee, K. S., Elebash, C., & Copeland, G. A. (1992). George C. Wallace's legacy: Thirty years of negative political advertising. Paper presented at the annual meeting of the Association of Education in Journalism and Mass Communication, Montreal, Canada.

Johnston, A. (1991). Political broadcasts: An analysis of form, content, and style in presidential communication. In L. L. Kaid, J. Gerstle, & K. R. Sanders (Eds.), *Mediated politics in two cultures* (pp. 59-72). New York: Praeger.

Jones, E. E. (1972). Introduction. In E. E. Jones et al. (Eds.), *Attribution: Perceiving the causes of behavior.* Morristown, NJ: General Learning Press.

Jordan, N. (1965). The "asymmetry" of "liking" and "disliking": A phenomenon meriting further replication and research. *Public Opinion Quarterly, 29,* 315-322.

Joslyn, R. (1986). Political advertising and the meaning of elections. In L. L. Kaid, D. Nimmo, & K. R. Sanders (Eds.), *New perspectives on political advertising,* (pp. 139-183). Carbondale, IL: Southern Illinois University Press.

Kahn, K. F., & Greer, J. G. (1994). Creating impressions: An experimental investigation of political advertising on television. *Political Behavior, 16,* 93-116

Kaid , L. L., & Boydston, J. (1987). An experimental study of the effectiveness of negative political advertisements. *Communication Quarterly, 35,* 193-201.

Kaid, L. L., & Davidson, D. K. (1986). Elements of videostyle: Candidate presentation through television advertising. In L.L. Kaid, D. Nimmo, & K. R. Sanders (Eds.), *New perspectives on political advertising,* (pp. 184-209). Carbondale, IL: Southern Illinois University Press.

Kaid, L. L., & Johnston, A. (1991). Negative versus positive television advertising in U. S. presidential campaigns, 1960-1988. *Journal of Communication, 41* (3), 53-64.

Kaid, L. L., Leland, C. M., & Whitney, S. (1992). The impact of televised political ads: Evoking viewer responses in the 1988 presidential campaign. *The Southern Communication Journal, 57,* 285-295.

Kanouse, D. E., & Hanson, L. R. (1972). Negativity in evaluation. In E. E. Jones, D. E. Kanouse, H. H. Kelley, R. E. Nisbett, S. Valins, & B. Weiner (Eds.), *Attribution: Perceiving the causes of behavior* (pp. 47-62). Morristown, NJ: General.

Kaplan, R. (1987, December 28). Political consultants & TV ads. "Nightline," (trans. pp. 2-7). New York: ABC News.

Katz, G. (1988, October 27). Viewers like feel of positive spots. *USA Today,* p. 7A.

Kellermann, K. (1984). The negativity effect and its implications for initial interaction. *Communication Monographs, 51,* 37-55.

Kelly, J. (1984, November 12). Packaging the presidency. *Time,* p. 36.

Kepplinger, H. M. (1991). The impact of presentational techniques: Theoretical Aspects and empirical findings. In F. Biocca (Ed.), *Television and Political*

Advertising, Vol. I: Psychological Processes (pp. 173-194). Hillsdale, NJ: Lawrence Erlbaum Associates.

Kern, M. (1989). *Thirty-second politics: Political advertising in the eighties.* New York: Praeger.

Kernell, S. (1977). Presidential popularity and negative voting: An alternative explanation of the midterm congressional decline of the president's party. *American Political Science Review, 71,* 44-66.

Kiesler, C. A., Collins, R. E., & Miller, N. (1969). *Attitude change: A critical analysis of theoretical approaches.* New York: John Wiley and Sons.

Kinder, D. R. (1978). Political person perception: The asymmetrical influence of sentiment and choice on perceptions of presidential candidates. *Journal of Personality and Social Psychology, 38,* 859-871.

Kirkwood, W. G. (1983). Storytelling and self-confrontation: Parables as communication strategies. *Quarterly Journal of Speech, 69,* 58-74.

Kitchens, J. T., & Stiteler, B. (1979). Challenge to the "rule of minimum effect": A case study of the in man-out man strategy. *The Southern Speech Communication Journal, 44,* 176-190.

Klein, J. G. (1991). Negativity effects in impression formation: A test in the political arena. *Personality and Social Psychology Bulletin, 17,* 412-418.

Kleinke, C. L. (1975). *First impressions: The psychology of encountering others.* Englewood Cliffs, NJ: Prentice-Hall.

Kouvenhaven, J. A. (1975). Living in a snapshot world. *Aperture, 19,* 106-108.

Krugman, H. E. (1966). The impact of television advertising: Learning without involvement. *Public Opinion Quarterly, 29,* 249-356.

Lang, A. (1991). Emotion, formal features, and memory for televised political advertisements. In F. Biocca (Ed.), *Television and Political Advertising Vol. I: Psychological Processes* (pp. 221-243). Hillsdale, NJ: Lawrence Erlbaum Associates.

Lanzetta, J. T., Sullivan, D. G., Masters, R. D., & McHugo, G. J. (1985). Emotional and cognitive responses to televised images of political leaders. In S. Kraus & R. M. Perlofff (Eds.), *Mass Media and political thought: An information-processing approach* (pp. 85-116). Beverly Hills, CA: Sage.

Lau, R. R. (1980). Negativity in political perceptions. Unpublished manuscript, University of California, Department of Psychology, Los Angeles.

Lau, R. R. (1982). Negativity in political perception. *Political Behavior, 4,* 353-378.

Lau, R. R. (1985). Two explanations for negativity effects in political behavior. *American Journal of Political Science, 29,* 119-138.

Lazarus, R. S. (1982). Thoughts on the relations between emotion and cognition. *American Psychologist, 37,* 1019-1024.

Lazarus, R. S., Coyne, J. C., & Folkman, S. (1982). Cognition, emotion, and motivation: The doctoring of Humpty-Dumpty. In R.W.J. Neufeld (Ed.), *Psychological stress and psychopathology* (pp. 218-239). New York: McGraw-Hill.

Lemert, J. B., Elliot, W. R., Bernstein, J. M., Rosenberg, W. L., & Nestvold, K. J. (1991). *News verdicts, the debates, and presidential campaigns.* New York: Praeger.

Letcher, M. (1991, June 11). *Confessions of a media consultant.* Video documentary, Alabama Public Television. Center for Public Television, University of Alabama.

Leventhal, H. (1970). Findings and theory in the study of fear communication. In L. Berkowitz (Ed.), *Advances in experimental and social psychology Vol. 5* (pp. 119-186). New York: Academic Press.

Leventhal, H. (1984). A perceptual motor theory of emotion. In K. R. Scherer & P. Ekman (Eds.), *Approaches to emotion*. Hillsdale, NJ: Lawrence Erlbaum Associates.

Leventhal, H., Meyers, D., & Nerenz, D. (1980). The common sense representation of illness danger. In S. Rachman (Ed.), *Medical Psychology, Vol. 2* (pp. 7-30). New York: Pergamon.

Leventhal, H., & Singer, D. (1964). Cognitive complexity, impression formation, and impression change. *Journal of Personality, 32*, 210-226.

Leventhal, H., Watts, J. C., & Pagano, F. (1967). Effects of fear and instructions on how to cope with danger. *Journal of Personality and Social Psychology, 6*, 313-332.

Levin, I. P., & Schmidt, C. F. (1969). Sequential effects in impression formation with binary intermittent responding. *Journal of Experimental Psychology, 79*, 283-287.

Leymore, V. L. (1975). *Hidden myth: Structure and symbolism in advertising*. New York: Basic.

Lieske, J. (1991). Cultural issues and images in the 1988 presidential campaign: Why the Democrats lost—again! *Political Science & Polity, 24*, 180-187.

Linden, G. W. (1970). *Reflections on the screen*. Belmont, CA: Wadsworth.

Lippmann, W. (1965 ed.). *Public opinion*. New York: Free Press.

Lumsdaine, A. A., & Janis, I. L. (1953). Resistence to "counter propaganda" produced by one-sided and two-sided "propaganda" presentation. *Public Opinion Quarterly, 17*, 311-318.

MacDonald, L. C. (1969). Myth, politics, and political science. *Western Political Quarterly, 22*, 141-150.

MacIntyre, A. (1981). *After virtue: A study in moral theory*. Notre Dame, IN: University of Notre Dame Press.

MacKenzie, S. B., & Lutz, R. J. (1989). An empirical examination of the structural antecedents of attitude toward the ad in an advertising pretesting context. *Journal of Marketing, 53*, 48-65.

Maddux, J. E., & Rogers, R. W. (1983). Protection motivation and self-efficacy: A revised theory of fear appeals and attitude change. *Journal of Experimental Social Psychology, 19*, 469-479.

Makay, J. J. (1970). The rhetorical strategies of Governor George Wallace in the 1964 Maryland primary. *Southern Speech Journal, 36*, 164-175.

Mandell, L. M., & Shaw, D. L. (1973). Judging people in the news unconsciously: Effect of camera angle and bodily activity. *Journal of Broadcasting, 17*, 353-362.

Manz, W., & Lueck, H. E. (1968). Influence of wearing glasses on personality ratings: Cross-cultural validation of an old experiment. *Perceptual and Motor Skills, 27*, 704.

Marcus, G. E. (1985). A theory and methodology for measuring emotions in politics. Paper presented at the annual meeting of the Political Methodology Society, Berkeley, CA.

Marcus, G. E. (1988). The structures of emotional response: 1984 presidential candidates. *American Political Science Review, 82*, 737-761.

Markerson, L., & Goldstein, J. (1994). *Open secrets: The encyclopedia of Congressional money & politics. The 1992 election*. Washington, DC: Center for Responsive Politics, Congressional Quarterly.

Mayo, C. W., & Crockett, W. H. (1964). Cognitive complexity and primacy-recency effects in impression formation. *Journal of Abnormal and Social Psychology, 68*, 335-338.

McBurney, J. H., & Mills, G. E. (1964). *Argumentation and debate: Techniques of a free society*. (2nd ed.) New York: Macmillan.

McCabe, E. (1988, December 12). The campaign you never saw. *New York*, pp. 33-48.

McCain, T. A., Chilberg, J., & Wakshlag, J. (1977). The effect of camera angle on source credibility and attraction. *Journal of Broadcasting, 21*, 35-46.

McCain, T. A., & Divers, L. (1973, November). The effect of body type and camera shot on interpersonal attraction and source credibility. Paper presented at the annual meeting of the Speech Communication Association, Chicago.

McCain, T. A., & Repensky, G. R. (1972, November). The effect of camera shot on interpersonal attraction for comedy performers. Paper presented at the annual meeting of the Speech Communication Association, New York.

McCain, T. A., & White, S. (1980, November). Channel effects and non-verbal properties of media messages: A state of the art review. Paper presented at the annual meeting of the Speech Communication Association, New York.

McCroskey, J. (1969). A summary of experimental research on the effects of evidence in persuasive communication. *Quarterly Journal of Speech, 55*, 169-176.

McCroskey, J. (1970). The effects of evidence as an inhibitor of counter-persuasion. *Speech Monographs, 37*, 188-194.

McGee, M. (1980). The "ideograph": A link between rhetoric and ideology. *Quarterly Journal of Speech, 66*, 1-16.

McGuire, W. J. (1961a). Resistance to persuasion conferred by active and passive prior refutation of the same and alternate counterarguments. *Journal of Abnormal and Social Psychology, 63*, 326-332.

McGuire, W. J. (1961b). The effectiveness of supportive and refutational defenses in immunizing and restoring beliefs against persuasion. *Sociometry, 24*, 184-197.

McGuire, W. J. (1962). Persistence of resistance to persuasion induced by various types of prior belief defenses. *Journal of Abnormal and Social Psychlogy, 64*, 241-248.

McGuire, W. J. (1964). Inducing resistance to persuasion: Some contemporary approaches. In L. Berkowitz (Ed.), *Advances in experimental social psychology, Vol.I* (pp. 191-229). New York: Academic Press.

McGuire, W. J. (1968). Personality and susceptibility to social influence. In E. F. Borgatta & W. W. Lambert (Eds.), *Handbook of Personality Theory and Research* (pp. 1130-1187). Chicago: Rand McNally.

McGuire, W. J. (1985). Attitudes and attitude change. In G. Lindzey & E. Aronson (Eds.), *The Handbook of Social Psychology Vol. II* (3rd. ed.), pp. 233-346. New York: Random.

McGuire, W. J., & Papageorgis, D. (1961). The relative efficacy of various types of prior belief defense in producing immunity against persuasion. *Journal of Abnormal and Social Psychology, 62*, 327-337.

McGuire, W. J., & Papageorgis, D. (1962). Effectiveness in forewarning in developing resistance to persuasion. *Public Opinion Quarterly, 26*, 24-34.

McKeachie, W. J. (1952). Lipstick as a determiner of first impressions of personality: An experiment for the general psychology course. *Journal of Social Psychology, 36*, 241-244.

McLuhan, M. (1967). *The mechanical bride: Folklore of industrial man*. Boston: Beacon Hill. (Originally published 1951.)

Mead, G. H. (1934). *Mind, self and society: From the standpoint of a social behaviorist*. Chicago: University of Chicago Press.

Mead, M., & Macgregor, F. C. (1951). *Growth and culture: A photographic study of Balinese childhood*. New York: Putnam.

Mendelsohn, H., & Crespi, I. (1970). *Polls, television and the new politics.* Scranton, PA: Chandler.

Merritt, S. (1984). Negative political advertising: Some empirical findings. *Journal of Advertising, 13,* 27-38.

Messaris, P., & Gross, L. (1977). Interpretations of a photographic narrative by viewers in four age groups. *Studies in the Anthropology of visual communication, 4,* 99-111.

Metallinos, N., & Tiemens, R. K. (1977). Asymmetry of the screen: The effect of left versus right placement of television images. *Journal of Broadcasting, 21,* 21-33.

Middleton, K. R., & Chamberlin, B. F. (1988). *The law of public communication.* White Plains, NY: Longman.

Miller, A. H., Wattenberg, M. P., & Malanchuk, O. (1986). Schematic assessments of presidential candidates. *American Political Science Review, 80,* 521-540.

Miller, J. W., & Rowe, R. M. (1967). Influence of favorable and unfavorable information upon assessment decisions. *Journal of Applied Psychology, 15,* 432-435.

Miller, M. D., & Burgoon, M. (1979). The relationship between violations of expectations and the induction of resistance to persuasion. *Human Communication Research, 5,* 301-312.

Moore, H. F., & Kalupa, F. B. (1985). *Public relations: Principles, cases, and problems.* (9th ed.) Homewood, IL: Richard D. Irwin.

Moran, E. G. (1973). Negative salience: Sex differences in a German population. Unpublished Master's thesis. St. Louis, MO: St. Louis University.

Morreale, J. (1991a). *A new beginning: A textual frame analysis of the political campaign film.* Albany, NY: State University of New York Press.

Morreale, J. (1991b). The political campaign film: Epideictic rhetoric in a documentary frame. In F. Biocca (Ed.), *Television and political advertising: Signs, codes, and images, Vol. II* (pp. 187-201). Hillsdale, NJ: Lawrence Erlbaum Associates.

Morris, D., & Gamache, M. (1994). *Handbook of campaign spending: Money in the 1992 congressional races.* Washington, DC: Congressional Quarterly.

Mullen, B., Futrell, D., Stairs, D. & others (1986). Newscasters' facial expressions and voting behavior of viewers: Can a smile elect a president. *Journal of Personality and Social Psychology, 51,* 291-295.

Mullins, W. A. (1972). On the concept of ideology in political science. *American Political Science Review, 66,* 498-510.

Murray-Brown, J. (1991). Video ergo sum. In A. M. Olson, C. Parr, & D. Parr (Eds.), *Video icons & values* (pp. 17-32). Albany, NY: State University of New York Press.

Musello, C. (1979). Family photography. In J. Wagner (Ed.), *Images of information: Still photography in the social sciences* (pp. 101-118). Beverly Hills, CA: Sage.

Nesbitt, D. (1988). *Videostyle: In senate campaigns.* Knoxville, TN: University of Tennessee Press.

New Campaign Techniques (1986). In *Elections '86* (pp. 29-35). Washington, DC: Congressional Quarterly.

Newhagen, J. E., & Reeves, B. (1991). Emotion and memory responses for negative political advertising: Study of television commercials used in the 1988 presidential election. In F. Biocca (Ed.), *Television and political advertising, Vol. I* (pp. 197-220). Hillsdale, NJ: Lawrence Erlbaum Associates.

Nichols, B. (1981). *Ideology and the image.* Bloomington, IN: Indiana University Press.

Nilsen, D.L.F. (1990). The social functions of political humor. *Journal of Popular Culture, 24*, 35-47.

Nimmo, D. (1978). *Political communication and public opinion in America*. Santa Monica, CA: Goodyear.

Nimmo, D., & Combs, J. (1980). *Subliminal politics: Myths and mythmakers in America*. Englewood Cliffs, NJ: Prentice-Hall.

Nimmo, D., & Combs, J. (1983). *Mediated political realities*. New York: Longman.

Nimmo, D., & Felsberg, A. J. (1986). Hidden myths in televised political advertising: An illustration. In L. L. Kaid, D. Nimmo, & K. R. Sanders (Eds.), *New perspectives on political advertising* (pp. 248-267). Carbondale, IL: Southern Illinois University Press.

O'Hara, R. (1961). *Media for the millions*. New York: Random House.

Oft-Rose, N. (1989). The importance of ethos. *Argumentation and Advocacy: Journal of the American Forensic Association, 25*, 197-199.

Orlik, P. (1990). Negative political commercials: A 1988 snapshot. *Feedback, 31*, 2-7.

Oskamp, S. (1991). *Attitudes and opinions*. (2nd ed.) Englewood Cliffs, NJ: Prentice Hall.

Osterhouse, R. A., & Brock, T. C. (1970). Distraction increases yielding to propaganda by inhibiting counterarguing. *Journal of Personality and Social Psychology, 15*, 344-358.

Owen, D. (1991). *Media messages in American presidential elections*. New York: Greenwood Press.

Page, B. I. (1976). The theory of political ambiguity. *American Political Science Review, 70*, 742-752.

Page, B. I. (1978). *Choices and echoes in presidential elections*. Chicago: University of Chicago Press.

Papageorgis, D., & McGuire, W. J. (1961). The generality of immunity to persuasion produced by pre-exposure to weakened counterarguments. *Journal of Abnormal and Social Psychology, 62*, 475-481.

Parsons, T., & Shils, E. (Eds.) (1951). *Toward a general theory of action*. New York: Harper and Row.

Patterson, T. (1980). *The mass media election*. New York: Praeger.

Patterson, T. E., & McClure, R. D. (1976). *The unseeing eye*. New York: Putnam.

Patti, C. H., & Frazer, C. F. (1988). *Advertising: A decision-making approach*. Chicago: Dryden.

Payne, J. G., & Baukus, R. A. (1988). Trend analysis of the 1984 GOP senatorial spots. *Political Communication and Persuasion, 5*, 161-177.

Payne, J. G., Marlier, J, & Baukus, R. A. (1989). Polispots in the 1988 presidential primaries: Separating the nominees from the rest of the guys. *American Behavioral Research, 32*, 365-381.

Penn, R. (1971). Effects of motion and cutting-rate in motion pictures. *AV Communication Review, 19*, 29-51.

Perloff, R. M. (1993). *The dynamics of persuasion*. Hillsdale, NJ: Lawrence Erlbaum Associates.

Perucci, R., & Knudsen, D. D. (1983). *Sociology*. New York: West.

Peterson, J. R., & Koulack, D. (1969). Attitude change as a function of latitudes of acceptance and rejection. *Journal of Personality and Social Psychology, 11*, 309-311.

Petty, R. E., & Cacioppo, J. T. (1984). The effects of involvement on responses to argument quantity and quality: Central and peripheral routes to persuasion. *Journal of Personality and Social Psychology, 46*, 69-81.

Petty, R. E., Cacioppo, J. T., & Heesacker, M. (1981). Effects of rhetorical questions on persuasion: A cognitive response analysis. *Journal of Personality and Social Psychology, 40,* 432-440.

Pfau, M. & Burgoon, M. (1988). Inoculation in political campaign communication. *Human Communication Research, 15,* 91-111.

Pfau, M., & Burgoon, M. (1989). The efficacy of issue and character attack message strategies in political campaign communication. *Communication Reports, 2,* 53-61.

Pfau, M., & Kenski, H. C. (1990). *Attack politics.* New York: Praeger.

Political TV Classics (Producer) (1984). *Campaigns & Elections* [Videotape]. Washington, DC.

Prasad, V. K. (1976). Communications-effectiveness of comparative advertising: A laboratory analysis. *Journal of Marketing Research, 13,* 128-137.

Priest, R. F. (1966). Election jokes: The effects of reference group membership. *Psychological Reports, 18,* 600-602.

Pryor, B., & Steinfatt, T. M. (1978). The effects of initial belief level on inoculation theory and its proposed mechanisms. *Human Communication Research, 4,* 216-230.

Ray, G. B. (1986). Vocally cued personality prototypes: An implicit personality theory approach. *Communication Monographs, 53,* 266-276.

Reeves, B., Thorson, E., & Schleuder, J. (1986). Attention to television: Psychological theories and chronometric measures. In J. Bryant & D. Zillmann (Eds.), *Perspectives on media effects* (pp. 251-279). Hillsdale, NJ: Lawrence Erlbaum Associates.

Responsibility, *The Tuscaloosa News.* Saturday, October 8, 1994, p. 4b.

Richey, M. H., & Dwyer, J. D. (1970). Negative salience in impressions of character: Sex differences. *Psychonomic Science , 20,* 77-79.

Richey, M. H., Koenigs, R. J., Richey, H. W., & Fortin, R. (1975). Negative salience on impressions of character: Effects of unequal proportions of positive and negative information. *Journal of Social Psychology, 97,* 233-241.

Richey, M. H., McClelland, L., & Shimkunas, A. M. (1967). Relative influence of positive and negative information in impression formation and persistence. *Journal of Personality and Social Psychology, 6,* 322-327.

Richey, M. H., Richey, H. W., & Thieman, G. (1972). Negative salience in impressions of character: Effects of new information on established relationships. *Psychonomic Science, 28,* 65-66.

Roberts, S. (1986, November, 2). Politicking goes high tech. *New York Times Magazine,* p. 38.

Robinson, M. J. (1981). The media in 1980: Was the message the message? In Austin Ranney (Ed.), *The American Elections of 1980* (pp. 171-211). Washington, DC: American Enterprise Institute.

Roering, K. J., & Paul, R. J. (1976). The effect of the consistency of product claims on the credibility of persuasive messages. *Journal of Advertising, 5,* 32-36.

Rogers, R. W. (1975). A protection motivation theory of fear appeals and attitude change. *Journal of Psychology, 91,* 93-114.

Rogers, R. W., & Mewborn, C. R. (1976). Fear appeals and attitude change: Effects of a threat's noxiousness, probability of occurrence, and efficacy of coping response. *Journal of Personality and Social Psychology, 34,* 54-61.

Root, R. L., Jr. (1987). *The rhetorics of popular culture: Advertising, advocacy, and entertainment.* Westport, CT: Greenwood Press.

Roper, E. (1957). *You and your leaders.* New York: William Morrow.

Rose, E. D., & Fuchs, D. (1968). Reagan vs. Brown: A TV image playback. *Journal of Broadcasting, 12,* 247-260.

Roseman, I. J. (1979). Cognitive aspects of emotion and emotional behavior. Paper presented at the annual meeting of the American Psychological Association, Washington, DC.

Roseman, I. J. (1984). Cognitive determinants of emotions: A structural theory. In P. Shaver (Ed.), *Review of personality and social psychology* (Vol. 5, pp. 11-36). Beverly Hills, CA: Sage.

Roseman, I., Abelson, R. P., & Ewing, M. F. (1986). Emotion and political cognition: Emotional appeals in political communication. In R. R. Lau and D. O. Sears (Eds.), *Political cognition* (pp. 279-294). Hillsdale, NJ: Lawrence Erlbaum Associates.

Rosenberg, M., & Rosenberg, D. (1962). The dirtiest election. *American Heritage, 13,* 4-9.

Rosenberg, S. W., Bohan, L., McCafferty, P., & Harris, K. (1986). The image and the vote: The effect of candidate presentation on voter preference. *American Journal of Political Science, 30,* 108-127.

Rosenberg, S. W., & McCafferty, P. (1987). The image and the vote: Manipulating voters' preferences. *Public Opinion Quarterly, 51,* 31-47.

Rosenfeld, H. M. (1966). Approval-seeking and approval-inducing functions of verbal and nonverbal responses in the dyad. *Journal of Personality and Social Psychology, 4,* 597-605.

Rossen, E. (1984, Sept. 6). The 30-second man. "20/20." (trans. pp. 10-15). New York: ABC News.

Sabato, L. (1981). *The rise of political consultants: New ways of winning elections.* New York: Basic Books.

Sale, K. (1975a, November 21). The cowboy challenge. *Commonweal, 12,* 555-559.

Sale, K. (1975b). *Power shift.* New York: Random House.

Salmore, S. A., & Salmore, B. G. (1985). *Candidates, parties, and campaigns: Electoral politics in America.* Washington, DC: Congressional Quarterly.

Sanford, D. L., & Roach, J. W. (1987, May). Imperative force in request forms: The demanding vs. pleading dimensions of directives. Paper presented at the annual meeting of the International Communication Association, Montreal, Canada.

Sapir, E. (1934). Symbolism. *Encyclopedia of the Social Sciences, 14,* 492-495.

Saussure, F. (1966). *Course in general linguistics.* New York: McGraw-Hill.

Sawyer, A. G. (1988). Can there be effective advertising without explicit conclusions? Decide for yourself. In S. Hecker & D. W. Stewart (Eds.), *Nonverbal communication in advertising* (pp. 159-184). Lexington, MA: D. C. Heath.

Scheflen, A. E. (1972). *Body language and social order: Communication as behavioral control.* Englewood Cliffs, NJ: Prentice-Hall.

Schneider, D. J., Hastoff, A. H., & Ellsworth, P. C. (1979). *Person perception.* (2nd ed.) Reading, PA: Addison-Wesley.

Schutz, A. (1962). Collected papers Vol. I., *The problem of social reality.* Maurice Natanson (Ed.), The Hague: Martinus Nyhoff.

Schutz, A. (1967). *The phenomenology of the social world.* Evanston, IL: Northwestern University Press.

Schwartz, T. (1972). *The responsive chord.* Garden City, NY: Anchor.

Schwartz, T. (1976). The inside of the outside. In R. Agranoff (Ed.), *The new style in election campaigns* (pp. 344-358). Boston: Holbrook.

Searle, J. R. (1976). A classification of illocutionary acts. *Language in Society, 5,* 1-23.

Secord, P. F. (1958). Facial featuires and inference processes in interpersonal perception. In R. Tangiuri & L. Petrultio (Eds.), *Person perception and interpersonal behavior* (pp. 300-315). Stanford, CA: Stanford University Press.

Seebok, T. A. (Ed.). (1958). *Myth: A symposium.* Bloomington, IN: Indiana University Press. (Original work published in 1955.)

Shapiro, M. A., & Rieger, R. H. (1989, May). Comparing positive and negative political advertising. Paper presented at the annual meeting of the International Communication Association, San Francisco.

Shapiro, M. A., & Rieger, R. H. (1992). Comparing positive and negative political advertising on radio. *Journalism Quarterly, 69,* 135-145.

Sheehan, M. R. (1971). The relative salience of negative information in life-like situations. Unpublished Doctoral dissertation, St. Louis, MO: St. Louis University.

Shepsle, K. A. (1972). The strategy of ambiguity: Uncertainty and electoral competition. *American Political Science Review, 66,* 555-568.

Shimanoff, S. B. (1980). *Communication rules: Theory and research.* Beverly Hills, CA: Sage.

Shyles, L. C. (1983). Defining the issues of a presidential election from televised political spot advertisements. *Journal of Broadcasting, 27,* 333-343.

Shyles, L. (1986). The televised political spot advertisement: Its structure, content, and role in the political system. In L. L. Kaid, D. Nimmo, & K. R. Sanders (Eds.), *New perspectives on political advertising* (pp. 107-138). Carbondale, IL: Southern Illinois University Press.

Shyles, L. (1988). Profiling candidate images in televised political spot advertisements for 1984: Roles and realities of presidential jousters at the height of the Reagan era. *Political Communication and Persuasion, 5,* 15-31.

Simons, H. W., & Aghazarian, A. A. (1986). Genres, rules, and political rhetoric: Toward a sociology of rhetorical choice. In H. W. Simons & A.A. Aghazarian (Eds.), *Form, genre, and the study of political discourse* (pp. 45-58). Columbia, SC: University of South Carolina.

Smelser, N. (1963). *Theory of collective behavior.* New York: Free Press.

Smith, L. D., & Golden, J. L. (1988). Electronic storytelling in electoral politics: An anecdotal analysis of television advertising in the Helms-Hunt Senate race. *The Southern Speech Communication Journal, 53,* 244-258.

Smith, L. D., & Johnston, A. (1991). Burke's sociological criticism applied to political advertising: An anecdotal taxonomy of presidential commercials. In F. Biocca (Ed.), *Television and political advertising, Vol. 2* (pp. 115-131). Hillsdale NJ: Lawrence Erlbaum Associates.

Smith, R. E., & Hunt, S. D. (1978). Attributional processes and effects in promotional situations. *Journal of Consumer Research, 5,* 149-158.

Sorauf, F. (1992). *Inside campaign finance: Myths and realities.* New Haven, CT: Yale University Press.

Stewart, C. J. (1975). Voter perception of mudslinging in political communication. *Central States Speech Journal, 26,* 279-286.

Street, R. L., Jr., & Brady, R. M. (1982). Speech rate acceptance ranges as a function of evaluative domain, listener speech rate, and communication context. *Communication Monographs, 49,* 290-308.

Strouse, J. C. (1975). *The mass media, public opinion and public policy analysis.* Columbus, OH: Charles E. Merrill.

Sullivan, D. G., & Masters, R. D. (1988). "Happy Warriors": Leaders' facial displays, viewers' emotions, and political support. *American Journal of Political Science, 32,* 345-368.

Surlin, S. H., & Gordon, T. F. (1977). How values affect attitudes toward direct reference political advertising. *Journalism Quarterly, 54*, 89-98.

Sutton, S. R., & Eiser, J. R. (1984). The effect of fear-arousing communications on cigarette smoking: An expectancy-value approach. *Journal of Behavioral Medicine, 7*, 13-33.

Sykes, A.J.M. (1965). Myth and attitude change. *Human Relations, 18*, 323-337.

Sykes, A.J.M. (1966). A study in attitude change. *Occupational Psychology, 40*, 31-41.

Sykes, A.J.M. (1970, March). Myth in communication. *Journal of Communication, 20*, 17-31.

Tannenbaum, P. H. (1967). The congruity principle revisited: Studies in the reduction, induction and generalization of attitude change. In L. Berkowitz (Ed.), *Advances in experimental social psychology, Vol. III* (pp. 271-320). New York: Academic Press.

Tannenbaum, P. H., McCauley, J. R., Norris, E. L. (1966). Principle of congruity and reduction of persuasion. *Journal of Personality and Social Psychology, 2*, 233-238.

Tarrance, V. L., Jr. (1982). *Negative campaigns and negative votes: The 1980 elections.* Washington, DC: Free Congress Research and Education Foundation.

Thornton, G. R. (1943). The effect upon judgments of personality traits of varying single factor in a photograph. *Journal of Social Psychology, 18*, 127-148.

Tiemens, R. (1965). Some relationships of camera angle to communicator credibility. *Journal of Broadcasting, 14*, 483-490.

Tiemens, R. K. (1978). Television's portrayal of the 1976 presidential debates: An analysis of visual content. *Communication Monographs, 45*, 362-370.

Tilly, C. (1979). Repertoires of contention in America and Britain, 1750-1830. In M. N. Zald & J. D. McCarthy (Eds.), *The dynamics of social movements: Resource mobilization, control, and tactics.* Cambridge: Winthrop.

Tinkham, S. F., & Weaver-Lariscy, R. A. (1993). A diagnostic approach to assessing the impact of negative political television commercials. *Journal of Broadcasting and Electronic Media, 37*, 377-399.

Trent, J. S., & Friedenberg, R. V. (1983). *Political campaign communication.* New York: Praeger.

Ullmann, W. R., & Bodaken, E. M. (1975). Inducing resistance to persuasive attack: A test of two strategies of communication. *Western Speech Communication, 39*, 240-248.

Vatz, R. (1973). The myth of the rhetorical situation. *Philosophy and Rhetoric, 6*, 154-161.

Wadsworth, A. J., & Kaid, L. L. (1987, May). Incumbent and challenger styles in presidential advertising. Paper presented at the annual meeting of the International Communication Association, Montreal, Canada.

Walker, E. E., Lindquist, J. H., Morey, R. D., & Walker, D. E. (1968). *Readings in American public opinion.* New York: American Book.

Warner, W. L. (1976). Mass media: The transformation of a political hero. In J. E. Combs & M. W. Mansfield (Eds.), *Drama in life: The uses of communication in society* (pp. 200-211). New York: Hastings House.

Warr, P., & Jackson, P. (1976). Three weighting criteria in impression formation. *European Journal of Social Psychology, 6*, 41-49.

Washburn, W. E. (1963). The great autumnal madness: Political symbolism in mid-nineteenth century America. *Quarterly Journal of Speech, 49*, 417-431.

Washburn, W. E. (1972). Campaign banners. *American Heritage, 23*, 8-13.

Weaver-Lariscy, R. A., & Tinkham, S. F. (1991). News coverage, endorsements and personal campaigning: The influence of non-paid activities in congressional elections. *Journalism Quarterly, 68*, 432-444.

Weiner, B. (1982). The emotional consequences of causal ascriptions. In M. S. Clark & S. T. Fiske (Eds.), *Affect and cognition: The 17th annual Carnegie symposium on cognition* (pp. 185-209). Hillsdale, NJ: Lawrence Erlbaum Associates.

Weiss, W. (1966). *Effects of the mass media of communication.* New York: Hunter College, Center for Research and Social Psychology.

Whillock, R. K. (1991). *Political Empiricism.* New York: Praeger.

Wilcox, D. L., Ault, P. H., & Agee, W.K. (1986). *Public relations: Strategies and tactics.* New York: Harper and Row.

Williamson, J. (1978). *Decoding advertisements: Ideology and meaning in advertising.* London: Marion Boyars.

Wilson, P. O. (1987). Presidential advertising in 1988. *Election Politics, 4*, 17-21.

Winnick, R. H., & Archer, J. (1974). The retrieval of positive and negative information from short-term memory storage for use in a concept-identification task. *Bulletin of the Psychonomic Society, 3*, 309-310.

Wisse, J. (1989). *Ethos and pathos from Aristotle to Cicero.* Amsterdam: Adolf M. Hakkert.

Wurtzel, A. (1979). *Television Production.* New York: McGraw-Hill.

Wyer, R. S. (1970). Information redundancy, inconsistency, and novelty and their role in impression formation. *Journal of Experimental Social Psychology, 6*, 111-127.

Zajonc, R. B. (1980). Feeling and thinking: Preferences need no inferences. *American Psychologist, 35*, 151-175.

Zajonc, R. B. (1984). On the primacy of affect. *American Psychologist, 39*, 117-123.

Zettl, H. (1973). *Sight-sound-motion: Applied media aesthetics.* Belmont, CA: Wadsworth.

Zettl, H. (1976). *Television production handbook.* (3rd ed.) Belmont, CA: Wadsworth.

Zettl, H. (1990). *Sight sound motion: Applied media aesthetics.* (2nd ed.) Belmont, CA: Wadsworth.

Zettl, H. (1992). *Television production handbook.* (5th ed.) Belmont, CA: Wadsworth.

Zillmann, D. (1983). Disparagement humor. In P. E. McGhee & J. H. Goldsteing (Eds.), *Handbook of humor research* Vol. 1 (pp. 85-107). New York: Springer-Verlag.

Zillmann, D., Bryant, J., & Cantor, J. (1974). Brutality of assault in political cartoons affecting humor appreciation. *Journal of Research in Personality, 7*, 334-345.

Zillmann, D., & Cantor, J. (1972). Directionality of transitory dominance as a communication variable affecting humor appreciation. *Journal of Personality and Social Psychology, 24*, 191-198.

Zillmann, D., & Cantor, J. (1976). A disposition theory of humour and mirth. In A. J. Chapman & H. C. Foote (Eds.), *Humour and laughter: Theory, research and applications* (pp. 93-115). London: John Wiley.

Index

About the Authors

KAREN S. JOHNSON-CARTEE is Professor of Advertising and Public Relations and Speech Communication at the University of Alabama.

GARY A. COPELAND is Professor of Telecommunication and Film and Speech Communication at the University of Alabama. They are the authors of *Negative Political Advertising* (1991) and *Inside Political Campaigns* (1997).